Why Don't Students *Like* School?

DANIEL T.
WILLINGHAM

WHY DON'T
STUDENTS

SCHOOL?

A COGNITIVE SCIENTIST
ANSWERS QUESTIONS ABOUT HOW
THE MIND WORKS AND WHAT IT
MEANS FOR YOUR CLASSROOM

JOSSEY-BASS
A Wiley Imprint
www.josseybass.com

Published by Jossey-Bass
A Wiley Imprint
989 Market Street, San Francisco, CA 94103-1741—www.josseybass.com

Jossey-Bass books and products are available through most bookstores. To contact Jossey-Bass directly call our Customer Care Department within the U.S. at 800-956-7739, outside the U.S. at 317-572-3986, or fax 317-572-4002.

Jossey-Bass also publishes its books in a variety of electronic formats. Some content that appears in print may not be available in electronic books.

Library of Congress Cataloging-in-Publication Data

Library of Congress Cataloging-in-Publication Data

Willingham, Daniel T.
    Why don't students like school?: a cognitive scientist answers questions about how the mind works and what it means for your classroom/Daniel T. Willingham.
        p.   cm.
    Includes bibliographical references and index.
    ISBN 978-0-470-27930-4 (alk. paper)
        1. Learning, Psychology of.   2. Effective teaching.   I. Title.
    LB1060.W5435   2009
    370.15'23—dc22
                                                                    2008043493

Printed in the United States of America

FIRST EDITION

HB Printing   10 9 8 7 6 5 4 3 2

Contents

Acknowledgments vii

The Author ix

Introduction 1

CHAPTER 1

Why Don't Students Like School? 3

CHAPTER 2

How Can I Teach Students the Skills They Need When
Standardized Tests Require Only Facts? 19

CHAPTER 3

Why Do Students Remember Everything That's on Television
and Forget Everything I Say? 41

CHAPTER 4

Why Is It So Hard for Students to Understand
Abstract Ideas? 67

CHAPTER 5

Is Drilling Worth It? 81

CHAPTER 6

What's the Secret to Getting Students to Think Like
Real Scientists, Mathematicians, and Historians? 97

CHAPTER 7
How Should I Adjust My Teaching for Different Types of
Learners? 113

CHAPTER 8
How Can I Help Slow Learners? 131

CHAPTER 9
What About My Mind? 147

Conclusion 161
Notes 167
Index 171
Credit Lines 177

Acknowledgments

Esmond Harmsworth, my literary agent, has been an asset every step of the way, starting with the initial concept. Lesley Iura, Amy Reed, and the whole team at Jossey-Bass showed great expertise and professionalism during the editing and production processes. Anne Carlyle Lindsay was an exceptional help with the artwork in the book. Special thanks go to two anonymous reviewers who went far above and beyond the call of duty in providing extensive and helpful comments on the entire manuscript. Finally, I thank my many friends and colleagues who have generously shared thoughts and ideas, and taught me so much about students and education, especially Judy Deloach, Jason Downer, Bridget Hamre, Lisa Hansel, Virkam Jaswal, Angel Lillard, Andy Mashburn, Susan Mintz, Bob Pianta, Ruth Wattenberg, and Trisha Thompson-Willingham.

For Trisha

The Author

Daniel T. Willingham earned his B.A. degree in psychology from Duke University in 1983 and his Ph.D. degree in cognitive psychology from Harvard University in 1990. He is currently professor of psychology at the University of Virginia, where he has taught since 1992. Until about 2000, his research focused solely on the brain basis of learning and memory. Today all of his research concerns the application of cognitive psychology to K–12 education. He writes the "Ask the Cognitive Scientist" column for *American Educator* magazine. His website is http://www.danielwillingham.com.

WHY DON'T STUDENTS *Like* SCHOOL?

Introduction

Arguably the greatest mysteries in the universe lie in the three-pound mass of cells, approximately the consistency of oatmeal, that reside in the skull of each of us. It has even been suggested that the brain is so complex that our species is smart enough to fathom everything except what makes us so smart; that is, the brain is so cunningly designed for intelligence that it is too stupid to understand itself. We now know that is not true. The mind is at last yielding its secrets to persistent scientific investigation. We have learned more about how the mind works in the last twenty-five years than we did in the previous twenty-five hundred.

It would seem that greater knowledge of the mind would yield important benefits to education—after all, education is based on change in the minds of students, so surely understanding the student's cognitive equipment would make teaching easier or more effective. Yet the teachers I know don't believe they've seen much benefit from what psychologists call "the cognitive revolution." We all read stories in the newspaper about research breakthroughs in learning or problem solving, but it is not clear how each latest advance is supposed to change what a teacher does on Monday morning.

The gap between research and practice is understandable. When cognitive scientists study the mind, they intentionally isolate mental processes (for example, learning or attention) in the laboratory in order to make them easier to study. But mental processes are not isolated in the classroom. They all operate simultaneously, and they often interact in difficult-to-predict ways. To provide an obvious example, laboratory studies show that repetition helps learning, but any teacher knows that you can't take that finding and pop it into a classroom by, for example, having students repeat long-division problems until they've mastered the process. Repetition is good for learning but terrible for motivation. With too much repetition, motivation plummets, students stop trying, and no learning takes place. The classroom application would not duplicate the laboratory result.

Why Don't Students Like School? began as a list of nine principles that are so fundamental to the mind's operation that they do *not* change as circumstances change. They are as true in the classroom as they are in the laboratory★ and therefore can reliably be applied to classroom situations. Many of these principles likely won't surprise you: factual knowledge is important, practice is necessary, and so on.

What may surprise you are the implications for teaching that follow. You'll learn why it's more useful to view the human species as *bad* at thinking rather than as cognitively gifted. You'll discover that authors routinely write only a fraction of what they mean, which I'll argue implies very little for reading instruction but a great deal for the factual knowledge your students must gain. You'll explore why you remember the plot of *Star Wars* without even trying, and you'll learn how to harness that ease of learning for your classroom. You'll follow the brilliant mind of television doctor Gregory House as he solves a case, and you'll discover why you should *not* try to get your students to think like real scientists. You'll see how people like Mary Kate and Ashley Olson have helped psychologists analyze the obvious truth that kids inherit their intelligence from their parents—only to find that it's not true after all, and you'll understand why it is so important that you communicate that fact to your students.

Why Don't Students Like School? ranges over a variety of subjects in pursuit of two goals that are straightforward but far from simple: to tell you how your students' minds work, and to clarify how to use that knowledge to be a better teacher.

Note

* There actually were three other criteria for inclusion: (1) using versus ignoring a principle had to have a big impact on student learning; (2) there had to be an enormous amount of data, not just a few studies, to support the principle; and (3) the principle had to suggest classroom applications that teachers might not already know. That's why there are nine principles rather than a nice round number like ten. I simply do not know more than nine.

1

Why Don't Students Like School?

Question: Most of the teachers I know entered the profession because they loved school as children. They want to help their students feel the same excitement and passion for learning that they felt. They are understandably dejected when they find that some of their pupils don't like school much, and that they, the teachers, have great difficulty inspiring them. Why is it difficult to make school enjoyable for students?

Answer: Contrary to popular belief, the brain is not designed for thinking. It's designed to save you from having to think, because the brain is actually not very good at thinking. Thinking is slow and unreliable. Nevertheless, people enjoy mental work if it is successful. People like to solve problems, but not to work on unsolvable problems. If schoolwork is always just a bit too difficult for a student, it should be no surprise that she doesn't like school much. The cognitive principle that guides this chapter is:

> People are naturally curious, but we are not naturally good thinkers; unless the cognitive conditions are right, we will avoid thinking.

The implication of this principle is that teachers should reconsider how they encourage their students to think, in order to maximize the likelihood that students will get the pleasurable rush that comes from successful thought.

The Mind Is Not Designed for Thinking

What is the essence of being human? What sets us apart from other species? Many people would answer that it is our ability to reason—birds fly, fish swim, and humans think. (By *thinking* I mean solving problems, reasoning, reading something complex, or doing any mental work that requires some effort.) Shakespeare extolled our cognitive ability in *Hamlet*: "What a piece of work is man! How noble in reason!" Some three hundred years later, however, Henry Ford more cynically observed, "Thinking is the hardest work there is, which is the probable reason why so few people engage in it."* They both had a point. Humans are good at certain types of reasoning, particularly in comparison to other animals, but we exercise those abilities infrequently. A cognitive scientist would add another observation: Humans don't think very often because our brains are designed not for thought but for the avoidance of thought. Thinking is not only effortful, as Ford noted, it's also slow and unreliable.

Your brain serves many purposes, and thinking is not the one it serves best. Your brain also supports the ability to see and to move, for example, and these functions operate much more efficiently and reliably than your ability to think. It's no accident that most of your brain's real estate is devoted to these activities. The extra brain power is needed because seeing is actually more difficult than playing chess or solving calculus problems.

You can appreciate the power of your visual system by comparing human abilities to those of computers. When it comes to math, science, and other traditional "thinking" tasks, machines beat people, no contest. Five dollars will get you a calculator that can perform simple calculations faster and more accurately than any human can. With fifty dollars you can buy chess software that can defeat more than 99 percent of the world's population. But the most powerful computer on the planet can't drive a truck. That's because computers can't see, especially not in complex, ever-changing environments like the one you face every time you drive. Robots are similarly limited in how they move. Humans are excellent at configuring our bodies as needed for tasks, even if the configuration is unusual, such as when you twist your torso and contort your arm in an effort to dust behind books on a shelf. Robots are not very good at figuring out novel ways to move, so they are useful mostly for repetitive work such as spray painting automotive parts, for which the required movements are always the same. Tasks that you take for granted—for example, walking on a rocky shore where the footing is uncertain— are much more difficult than playing top-level chess. No computer can do it (Figure 1).

Compared to your ability to see and move, thinking is slow, effortful, and uncertain. To get a feel for why I say this, try solving this problem:

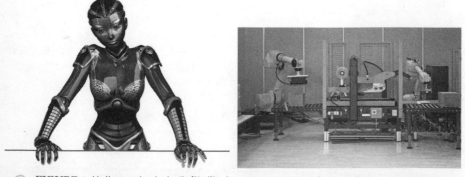

FIGURE 1: Hollywood robots (left), like humans, can move in complex environments, but that's true only in the movies. Most real-life robots (right) move in predictable environments. Our ability to see and move is a remarkable cognitive feat.

In an empty room are a candle, some matches, and a box of tacks. The goal is to have the lit candle about five feet off the ground. You've tried melting some of the wax on the bottom of the candle and sticking it to the wall, but that wasn't effective. How can you get the lit candle five feet off the ground without having to hold it there?[1]

Twenty minutes is the usual maximum time allowed, and few people are able to solve it by then, although once you hear the answer you will realize it's not especially tricky. You dump the tacks out of the box, tack the box to the wall, and use it as a platform for the candle.

This problem illustrates three properties of thinking. First, thinking is *slow.* Your visual system instantly takes in a complex scene. When you enter a friend's backyard you don't think to yourself, "Hmmm, there's some green stuff. Probably grass, but it could be some other ground cover—and what's that rough brown object sticking up there? A fence, perhaps?" You take in the whole scene—lawn, fence, flowerbeds, gazebo—at a glance. Your thinking system does not instantly calculate the answer to a problem the way your visual system immediately takes in a visual scene. Second, thinking is *effortful;* you don't have to try to see, but thinking takes concentration. You can perform other tasks while you are seeing, but you can't think about something else while you are working on a problem. Finally, thinking is *uncertain.* Your visual system seldom makes mistakes, and when it does you usually think you see something similar to what is actually out there—you're close, if not exactly right. Your thinking system might not even get you close; your solution to a problem may be far from correct. In fact, your thinking system may not produce an answer at all, which is what happens to most people when they try to solve the candle problem.

If we're all so bad at thinking, how does anyone get through the day? How do we find our way to work or spot a bargain at the grocery store? How does a teacher make the hundreds of decisions necessary to get through her day? The answer is that when we can get away with it, we don't think. Instead we rely on memory. Most of the problems we face are ones we've solved before, so we just do what we've done in the past. For example, suppose that next week a friend gives you the candle problem. You immediately say, "Oh, right. I've heard this one. You tack the box to the wall." Just as your visual system takes in a scene and, without any effort on your part, tells you what is in the environment, so too your memory system immediately and effort-lessly recognizes that you've heard the problem before and provides the answer. You may think you have a terrible memory, and it's true that your memory system is not as reliable as your visual or movement system—sometimes you forget, sometimes you *think* you remember when you don't—but your memory system is much more reliable than your thinking system, and it provides answers quickly and with little effort.

We normally think of memory as storing personal events (memories of my wedding) and facts (George Washington was the first president of the United States).

FIGURE 2: Your memory system operates so quickly and effortlessly that you seldom notice it working. For example, your memory has stored away information about what things look like (Hillary Clinton's face) and how to manipulate objects (turn the left faucet for hot water, the right for cold), and strategies for dealing with problems you've encountered before (such as a pot boiling over).

Our memory also stores strategies to guide what we should do: where to turn when driving home, how to handle a minor dispute when monitoring recess, what to do when a pot on the stove starts to boil over (Figure 2). For the vast majority of decisions we make, we don't stop to consider what we might do, reason about it, anticipate possible consequences, and so on. For example, when I decide to make spaghetti for dinner, I don't pore over my cookbooks, weighing each recipe for taste, nutritional value, ease of preparation, cost of ingredients, visual appeal, and so on—I just make spaghetti sauce the way I usually do. As two psychologists put it, "Most of the time what we do is what we do most of the time."[2] When you feel as though you are "on autopilot," even if you're doing something rather complex, such as driving home from school, it's because you are using memory to guide your behavior. Using memory doesn't require much of your attention, so you are free to daydream, even as you're stopping at red lights, passing cars, watching for pedestrians, and so on.

Of course you *could* make each decision with care and thought. When someone encourages you to "think outside the box" that's usually what he means—don't go on autopilot, don't do what you (or others) have always done. Consider what life would be like if you *always* strove to think outside the box. Suppose you approached every task afresh and tried to see all of its possibilities, even daily tasks like chopping an onion, entering your office building, or buying a soft drink at lunch. The novelty might be fun for a while, but life would soon be exhausting (Figure 3).

You may have experienced something similar when traveling, especially if you've traveled where you don't speak the local language. Everything is unfamiliar and even trivial actions demand lots of thought. For example, buying a soda from a vendor requires figuring out the flavors from the exotic packaging, trying to communicate with the vendor, working through which coin or bill to use, and so on. That's one reason that traveling is so tiring: all of the trivial actions that at home could be made on autopilot require your full attention.

So far I've described two ways in which your brain is set up to save you from having to think. First, some of the most important functions (for example, vision and movement) don't require thought: you don't have to reason about what you see; you just immediately know what's out in the world. Second, you are biased to use memory to guide your actions rather than to think. But your brain doesn't leave it there; it is capable of changing in order to save you from having to think. If you repeat the same thought-demanding task

FIGURE 3: "Thinking outside the box" for a mundane task like selecting bread at the supermarket would probably not be worth the mental effort.

again and again, it will eventually become automatic; your brain will change so that you can complete the task without thinking about it. I discuss this process in more detail in Chapter Five, but a familiar example here will illustrate what I mean. You can probably recall that learning to drive a car was mentally very demanding. I remember focusing on how hard to depress the accelerator, when and how to apply the brake as I approached a red light, how far to turn the steering wheel to execute a turn, when to check my mirrors, and so forth. I didn't even listen to the radio while I drove, for fear of being distracted. With practice, however, the process of driving became automatic, and now I don't need to think about those small-scale bits of driving any more than I need to think about how to walk. I can drive while simultaneously chatting with friends, gesturing with one hand, and eating French fries—an impressive cognitive feat, if not very attractive to watch. Thus a task that initially takes a great deal of thought becomes, with practice, a task that requires little or no thought.

The implications for education sound rather grim. If people are bad at thinking and try to avoid it, what does that say about students' attitudes toward school? Fortunately, the story doesn't end with people stubbornly refusing to think. Despite the fact that we're not that good at it, we actually *like* to think. We are naturally curious, and we look for opportunities to engage in certain types of thought. But because thinking is so hard, the conditions have to be right for this curiosity to thrive, or we quit thinking rather readily. The next section explains when we like to think and when we don't.

People Are Naturally Curious, but Curiosity Is Fragile

Even though the brain is not set up for very efficient thinking, people actually enjoy mental activity, at least in some circumstances. We have hobbies like solving crossword puzzles or scrutinizing maps. We watch information-packed documentaries. We pursue careers—such as teaching—that offer greater mental challenge than competing careers, even if the pay is lower. Not only are we willing to think, we intentionally seek out situations that demand thought.

Solving problems brings pleasure. When I say "problem solving" in this book, I mean any cognitive work that succeeds; it might be understanding a difficult passage of prose, planning a garden, or sizing up an investment opportunity. There is a sense of satisfaction, of fulfillment, in successful thinking. In the last ten years neuroscientists have discovered that there is overlap between the brain areas and chemicals that are important in learning and those that are important in the brain's natural reward system. Many neuroscientists suspect that the two systems are related. Rats in a maze learn better when rewarded with cheese. When you solve a problem, your brain may reward itself with a small dose of dopamine, a naturally occurring chemical that is important to the brain's pleasure system. Neuroscientists know that dopamine is important in both systems—learning and pleasure—but haven't yet worked out the explicit tie between them. Even though the neurochemistry is not completely understood, it seems undeniable that people take pleasure in solving problems.

It's notable too that the pleasure is in the *solving* of the problem. Working on a problem with no sense that you're making progress is not pleasurable. In fact, it's frustrating. Then too, there's not great pleasure in simply knowing the answer. I told you the solution to the candle problem; did you get any fun out of it? Think how much more fun it would have been if you had solved it yourself—in fact, the problem would have seemed more clever, just as a joke that you get is funnier than a joke that has to be explained. Even if someone doesn't tell you the answer to a problem, once you've had too many hints you lose the sense that *you've* solved the problem, and getting the answer doesn't bring the same mental snap of satisfaction.

Mental work appeals to us because it offers the opportunity for that pleasant feeling when it succeeds. But not all types of thinking are equally attractive. People choose to work crossword puzzles but not algebra problems. A biography of Bono is more likely to sell well than a biography of Keats. What characterizes the mental activity that people enjoy (Figure 4)?

The answer that most people would give may seem obvious: "I think crossword puzzles are fun and Bono is cool, but math is boring and so is Keats." In other words, it's the content that matters. We're curious about some stuff but not about other stuff. Certainly that's the way people describe our own interests—"I'm a stamp collector" or "I'm into medieval symphonic music." But I don't think content drives interest. We've all attended a lecture or watched a TV show (perhaps against our will) about a subject we thought we weren't interested in, only to find ourselves fascinated; and it's easy to get bored even when you usually like the topic. I'll never forget my eagerness for the day my middle school teacher was to talk about sex. As a teenage boy in a staid 1970s suburban culture, I fizzed with anticipation of any talk about sex, anytime, anywhere. But when the big day came, my friends and I were absolutely disabled with boredom. It's not that the teacher talked about flowers and pollination—he really did talk about human sexuality—but somehow it was still dull. I actually wish I could remember how he did it; boring a bunch of hormonal teenagers with a sex talk is quite a feat.

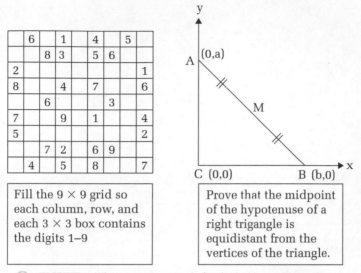

Fill the 9 × 9 grid so each column, row, and each 3 × 3 box contains the digits 1–9

Prove that the midpoint of the hypotenuse of a right triangle is equidistant from the vertices of the triangle.

FIGURE 4: Why are many people fascinated by problems like the one shown on the left, but very few people willingly work on problems like the one on the right?

I once made this point to a group of teachers when talking about motivation and cognition. About five minutes into the talk I presented a slide depicting the model of motivation shown in Figure 5. I didn't prepare the audience for the slide in any way; I just put it up and started describing it. After about fifteen seconds I stopped and said to the audience, "Anyone who is still listening to me, please raise your hand." One person did. The other fifty-nine were also attending voluntarily; it was a topic in which they were presumably interested, and the talk had only just started—but in fifteen seconds their minds were somewhere else. The content of a problem—whether it's about sex or human motivation—may be sufficient to prompt your interest, but it won't maintain it.

So, if content is not enough to keep your attention, when does curiosity have staying power? The answer may lie in the difficulty of the problem. If we get a little burst of pleasure from solving a problem, then there's no point in working on a problem that is too easy—there'll be no pleasure when it's solved because it didn't feel like much of a problem in the first place. Then too, when you size up a problem as very difficult, you are judging that you're unlikely to solve it, and are therefore unlikely to get the satisfaction that comes with the solution. A crossword puzzle that is too easy is just mindless work: you fill in the squares, scarcely thinking about it, and there's no gratification, even though you're getting all the answers. But you're unlikely to work long at a crossword puzzle that's too difficult. You know you'll solve very little of it, so it will just be frustrating. The slide in Figure 5 is too detailed to be absorbed with minimal introduction; my audience quickly concluded that it was overwhelming and mentally checked out of my talk.

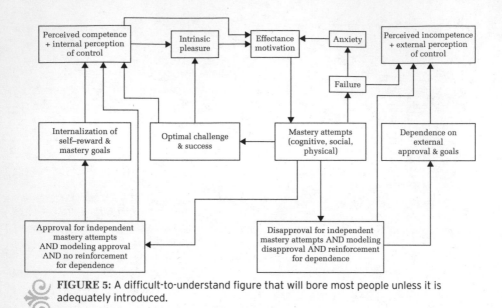

FIGURE 5: A difficult-to-understand figure that will bore most people unless it is adequately introduced.

To summarize, I've said that thinking is slow, effortful, and uncertain. Nevertheless, people like to think—or more properly, we like to think if we judge that the mental work will pay off with the pleasurable feeling we get when we solve a problem. So there is no inconsistency in claiming that people avoid thought and in claiming that people are naturally curious—curiosity prompts people to explore new ideas and problems, but when we do, we quickly evaluate how much mental work it will take to solve the problem. If it's too much or too little, we stop working on the problem if we can.

This analysis of the sorts of mental work that people seek out or avoid also provides one answer to why more students don't like school. Working on problems that are of the right level of difficulty is rewarding, but working on problems that are too easy or too difficult is unpleasant. Students can't opt out of these problems the way adults often can. If the student routinely gets work that is a bit too difficult, it's little wonder that he doesn't care much for school. I wouldn't want to work on the Sunday *New York Times* crossword puzzle for several hours each day.

So what's the solution? Give the student easier work? You could, but of course you'd have to be careful not to make it so easy that the student would be bored. And anyway, wouldn't it be better to boost the student's ability a little bit? Instead of making the work easier, is it possible to make thinking easier?

How Thinking Works

Understanding a bit about how thinking happens will help you understand what makes thinking hard. That will in turn help you understand how to make thinking easier for your students, and therefore help them enjoy school more.

Let's begin with a very simple model of the mind. On the left of Figure 6 is the environment, full of things to see and hear, problems to be solved, and so on. On the right is one component of your mind that scientists call *working memory.* For the moment, consider it to be synonymous with consciousness; it holds the stuff you're thinking about. The arrow from the environment to working memory shows that working memory is the part of your mind where you are aware of what is around you: the sight of a shaft of light falling onto a dusty table, the sound of a dog barking in the distance, and so forth. Of course you can also be aware of things that are not currently in the environment; for example, you can recall the sound of your mother's voice, even if she's not in the room (or indeed no longer living). *Long-term memory* is the vast storehouse in which you maintain your factual knowledge of the world: that ladybugs have spots, that your favorite flavor of ice cream is chocolate, that your three-year-old surprised you yesterday by mentioning kumquats, and so on. Factual knowledge can be abstract; for example, it would include the idea that triangles are closed figures with three sides, and your knowledge of what a dog generally looks like. All of the information in long-term memory resides outside of awareness. It lies quietly until it is needed, and then enters working memory and so becomes conscious. For example, if I asked you, "What color is a polar bear?" you would say, "white" almost immediately. That information was in long-term memory thirty second ago, but you weren't aware of it until I posed the question that made it relevant to ongoing thought, whereupon it entered working memory.

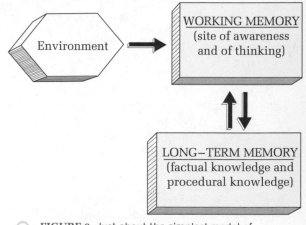

FIGURE 6: Just about the simplest model of the mind possible.

Thinking occurs when you combine information (from the environment and long-term memory) in new ways. That combining happens in working memory. To get a feel for this process, read the problem depicted in Figure 7 and try to solve it. (The point is not so much to solve it as to experience what is meant by thinking and working memory.)

With some diligence you might be able to solve this problem,[†] but the real point is to feel what it's like to have working memory absorbed by the problem. You begin by taking information from the environment—the rules and the configuration of the game board—and then imagine moving the discs to try to reach the goal. Within working memory you must maintain your current state in the puzzle—where the discs are—and imagine and evaluate potential moves. At the same time you have to remember the rules regarding which moves are legal, as shown in Figure 8.

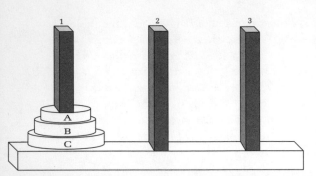

FIGURE 7: The figure depicts a playing board with three pegs. There are three rings of decreasing size on the leftmost peg. The goal is to move all three rings from the leftmost peg to the rightmost peg. There are just two rules about how you can move rings: you can move only one ring at a time, and you can't place a larger ring on top of a smaller ring.

The description of thinking makes it clear that knowing *how* to combine and rearrange ideas in working memory is essential to successful thinking. For example, in the discs and pegs problem, how do you know where to move the discs? If you hadn't seen the problem before, you probably felt like you were pretty much guessing. You didn't have any information in long-term memory to guide you, as depicted in Figure 8. But if you have had experience with this particular type of problem, then you likely have information in long-term memory about how to solve it, even if the information is not foolproof. For example, try to work this math problem in your head:

$$18 \times 7$$

You know just what to do for this problem. I'm confident that the sequence of your mental processes was something close to this:

1. Multiple 8 and 7.
2. Retrieve the fact that $8 \times 7 = 56$ from long-term memory.
3. Remember that the 6 is part of the solution, then carry the 5.
4. Multiply 7 and 1.
5. Retrieve the fact that $7 \times 1 = 7$ from long-term memory.
6. Add the carried 5 to the 7.
7. Retrieve the fact that $5 + 7 = 12$ from long-term memory.
8. Put the 12 down, append the 6.
9. The answer is 126.

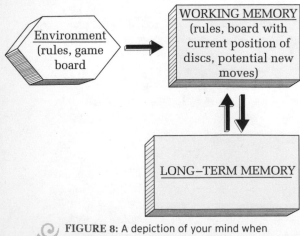

FIGURE 8: A depiction of your mind when you're working on the puzzle shown in Figure 7.

Your long-term memory contains not only factual information, such as the color of polar bears and the value of 8 × 7, but it also contains what we'll call *procedural knowledge*, which is your knowledge of the mental procedures necessary to execute tasks. If thinking is combining information in working memory, then procedural knowledge is a list of what to combine and when—it's like a recipe to accomplish a particular type of thought. You might have stored procedures for the steps needed to calculate the area of a triangle, or to duplicate a computer file using Windows, or to drive from your home to your office.

It's pretty obvious that having the appropriate procedure stored in long-term memory helps a great deal when we're thinking. That's why it was easy to solve the math problem and hard to solve the discs-and-pegs problem. But how about factual knowledge? Does that help you think as well? It does, in several different ways, which are discussed in Chapter Two. For now, note that solving the math problem required the retrieval of factual information, such as the fact that 8 × 7 = 56. I've said that thinking entails combining information in working memory. Often the information provided in the environment is not sufficient to solve a problem, and you need to supplement it with information from long-term memory.

There's a final necessity for thinking, which is best understood through an example. Have a look at this problem:

In the inns of certain Himalayan villages is practiced a refined tea ceremony. The ceremony involves a host and exactly two guests, neither more nor less. When his guests have arrived and seated themselves at his table, the host performs three services for them. These services are listed in the order of the nobility the Himalayans attribute to them: stoking the fire, fanning the flames, and pouring the tea. During the ceremony, any of those present may ask another, "Honored Sir, may I perform this onerous task for you?" However, a person may request of another only the least noble of the tasks which the other is performing. Furthermore, if a person is performing any tasks, then he may not request a task that is nobler than the least noble task he is already performing. Custom requires that by the time the tea ceremony is over, all the tasks will have been transferred from the host to the most senior of the guests. How can this be accomplished?[3]

Your first thought upon reading this problem was likely "Huh?" You could probably tell that you'd have to read it several times just to understand it, let alone begin

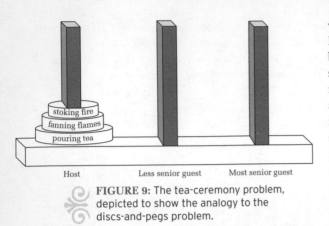

FIGURE 9: The tea-ceremony problem, depicted to show the analogy to the discs-and-pegs problem.

working on the solution. It seemed overwhelming because you did not have sufficient space in working memory to hold all of the aspects of the problem. Working memory has limited space, so thinking becomes increasingly difficult as working memory gets crowded.

The tea-ceremony problem is actually the same as the discs-and-pegs problem presented in Figure 7. The host and two guests are like the three pegs, and the tasks are the three discs to be moved among them, as shown in Figure 9. (The fact that very few people see this analogy and its importance for education is taken up in Chapter Four.)

This version of the problem seems much harder because some parts of the problem that are laid out in Figure 7 must be juggled in your head in this new version. For example, Figure 7 provides a picture of the pegs you can use to help maintain a mental image of the discs as you consider moves. The rules of the problem occupy so much space in working memory that it's difficult to contemplate moves that might lead to a solution.

In sum, successful thinking relies on four factors: information from the environment, facts in long-term memory, procedures in long-term memory, and the amount of space in working memory. If any one of these factors is inadequate, thinking will likely fail.

✵

Let me summarize what I've said in this chapter. People's minds are not especially well-suited to thinking; thinking is slow, effortful, and uncertain. For this reason, deliberate thinking does not guide people's behavior in most situations. Rather, we rely on our memories, following courses of action that we have taken before. Nevertheless, we find *successful* thinking pleasurable. We like solving problems, understanding new ideas, and so forth. Thus, we will seek out opportunities to think, but we are selective in doing so; we choose problems that pose some challenge but that seem likely to be solvable, because these are the problems that lead to feelings of pleasure and satisfaction. For problems to be solved, the thinker needs adequate information from the environment, room in working memory, and the required facts and procedures in long-term memory.

Implications for the Classroom

Let's turn now to the question that opened this chapter: Why don't students like school, or perhaps more realistically, why don't more of them like it? Any teacher knows that there are lots of reasons that a student might or might not enjoy school. (My wife loved it, but primarily for social reasons.) From a cognitive perspective, an important factor is whether or not a student consistently experiences the pleasurable rush of solving a problem. What can teachers do to ensure that each student gets that pleasure?

Be Sure That There Are Problems to Be Solved

By *problem* I don't necessarily mean a question addressed to the class by the teacher, or a mathematical puzzle. I mean cognitive work that poses moderate challenge, including such activities as understanding a poem or thinking of novel uses for recyclable materials. This sort of cognitive work is of course the main stuff of teaching—we want our students to think. But without some attention, a lesson plan can become a long string of teacher explanations, with little opportunity for students to solve problems. So scan each lesson plan with an eye toward the cognitive work that students will be doing. How often does such work occur? Is it intermixed with cognitive breaks? When you have identified the challenges, consider whether they are open to negative outcomes such as students failing to understand what they are to do, or students being unlikely to solve the problem, or students simply trying to guess what you would like them to say or do.

Respect Students' Cognitive Limits

When trying to develop effective mental challenges for your students, bear in mind the cognitive limitations discussed in this chapter. For example, suppose you began a history lesson with a question: "You've all heard of the Boston Tea Party; why do you suppose the colonists dressed as Indians and dumped tea into the Boston harbor?" Do your students have the necessary background knowledge in memory to consider this question? What do they know about the relationship of the colonies and the British crown in 1773? Do they know about the social and economic significance of tea? Could they generate reasonable alternative courses of action? If they lack the appropriate background knowledge, the question you pose will quickly be judged as "boring." If students lack the background knowledge to engage with a problem, save it for another time when they have that knowledge.

Equally important is the limit on working memory. Remember that people can keep only so much information in mind at once, as you experienced when you read the tea-ceremony version of the discs-and-pegs problem. Overloads of working memory are caused by such things as multistep instructions, lists of unconnected facts, chains of logic more than two or three steps long, and the application of a just-learned concept to new material (unless the concept is quite simple). The solution to working memory overloads is straightforward: slow the pace, and use memory aids such as writing on the blackboard that save students from keeping too much information in working memory.

Clarifying the Problems to Be Solved

How can you make the problem interesting? A common strategy is to try to make the material "relevant" to students. This strategy sometimes works well, but it's hard to use for some material. Another difficulty is that a teacher's class may include two football fans, a doll collector, a NASCAR enthusiast, a horseback riding competitor—you get the idea. Mentioning a popular singer in the course of a history lesson may give the class a giggle, but it won't do much more than that. I have emphasized that our curiosity is provoked when we perceive a problem that we believe we can solve. What is the question that will engage students and make them want to know the answer?

One way to view schoolwork is as a series of *answers*. We want students to know Boyle's law, or three causes of the U.S. Civil War, or why Poe's raven kept saying, "Nevermore." Sometimes I think that we, as teachers, are so eager to get to the answers that we do not devote sufficient time to developing the question. But as the information in this chapter indicates, it's the question that piques people's interest. Being *told* an answer doesn't do anything for you. You may have noted that I could have organized this book around principles of cognitive psychology. Instead I organized it around questions that I thought teachers would find interesting.

When you plan a lesson, you start with the information you want students to know by its end. As a next step, consider what the key question for that lesson might be and how you can frame that question so it will have the right level of difficulty to engage your students and so you will respect your students' cognitive limitations.

Reconsider When to Puzzle Students

Teachers often seek to draw students into a lesson by presenting a problem that we believe will interest the students (for example, asking, "Why is there a law that you have to go to school?" could introduce the process by which laws are passed), or by conducting a demonstration or presenting a fact that we think students will find surprising. In either case, the goal is to puzzle students, to make them curious. This is a useful technique, but it's worth considering whether these strategies might be used not only at the beginning of a lesson but also *after* the basic concepts have been learned. For example, a classic science demonstration is to put a burning piece of paper in a milk bottle and then put a boiled egg over the bottle's opening. After the paper burns, the egg is sucked into the bottle. Students will no doubt be astonished, but if they don't know the principle behind it, the demonstration is like a magic trick—it's a momentary thrill, but their curiosity to understand may not be long-lasting. Another strategy would be to conduct the demonstration after students know that warm air expands and cooling air contracts, potentially forming a vacuum. Every fact or demonstration that would puzzle students before they have the right background knowledge has the potential to be an experience that will puzzle students *momentarily,* and then lead to the pleasure of problem solving. It is worth thinking about when to use a marvelous device like the egg-in-the-bottle trick.

Accept and Act on Variation in Student Preparation

As I describe in Chapter Eight, I don't accept that some students are "just not very bright" and ought to be tracked into less demanding classes. But it's naïve to pretend that all students come to your class equally prepared to excel; they have had different preparations, as well as different levels of support at home, and they will therefore differ in their abilities. If that's true, and if what I've said in this chapter is true, it is self-defeating to give all of your students the same work. The less capable students will find it too difficult and will struggle against their brain's bias to mentally walk away from schoolwork. To the extent that you can, it's smart, I think, to assign work to individuals or groups of students that is appropriate to their current level of competence. Naturally you will want to do this in a sensitive way, minimizing the extent to which some students will perceive themselves as behind others. But the fact is that they *are* behind the others, and giving them work that is beyond them is unlikely to help them catch up, and is likely to make them fall still further behind.

Change the Pace

We all inevitably lose the attention of our students, and as this chapter has described, it's likely to happen if they feel somewhat confused. They will mentally check out. The good news is that it's relatively easy to get them back. Change grabs attention, as you no doubt know. When there's a bang outside your classroom, every head turns to the windows. When you change topics, start a new activity, or in some other way show that you are shifting gears, virtually every student's attention will come back to you, and you will have a new chance to engage them. So plan shifts and monitor your class's attention to see whether you need to make them more often or less frequently.

Keep a Diary

The core idea presented in this chapter is that solving a problem gives people pleasure, but the problem must be easy enough to be solved yet difficult enough to take some mental effort. Finding this sweet spot of difficulty is not easy. Your experience in the classroom is your best guide—whatever works, do again; whatever doesn't, discard. But don't expect that you will really remember how well a lesson plan worked a year later. Whether a lesson goes brilliantly well or down in flames, it feels at the time that we'll never forget what happened; but the ravages of memory can surprise us, so write it down. Even if it's just a quick scratch on a sticky note, try to make a habit of recording your success in gauging the level of difficulty in the problems you pose for your students.

One of the factors that contributes to successful thought is the amount and quality of information in long-term memory. In Chapter Two I elaborate on the importance of background knowledge—on why it is so vital to effective thinking.

Notes

*A more eloquent version comes from eighteenth-century British painter Sir Joshua Reynolds: "There is no expedient to which a man will not resort to avoid the real labor of thinking."

†If you couldn't solve it, here's a solution. As you can see, the rings are marked A, B, and C, and the pegs are marked 1, 2, and 3. The solution is A3, B2, A2, C3, A1, B3, A3.

Bibliography

Less Technical

Csikszentmihalyi, M. (1990). *Flow: The psychology of optimal experience.* New York: Harper Perennial. The author describes the ultimate state of interest, when one is completely absorbed in what one is doing, to the point that time itself stops. The book does not tell you how to enter this state, but it is an interesting read in its own right.

Pinker, S. (1997). *How the mind works.* New York: Basic Books. This book covers not only thinking but also emotion, visual imagery, and other related topics. Pinker is a wonderful writer and draws in references from many academic fields and from pop culture. Not for the fainthearted, but great fun if the topic appeals to you.

More Technical

Baddeley, A. (2007). *Working memory, thought, and action.* London: Oxford University Press. Written by the originator of the working memory theory, this book summarizes an enormous amount of research that is consistent with that theory.

Schultz, W. (2007) Behavioral dopamine signals. *Trends in Neurosciences, 30,* 203–210. A review of the role of dopamine, a neurochemical, in learning, problem solving, and reward.

Silvia, P. J. (2008). Interest: The curious emotion. *Current Directions in Psychological Science, 17,* 57–60. The author provides a brief overview of theories of interest, highlighting his own, which is similar to the account provided here: we evaluate situations as interesting if they are novel, complex, and comprehensible.

Willingham, D. T. (2007). *Cognition: The thinking animal.* Upper Saddle River, NJ: Prentice Hall. This is a college-level textbook on cognitive psychology that can serve as an introduction to the field. It assumes no background, but it is a textbook, so although it is thorough, it might be a bit more detailed than you want.

2

How Can I Teach Students
the Skills They Need When
Standardized Tests Require
Only Facts?

Question: Much has been written about fact learning, most of it negative. The narrow-minded schoolmaster demanding that students parrot facts they do not understand has become a cliché of American education, although the stereotype is neither new nor exclusively American—Dickens used it in *Hard Times*, published in 1854. Concern about fact learning has intensified in the last ten years as the new emphasis on accountability in education has brought an increase in the use of standardized tests. It is too often true that standardized tests offer little opportunity for students to analyze, synthesize, or critique and instead demand the regurgitation of isolated facts. Many teachers feel that time for teaching skills is crowded out by preparation for standardized tests. Just how useful or useless is fact learning?

Answer: There is no doubt that having students memorize lists of dry facts is not enriching. It is also true (though less often appreciated) that trying to teach students skills such as analysis or synthesis in the absence of factual knowledge is impossible. Research from cognitive science has shown that the sorts of skills that teachers want for students—such as the ability to analyze and to think critically—*require* extensive factual knowledge. The cognitive principle that guides this chapter is:

> Factual knowledge must precede skill.

The implication is that facts must be taught, ideally in the context of skills, and ideally beginning in preschool and even before.

> There is a great danger in the present day lest science-teaching should degenerate into the accumulation of disconnected facts and unexplained formulae, which burden the memory without cultivating the understanding.
>
> —*J. D. Everett, writing in 1873*[1]

When I was a freshman in college a guy down the hall from me had a poster depicting Einstein and a quotation from the brilliant, frowsy-haired physicist: "Imagination is more important than knowledge." I could not have said why, but I thought this was very deep. Perhaps I was anticipating what I might say to my parents if my grades were poor: "Sure, I got Cs, but I have *imagination!* And according to Einstein..."

Some thirty years later teachers have a different reason to be wary and weary of "knowledge." The national watchword in education is *accountability,* which has translated into state tests. In most states these tests are heavy on multiple-choice questions and usually require straightforward recall of facts. Here are two examples of

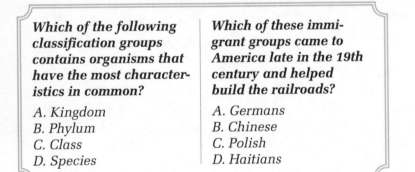

Which of the following classification groups contains organisms that have the most character-istics in common?

A. Kingdom
B. Phylum
C. Class
D. Species

Which of these immi-grant groups came to America late in the 19th century and helped build the railroads?

A. Germans
B. Chinese
C. Polish
D. Haitians

eighth-grade test items from my home state of Virginia, one from the science test and one from the history test.

It's easy to see why a teacher, parent, or student would protest that knowing the answer to a lot of these questions doesn't prove that one really *knows* science or history. We want our students to think, not simply to memorize. When someone shows evidence of thinking critically, we consider her smart and well educated. When someone spouts facts without context, we consider her boring and a show-off.

That said, there are obvious cases in which everyone would agree that factual knowledge is necessary. When a speaker uses unfamiliar vocabulary, you may not understand what he means. For example, if a friend sent you an e-mail telling you she thought your daughter was dating a "yegg," you'd certainly want to know the definition of the word (Figure 1). Similarly, you may know all of the vocabulary

FIGURE 1: If someone said your daughter is dating a *yegg*, you'd certainly want to know whether the word meant "nice-looking fellow," "slob," or "burglar."

words but lack the conceptual knowledge to knit the words together into something comprehensible. For example, a recent copy of the technical journal *Science* contained an article titled "Physical Model for the Decay and Preservation of Marine Organic Carbon." I know what each of these words means, but I don't know enough about organic carbon to understand why its decay or preservation is important, nor why you might want to model it.

The necessity of background knowledge for comprehension is pretty obvious, at least as I've described it so far. You could summarize this view by noting that *to think* is a transitive verb. You need something to think *about*. But you could counter (and I've heard the argument often) that you don't need to have this information memorized—you can always look it up. Recall the figure of the mind in Chapter One (Figure 2, below).

I defined *thinking* as combining information in new ways. The information can come from long-term memory—facts you've memorized—or from the environment. In today's world, is there a reason to memorize anything? You can find any factual information you need in seconds via the Internet—including the definition of *yegg*. Then too, things change so quickly that half of the information you commit to memory will be out of date in five years—or so the argument goes. Perhaps instead of learning facts, it's better to practice critical thinking, to have students work at *evaluating* all the information available on the Internet rather than trying to commit some small part of it to memory.

In this chapter I show that this argument is false. Data from the last thirty years lead to a conclusion that is not scientifically challengeable: thinking well requires knowing facts, and that's true not simply because you need

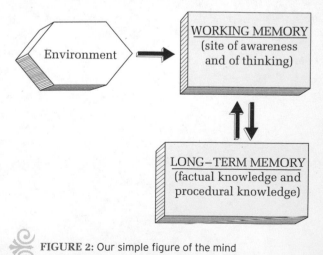

FIGURE 2: Our simple figure of the mind

something to think *about*. The very processes that teachers care about most—critical thinking processes such as reasoning and problem solving—are intimately intertwined with factual knowledge that is stored in long-term memory (not just found in the environment).

It's hard for many people to conceive of thinking processes as intertwined with knowledge. Most people believe that thinking processes are akin to the functions of a calculator (Figure 3). A calculator has available a set of procedures (addition, multiplication, and so on) that can manipulate numbers, and these procedures can be applied to *any set of numbers*. The data (the numbers) and the operations that manipulate the data are separate. Thus, if you learn a new thinking operation (for example, how to critically analyze historical documents), that operation should be applicable to all historical documents, just as a fancier calculator that computes sines can do so for all numbers.

But the human mind does not work that way. When we learn to think critically about, say, the start of the Second World War, it does not mean we can also think critically about a chess game or about the current situation in the Middle East or even about the start of the American Revolutionary War. Critical thinking processes are tied to background knowledge (although they become much less so when we become quite experienced, as I describe in Chapter Six). The conclusion from this work in cognitive science is straightforward: we must ensure that students acquire background knowledge parallel with practicing critical thinking skills.

In this chapter I describe how cognitive scientists know that thinking skills and knowledge are bound together.

FIGURE 3:
A calculator can apply the same set of functions to any data. The mind does not work that way.

Knowledge Is Essential to Reading Comprhension

Background knowledge helps you understand what someone is talking about or writing. In the last section I gave a couple of rather obvious examples: if a vocabulary word (for example, *yegg*) or a concept (for example, *marine organic compound*) is missing from your long-term memory, you'll likely be confused. But the need for background knowledge is deeper than the need for definitions.

Suppose a sentence contains two ideas—call them A and B. Even if you know the vocabulary and you understand A and B, you still might need background knowledge to understand the sentence. For example, suppose you read the following sentence in a novel:

> "I'm not trying out my new barbecue when the boss comes to dinner!" Mark yelled.

You could say that idea A is Mark trying out his new barbecue, and idea B is that he won't do it when his boss comes to dinner. To understand the sentence, you need to understand the *relationship* between A and B, but not provided here are the two pieces of information that would help you bridge A and B: that people often make mistakes the first time they use a new appliance and that Mark would like to impress his boss. Putting these facts together would help you understand that Mark is afraid he'll ruin the food the first time he uses his new barbecue, and he doesn't want that to be the meal he serves to his boss.

Reading comprehension depends on combining the ideas in a passage, not just comprehending each idea on its own. And writing contains gaps—lots of gaps—from which the writer omits information that is necessary to understand the logical flow of ideas. Writers assume that the reader has the knowledge to fill the gaps. In the example just given, the writer assumed that the reader would know the relevant facts about new appliances and about bosses.

Why do writers leave gaps? Don't they run the risk that the reader *won't* have the right background knowledge and so will be confused? That's a risk, but writers can't include all the factual details. If they did, prose would be impossibly long and tedious. For example, imagine reading this:

> "I'm not trying out my new barbecue when the boss comes to dinner!" Mark yelled. Then he added, "Let me make clear that by *boss* I mean our immediate supervisor. Not the president of the company, nor any of the other supervisors intervening. And I'm using *dinner* in the local vernacular, not to mean 'noontime meal,' as it is used in some parts of the United States. And when I said *barbecue*, I was speaking imprecisely, because I really meant grill, because *barbecue* generally refers to slower roasting, whereas I plan to cook over high heat. Anyway, my concern, of course, is that

my inexperience with the barbecue (that is, grill) will lead to inferior food, and I hope to impress the boss."

We've all known someone who talks that way (and we try to avoid him or her), but not many; most writers and speakers feel safe omitting some information.

How do writers (and speakers) decide what to omit? It depends on whom they're writing for (or speaking to). Have a look at Figure 4. What would the woman pictured there say if someone asked her, "What are you doing?"

If she were talking to a two-year-old she might say, "I'm typing on a computer." But that would be a ridiculous answer for an adult. Why? Because the typist should assume that the adult knows she's typing. A more appropriate response might be, "I'm filling out a form." Thus we calibrate our answers, providing more or less (or different) information depending on our judgment of what the other person knows, thereby deciding what we can safely leave out and what needs to be explained.★

FIGURE 4:
What would this woman say if someone asked her, "What are you doing?" The answer depends on who asked.

What happens when the knowledge is missing? Suppose you read the following sentence:

I believed him when he said he had a lake house, until he said it's only forty feet from the water at high tide.

If you're like me, you're confused. When I read a similar passage, my mother-in-law later explained to me that lakes don't have appreciable tides. I didn't have that bit of background knowledge that the author assumed I had, so I didn't understand the passage.

So, background knowledge in the form of vocabulary is not only necessary in order to understand a single idea (call it A), but it's also necessary in order to understand the connection between two ideas (A and B). In still other situations, writers present multiple ideas at the same time—A, B, C, D, E, and F—expecting that the reader will knit them together into a coherent whole. Have a look at this sentence from Chapter Thirty-Five of *Moby-Dick:*

Now, it was plainly a labor of love for Captain Sleet to describe, as he does, all the little detailed conveniences of his crow's-nest; but though he so enlarges upon many of these, and though he treats us to a very scientific account of his experiments in this crow's-nest, with a small compass he kept there for the purpose of counteracting the errors resulting from what is called the "local attraction" of all binnacle magnets; an error ascribable to the horizontal vicinity of the iron in the ship's planks, and in the Glacier's case, perhaps, to there having been so many broken-down blacksmiths among her crew; I say, that though the Captain is very discreet and scientific here, yet, for all his learned "binnacle deviations," "azimuth compass observations," and "approximate errors," he knows very well, Captain Sleet, that he was not so much immersed in those profound magnetic meditations, as to fail being attracted occasionally towards that well replenished little case-bottle, so nicely tucked in on one side of his crow's-nest, within easy reach of his hand.

Why is this sentence so hard to understand? You run out of room. It has a lot of ideas in it, and because it's one sentence, you try to keep them all in mind at once and to relate them to one another. But there are so many ideas, you can't keep them all in mind simultaneously. To use the terminology from Chapter One, you don't have sufficient capacity in working memory. In some situations, background knowledge can help with this problem.

To understand why, let's start with a demonstration. Read the following list of letters once, then cover the list and see how many letters you can remember.

X C N

N P H

D F B

I C I

A N C

A A X

Okay, how many could you remember? If you're like most people, the answer would perhaps be seven. Now try the same task with this list:

X

C N N

P H D

F B I

C I A

N C A A

X

You probably got many more letters correct with this second list, and you no doubt noticed that it's easier because the letters form acronyms that are familiar. But did you notice that the first and second lists are the same? I just changed the spacing to make the acronyms more apparent in the second list.

This is a working memory task. You'll remember from Chapter One that working memory is the part of your mind in which you combine and manipulate information—it's pretty much synonymous with consciousness. Working memory has a limited capacity (as discussed in Chapter One), so you can't maintain in your working memory all of the letters from list one. But you can for list two. Why? Because the amount of space in working memory doesn't depend on the number of letters; it depends on the number of meaningful objects. If you can remember seven individual letters, you can remember seven (or just about seven) meaningful acronyms or words. The letters *F, B,* and *I* together count as only one object because combined they are meaningful.

The phenomenon of tying together separate pieces of information from the environment is called *chunking.* The advantage is obvious: you can keep more stuff in working memory if it can be chunked. The trick, however, is that chunking works only when you have applicable factual knowledge in long-term memory. You will see *CNN* as meaningful only if you already know what CNN is. In the first list, one of the three-letter groups was *ICI.* If you speak French, you may have treated this group as a chunk, because *ici* is French for "here." If you don't have French vocabulary in your long-term memory, you would not treat *ICI* as a chunk. This basic effect—using background knowledge to group things in working memory—doesn't work only for letters. It works for anything. Bridge players can do it with hands of cards, dancing experts can do it with dance moves, and so forth.

So factual knowledge in long-term memory allows chunking, and chunking increases space in working memory. What does the ability to chunk have to do with reading comprehension? Well, I was saying before that if you read ideas A, B, C, D, E, and F, you would need to relate them to one another in order to comprehend their meaning. That's a lot of stuff to keep in working memory. But suppose you could *chunk* A through E into a single idea? Comprehension would be much easier. For example, consider this passage:

> Ashburn hit a ground ball to Wirtz, the shortstop, who threw it to Dark, the second baseman. Dark stepped on the bag, forcing out Cremin, who was running from first, and threw it to Anderson, the first baseman. Ashburn failed to beat the throw.

If you're like me this passage is hard to comprehend. There are a number of individual actions, and they are hard to tie together. But for someone who knows about baseball, it's a familiar pattern, like *CNN.* The sentences describe a double play.

A number of studies have shown that people understand what they read much better if they already have some background knowledge about the subject. Part of the reason is chunking. A clever study on this point was conducted with junior high school students.[2] Half were good readers and half were poor readers, according to standard reading tests. The researchers asked the students to read a story that described half an inning of a baseball game. As they read, the students were periodically stopped and asked to show that they understood what was happening in the story by using a model of a baseball field and players. The interesting thing about this study was that some of the students knew a lot about baseball and some knew just a little. (The researchers made sure that everyone could comprehend individual actions, for example, what happened when a player got a double.) The dramatic finding, shown in Figure 5, was that the students' knowledge of baseball determined how much they understood of the story. Whether they were "good readers" or "bad readers" didn't matter nearly as much as what they knew.

Thus, background knowledge allows chunking, which makes more room in working memory, which makes it easier to relate ideas, and therefore to comprehend.

Background knowledge also clarifies details that would otherwise be ambiguous and confusing. In one experiment illustrating this effect,[3] subjects read the following passage:

The procedure is actually quite simple. First, you arrange items into different groups. Of course one pile may be sufficient depending on how much there is to do. If you have to go somewhere else due to lack of facilities, that is the next step; otherwise, you are pretty well set. It is important not to overdo things. That is, it is better to do too few things at once than too many.

The passage went on in this vein, vague and meandering, and therefore very difficult to understand. It's not that

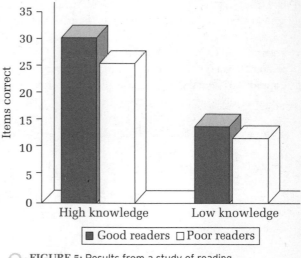

FIGURE 5: Results from a study of reading. As you would predict, the good readers (shaded bars) understood more than the poor readers (unshaded bars), but this effect is modest compared to the effect of knowledge. The people who knew a lot about baseball (leftmost columns) understood the passage much better than the people who didn't know a lot, regardless of whether they were "good" or "poor" readers, as measured by standard reading tests.

you're missing vocabulary. Rather, everything seems really vague. Not surprisingly, people couldn't remember much of this paragraph when asked about it later. They remembered much more, however, if they had first been told that the passage's title is "Washing Clothes." Have another look at the passage now that you know the title. The title tells you which background knowledge is relevant, and you recruit that knowledge to clarify ambiguities. For example, "Arrange items into groups" is interpreted as sorting darks, bright colors, and whites. This experiment indicates that we don't take in new information in a vacuum. We interpret new things we read in light of other information we already have on the topic. In this case, the title, "Washing Clothes," tells the reader which background knowledge to use to understand the passage. Naturally, most of what we read is not so vague, and we usually know which background information is relevant. Thus, when we read an ambiguous sentence, we seamlessly use background knowledge to interpret it, and likely don't even notice the potential ambiguities.

I've listed four ways that background knowledge is important to reading comprehension: (1) it provides vocabulary; (2) it allows you to bridge logical gaps that writers leave; (3) it allows chunking, which increases room in working memory and thereby makes it easier to tie ideas together; and (4) it guides the interpretation of ambiguous sentences. There are in fact other ways that background knowledge helps reading, but these are some of the highlights.

It's worth noting that some observers believe that this phenomenon—that knowledge makes you a good reader—is a factor in the fourth-grade slump. If you're unfamiliar with that term, it refers to the fact that students from underprivileged homes often read at grade level through the third grade, but then suddenly in the fourth grade they fall behind, and with each successive year they fall even farther behind. The interpretation is that reading instruction through third grade focuses mostly on decoding—figuring out how to sound out words using the printed symbols—so that's what reading tests emphasize. By the time the fourth grade rolls around, most students are good decoders, so reading tests start to emphasize *comprehension*. As described here, comprehension depends on background knowledge, and that's where kids from privileged homes have an edge. They come to school with a bigger vocabulary and more knowledge about the world than underprivileged kids. And because knowing things makes it easier to learn new things (as described in the next section), the gap between privileged and underprivileged kids widens.

Background Knowledge Is Necessary for Cognitive Skills

Not only does background knowledge make you a better reader, but it also is necessary to be a good thinker. The processes we most hope to engender in our students—thinking critically and logically—are not possible without background knowledge.

First, you should know that much of the time when we see someone apparently engaged in logical thinking, he or she is actually engaged in memory retrieval. As

I described in Chapter One, memory is the cognitive process of *first* resort. When faced with a problem, you will first search for a solution in memory, and if you find one, you will very likely use it. Doing so is easy and fairly likely to be effective; you probably remember the solution to a problem because it worked the last time, not because it failed. To appreciate this effect, first try a problem for which you *don't* have relevant background knowledge, such as the one shown in Figure 6.[4]

The problem depicted in Figure 6 is more difficult than it first appears. In fact, only about 15 or 20 percent of college students get it right. The correct answer is to turn over the A card and the 3 card. Most people get A—it's clear that if there is not an even number on the other side, the rule has been violated. Many people incorrectly think they need to turn over the 2 card. The rule does not, however, say what must be on the other side of a card with an even number. The 3 card must be flipped because if there is a vowel on the other side, the rule has been violated.

Now let's look at another version of the problem, shown in Figure 7.[5]

If you're like most people, this problem is relatively easy: you flip the beer card (to be sure this patron is over twenty-one) and you flip the 17 card (to be sure this kid isn't drinking beer). Yet logically the 17 card has the same role in the problem that the 3 card did in the previous version, and it was the 3 card that everyone missed. Why is it so much easier this time? One reason (but not the only one) is that the topic is familiar. You have background knowledge about the idea of a drinking age, and you know what's involved in enforcing that rule. Thus you don't need to reason logically. You have experience with the problem and you remember what to do rather than needing to reason it out.

In fact, people draw on memory to solve problems more often than you might expect. For example, it appears that much of the difference among the world's best chess players is *not* their ability to reason about the game or to plan the best move; rather, it is their memory for game positions. Here's a key finding that led to that conclusion. Chess matches are timed, with each player getting an hour to complete his or her moves in the game. On occasion there are so-called blitz tournaments in which players get just five minutes to make all of their moves in a match (Figure 8). It's no surprise that everyone plays a little bit worse in a blitz tournament. What's surprising is that the best players are still the best, the nearly best are still nearly best, and so on.[†] This finding indicates that whatever makes the best players better than everyone else is still present in blitz tournaments; whatever gives them their edge is *not* a process that takes a lot of time, because if it were they would have lost their edge in blitz tournaments.

It seems that it is memory that creates the differences among the best players. When

FIGURE 6: Each card has a letter on one side and a digit on the other. There is a rule: *If there is a vowel on one side, there must be an even number on the other side.* Your job is to verify whether this rule is met for this set of four cards, and to turn over the minimum number of cards necessary to do so. Which cards would you turn over?

FIGURE 7: You are to imagine that you are a bouncer in a bar. Each card represents a patron, with the person's age on one side and their drink on the other. You are to enforce this rule: *If you're drinking beer, then you must be twenty-one or over.* Your job is to verify whether this rule is met for this set of four people. You should turn over the minimum number of cards necessary to do so. Which cards would you turn over?

FIGURE 8: A device used to time a chess match. The black hand on each clock counts down the minutes remaining. After making a move, the player pushes the button above his clock, which stops it and causes his opponent's clock to restart. Players set identical amounts of time to elapse on each clock—just five minutes in a blitz tournament—representing the total time the player can take for all moves in the game. The flag near the twelve on each clock is pushed aside by the black hand as it approaches twelve. When the flag falls, the player has exceeded his allotted time, and so forfeits the match.

tournament-level chess players select a move, they first size up the game, deciding which part of the board is the most critical, the location of weak spots in their defense and that of their opponents, and so on. This process relies on the player's memory for similar board positions and, because it's a memory process, it takes very little time, perhaps a few seconds. This assessment greatly narrows the possible moves the player might make. Only then does the player engage slower reasoning processes to select the best among several candidate moves. This is why top players are still quite good even in a blitz tournament. Most of the heavy lifting is done by memory, a process that takes very little time. On the basis of this and other research, psychologists estimate that top chess players may have fifty thousand board positions in long-term memory. Thus background knowledge is decisive even in chess, which we might think is the prototypical game of reasoning.

That's not to say that all problems are solved by comparing them to cases you've seen in the past. You do, of course, sometimes reason, and even when you do, background knowledge can help. Earlier in this chapter I discussed chunking, the process that allows us to think of individual items as a single unit (for example, when C, N, and N become CNN), thereby creating more room in working memory. I emphasized that in reading, the extra mental space afforded by chunking can be used to relate the meaning of sentences to one another. This extra space is also useful when reasoning.

Here's an example. Do you have a friend who can walk into someone else's kitchen and rapidly produce a nice dinner from whatever food is around, usually to the astonishment of whoever's kitchen it is? When your friend looks in a cupboard, she doesn't see ingredients, she see recipes. She draws on extensive background knowledge about food and cooking. For example, have a look at the pantry in Figure 9.

A food expert will have the background knowledge to see many recipes here, for

FIGURE 9: Suppose you were at a friend's house and she asked you to make dinner with some chicken and whatever else you could find. What would you do?

example, wild rice cranberry stuffing or chicken with salsa over pasta. The necessary ingredients will then become a chunk in working memory, so the expert will have room in working memory to devote to other aspects of planning, for example, to consider other dishes that might complement this one, or to begin to plan the steps of cooking.

Chunking applies to classroom activities as well. For example, take two algebra students. One is still a little shaky on the distributive property, the other knows it cold. When the first student is trying to solve a problem and sees $a(b + c)$, he's unsure whether that's the same as $ab + c$, or $b + ac$, or $ab + ac$. So he stops working on the problem and substitutes small numbers into $a(b + c)$ to be sure he's got it right. The second student recognizes $a(b + c)$ as a chunk and doesn't need to stop and occupy working memory with this subcomponent of the problem. Clearly the second student is more likely to complete the problem successfully.

There is a final point to be made about knowledge and thinking skills. Much of what experts tell us they do in the course of thinking about their field *requires* background knowledge, even if it's not described that way. Let's take science as an example. We could tell students a lot about how scientists think, and they could memorize those bits of advice. For example, we could tell students that when interpreting the results of an experiment, scientists are especially interested in anomalous (that is, unexpected) outcomes. Unexpected outcomes indicate that their knowledge is incomplete and that this experiment contains hidden seeds of new knowledge. But for results to be unexpected, you must have an expectation! An expectation about the outcome would be based on your knowledge of the field. Most or all of what we tell students about scientific thinking strategies is impossible to use without appropriate background knowledge. (See Figure 10.)

The same holds true for history, language arts, music, and so on. Generalizations that we can offer to students about how to think and reason successfully in the field may *look* like

FIGURE 10: Scientists are good at "thinking like scientists," but doing so depends not just on knowing and practicing the thinking strategies, but also on having background knowledge that allows them to use the thinking strategies. This may be why a well-known geologist, H. H. Read, said, "The best geologist is the one who has seen the most rocks."

they don't require background knowledge, but when you consider how to apply them, they actually do.

Factual Knowledge Improves Your Memory

When it comes to knowledge, those who have more gain more. Many experiments have confirmed the benefit of background knowledge to memory using the same basic method. The researchers bring into the laboratory some people who have some expertise in a field (for example, football or dance or electronic circuitry) and some who do not. Everyone reads a story or a brief article. The material is simple enough that the people without expertise have no difficulty understanding it; that is, they can tell you what each sentence means. But the next day the people with background knowledge remember substantially more of the material than the people who do not have background knowledge.

You might think this effect is really due to attention. If I'm a basketball fan, I'll enjoy reading about basketball and will pay close attention, whereas if I'm not a fan, reading about basketball will bore me. But other studies have actually *created* experts. The researchers had people learn either a lot or just a little about subjects that were new to them (for example, Broadway musicals). Then they had them read other, new facts about the subject, and they found that the "experts" (those who had earlier learned a lot of facts about the subject) learned new facts more quickly and easily than the "novices" (who had earlier learned just a few facts about the subject).[6]

Why is it easier to remember material if you already know something about the topic? I've already said that if you know more about a particular topic, you can better understand new information about that topic; for example, people who know about baseball *understand* a baseball story better than people who don't. We remember much better if something has meaning. That generalization is discussed and refined in the next chapter, but to get a sense of this effect, read each of the following two brief paragraphs:

Motor learning is the change in capacity to perform skilled movements that achieve behavioral goals in the environment. A fundamental and unresolved question in neuroscience is whether there is a separate neural system for representing learned sequential motor responses. Defining that system with brain imaging and other methods requires a careful description of what specifically is being learned for a given sequencing task.

A chiffon cake replaces butter—the traditional fat in cakes—with oil. A fundamental and unresolved question in baking is when to make a butter cake and when to make a chiffon cake. Answering this question with expert tasting panels and other methods requires a careful description of what characteristics are desired for a cake.

The paragraph on the left is taken from a technical research article.[7] Each sentence is likely comprehensible, and if you take your time, you can see how they are connected: The first sentence provides a definition, the second sentence poses a problem, and the third states that a description of the thing under study (skills) is necessary before the problem can be addressed. I wrote the paragraph on the right to parallel the motor-skill paragraph. Sentence by sentence, the structure is the same. Which do you think you will remember better tomorrow?

The paragraph on the right is easier to understand (and therefore will be better remembered) because you can tie it to things you already know. Your experience tells you that a good cake tastes buttery, not oily, so the interest value of the fact that some are made with oil is apparent. Similarly, when the final sentence refers to "what characteristics are desired for a cake," you can imagine what those characteristics might be—fluffiness, moistness, and so on. Note that these effects aren't about comprehension; you can comprehend the paragraph on the left pretty well despite a lack of background knowledge. But some richness, some feeling of depth to the comprehension is missing. That's because when you have background knowledge your mind connects the material you're reading with what you already know about the topic, even if you're not aware that it's happening.

It's those connections that will help you remember the paragraph tomorrow. Remembering things is all about *cues* to memory. We dredge up memories when we think of things that are related to what we're trying to remember. Thus, if I said, "Try to remember that paragraph you read yesterday," you'd say to yourself, "Right, it was about cakes," and automatically (and perhaps outside of awareness) information about cakes would start to flit through your mind—they are baked . . . they are frosted . . . you have them at birthday parties . . . they are made with flour and eggs and butter . . . and suddenly, that background knowledge (that cakes are made with butter) provides a toehold for remembering the paragraph: "Right, it was about a cake that uses oil instead of butter." It's adding these lines from the paragraph to your background knowledge that makes the paragraph seem both better understood and easier to remember. The motor-skills paragraph, alas, is marooned, removed from any background knowledge, and so is more difficult to remember later.

This final effect of background knowledge—that having factual knowledge in long-term memory makes it easier to acquire still more factual knowledge—is worth contemplating for a moment. It means that the amount of information you retain depends on what you already have. So, if you have more than I do, you retain more than I do, which means you gain more than me. To make the idea concrete (but the numbers manageable), suppose you have ten thousand facts in your memory but I have only nine thousand. Let's say we each remember a percentage of new stuff, and that percentage is based on what's already in our memories. You remember 10 percent of the new facts you hear, but because I have less knowledge in long-term memory, I remember only 9 percent of new facts. Table 1 shows how many facts each of us has in long-term memory over the course of ten months, assuming we're each exposed to five hundred new facts each month.

By the end of ten months, the gap between us has widened from 1,000 facts to 1,043 facts. Because people who have more in long-term memory learn more easily, the gap

TABLE 1: A demonstration that, when it comes to knowledge, the rich get richer.

Months	Facts in your memory	% of new facts you remember	Facts in my memory	% of new facts I remember
1	10,000	10.000	9,000	9.000
2	10,050	10.050	9,045	9.045
3	10,100	10.100	9,090	9.090
4	10,151	10.151	9,135	9.135
5	10,202	10.202	9,181	9.181
6	10,253	10.253	9,227	9.227
7	10,304	10.304	9,273	9.273
8	10,356	10.356	9,319	9.319
9	10,408	10.408	9,366	9.366
10	10,460	10.460	9,413	9.413

is only going to get wider. The only way I could catch up is to make sure I am exposed to more facts than you are. In a school context, I have some catching up to do, but it's very difficult because you are pulling away from me at an ever-increasing speed.

I have of course made up all of the numbers in the foregoing example, but we know that the basics are correct—the rich get richer. We also know where the riches lie. If you want to be exposed to new vocabulary and new ideas, the places to go are books, magazines, and newspapers. Television, video games, and the sorts of Internet content that students lean toward (for example, social networking sites, music sites, and the like) are for the most part unhelpful. Researchers have painstakingly analyzed the contents of the many ways that students can spend their leisure time. Books, newspapers, and magazines are singularly helpful in introducing new ideas and new vocabulary to students.

❧ ❧

I began this chapter with a quotation from Einstein: "Imagination is more important than knowledge." I hope you are now persuaded that Einstein was wrong. Knowledge is more important, because it's a prerequisite for imagination, or at least for the sort of imagination that leads to problem solving, decision making, and creativity. Other great minds have made similar comments that denigrate the importance of knowledge, as shown in Table 2.

I don't know why some great thinkers (who undoubtedly knew many facts) took delight in denigrating schools, often depicting them as factories for the useless memorization of information. I suppose we are to take these remarks as ironic, or at least as interesting, but I for one don't need brilliant, highly capable minds telling me (and my children) how silly it is to know things. As I've shown in this chapter, the

TABLE 2: Quotations from great thinkers denigrating the importance of factual knowledge.

Education is what survives when what has been learned has been forgotten.	Psychologist B. F. Skinner
I have never let my schooling interfere with my education.	Writer Mark Twain
Nothing in education is so astonishing as the amount of ignorance it accumulates in the form of inert facts.	Writer Henry Brooks Adams
Your learning is useless to you till you have lost your textbooks, burnt your lecture notes, and forgotten the minutiae which you learned by heart for the examination.	Philosopher Alfred North Whitehead
We are shut up in schools and college recitation rooms for ten or fifteen years, and come out at last with a bellyful of words and do not know a thing.	Poet Ralph Waldo Emerson

cognitive processes that are most esteemed—logical thinking, problem solving, and the like—are intertwined with knowledge. It is certainly true that facts without the skills to use them are of little value. It is equally true that one cannot deploy thinking skills effectively without factual knowledge.

As an alternative to the quotations in Table 2, I offer a Spanish proverb that emphasizes the importance of experience and, by inference, knowledge: *Mas sabe El Diablo por viejo que por Diablo.* Roughly translated: "The Devil is not wise because he's the Devil. The Devil is wise because he's *old.*"

Implications for the Classroom

If factual knowledge makes cognitive processes work better, the obvious implication is that we must help children learn background knowledge. How can we ensure that that happens?

How to Evaluate Which Knowledge to Instill

We might well ask ourselves, *Which knowledge should students be taught?* This question often becomes politically charged rather quickly. When we start to specify what must be taught and what can be omitted, it appears that we are grading information on its importance. The inclusion or omission of historical events and figures, playwrights, scientific achievements, and so on, leads to charges of cultural bias. A cognitive scientist sees these issues differently. The question, *What should students be taught?* is equivalent not to *What knowledge is important?* but rather to *What knowledge yields the greatest cognitive benefit?* This question has two answers.

For reading, students must know whatever information writers assume they know and hence leave out. The necessary knowledge will vary depending on what students read, but most observers would agree that a reasonable minimum target would be to read a daily newspaper and to read books written for the intelligent layman on serious topics such as science and politics. Using that criterion, we may still be distressed that much of what writers assume their readers know seems to be touchstones of the culture of dead white males. From the cognitive scientist's point of view, the only choice in that case is to try to persuade writers and editors at the *Washington Post, Chicago Tribune,* and so on to assume different knowledge on the part of their readers. I don't think anyone would claim that change would be easy to bring about. It really amounts to a change in culture. Unless and until that happens, I advocate teaching that material to our students. The simple fact is that without that knowledge, they cannot read the breadth of material that their more knowledgeable schoolmates can, nor with the depth of comprehension.

The second answer to the question applies to core subject matter courses. *What should students know of science, of history, of mathematics?* This question is different than the first because the uses of knowledge in these subject areas are different than the uses of knowledge for general reading. Reading requires relatively shallow knowledge. I don't need to know much about a nebula to understand the word when it's used in a newspaper article; but if I'm studying astrophysics, I need to know much more.

Students can't learn everything, so what should they know? Cognitive science leads to the rather obvious conclusion that students must learn the concepts that come up again and again—the unifying ideas of each discipline. Some educational thinkers have suggested that a limited number of ideas should be taught in great depth, beginning in the early grades and carrying through the curriculum for years as different topics are taken up and viewed through the lens of one or more of these ideas. From the cognitive perspective, that makes sense.

Be Sure That the Knowledge Base Is Mostly in Place When You Require Critical Thinking

Our goal is not simply to have students know a lot of stuff—it's to have them know stuff in service of being able to think effectively. As emphasized in this chapter, thinking critically requires background knowledge. Critical thinking is not a set of procedures that can be practiced and perfected while divorced from background knowledge. Thus it makes sense to consider whether students have the necessary background knowledge to carry out a critical thinking task you might assign. For example, I once observed a teacher ask her fourth-grade class what they thought it would be like to live in a rain forest. Although the students had spent a couple of days talking about rain forests, they didn't have the background knowledge to give anything beyond rather shallow responses (such as "It would be rainy"). She asked the same question at the end of the unit, and the student's answers were much richer. One student immediately said she wouldn't want to live there because the poor soil and constant shade would mean she would probably have to include meat in her diet—and she was a vegetarian.

Shallow Knowledge Is Better Than No Knowledge

Some of the benefits of factual knowledge require that the knowledge be fairly deep—for example, we need detailed knowledge to be able to chunk. But other benefits accrue from shallow knowledge. As has been noted, we usually do not need to have detailed knowledge of a concept to be able to understand its meaning in context when we're reading. For example, I know almost nothing about baseball, but for general reading, a shallow definition such as "a sport played with a bat and ball, in which two teams oppose one another" will often do. Of course deep knowledge is better than shallow knowledge. But we're not going to have deep knowledge of everything, and shallow knowledge is certainly better than no knowledge.

Do Whatever You Can to Get Kids to Read

The effects of knowledge described in this chapter also highlight why reading is so important. Books expose children to more facts and to a broader vocabulary than virtually any other activity, and persuasive data indicate that people who read for pleasure enjoy cognitive benefits throughout their lifetime. I don't believe it is quite the case that any book is fine "as long as they're reading." Naturally, if a child has a history of resisting reading, I'd be happy if she picked up any book at all. But once she is over that hump, I'd start trying to nudge her toward books at the appropriate reading level. It's rather obvious that a student doesn't gain much from reading books several grades below her reading level. I'm all for reading for pleasure, but there are fun, fascinating books at every reading level, so why not encourage age-appropriate materials? It's just as obvious that a too difficult book is a bad idea. The student won't understand it and will just end up frustrated. The school librarian should be a tremendous resource and ally in helping children learn to love reading, and she is arguably the most important person in any school when it comes to reading.

Knowledge Acquisition Can Be Incidental

The learning of factual knowledge can be incidental—that is, it can happen simply by exposure rather than only by concentrated study or memorization. Think about all you have learned by reading books and magazines for pleasure, or by watching documentaries and the news on television, or through conversation with friends. School offers many of the same opportunities. Students can learn information from math problems, or through sample sentences when they are learning grammar, or from the vocabulary you use when you select a classroom monitor. Every teacher knows so much that students don't. There are opportunities to fold this knowledge into each school day.

Start Early

At the end of the last section I noted that a child who starts behind in terms of knowledge will fall even farther behind unless there is some intervention. There seems to be little doubt that this is a major factor in why some children fare poorly in school. Home environments vary a great deal. What sort of vocabulary do parents use? Do the parents ask the children questions and listen to the children's answers? Do they take their child to the museum or aquarium? Do they make books available to their children? Do the children observe their parents reading? All of these factors (and others) likely play a role in what children know on their first day of school. In other words, before a child meets her first teacher, she may be quite far behind the child sitting next to her in terms of how easy it is going to be for her to learn. Trying to level this playing field is a teacher's greatest challenge. There are no shortcuts and no alternatives to trying to increase the factual knowledge that the child has not picked up at home.

Knowledge Must Be Meaningful

Teachers should not take the importance of knowledge to mean that they should create lists of facts—whether shallow or detailed—for students to learn. Sure, some benefit might accrue, but it would be small. Knowledge pays off when it is conceptual and when the facts are related to one another, and that is not true of list learning. Also, as any teacher knows, such drilling would do far more harm by making students miserable and by encouraging the belief that school is a place of boredom and drudgery, not excitement and discovery. Most teachers also know that learning lists of unconnected facts is pretty hard to do. But what is a better way to ensure that students acquire factual knowledge, now that we've concluded it's so important? In other words, why do some things stick in our memory whereas other things slip away? That is the topic of the next chapter.

Notes

★ One of the pleasures of the experiences shared with a close friend is the "inside joke," a reference that only the two of you understand. Hence, if her best friend asked what she was doing, the typist might say, "I'm painting a gravel road"—their personal code, based on a shared experience, for a long, pointless task. That's one extreme of assuming information on the part of your audience.

† Tournament-level chess players all have rankings—a number representing their skill level—based on whom they have beaten and who has beaten them.

Bibliography

Less Technical

Chall, J. S., & Jacobs, V. A. (2003). Poor children's fourth-grade slump. *American Educator,* Spring, 14. This article makes the case that the precipitous drop in reading scores for disadvantaged children is due in part to a lack of background knowledge.

Lareau, A. (2003). *Unequal childhoods.* Berkeley: University of California Press. Fascinating ethnographic study of childhood in homes of different socioeconomic status.

More Technical

Alexander, P. A., Kulikowich, J. M., & Schulze, S. K. (1994). How subject matter knowledge affects recall and interest. *American Educational Research Journal, 31,* 313–337. One of many articles that show that people remember a lot of new information if they already know a lot about the domain.

Gobet, F., & Charness, N. (2006). Expertise in chess. In K. A. Ericsson, N. Charness, P. J. Feltovich, & R. R. Hoffman (Eds.), *The Cambridge handbook of expertise and expert performance* (pp. 523–539). Cambridge, UK: Cambridge University Press. This chapter summarizes much of the important research showing that knowledge is fundamental to chess skill.

Rosenshine, B., Meister, C., & Chapman, S. (1996). Teaching students to generate questions: A review of the intervention studies. *Review of Educational Research, 66,* 181–221. A review of studies of one type of reading comprehension strategy. The upshot is that the intervention works, but a few sessions of practice are just as effective as fifty sessions, which indicates that reading comprehension strategies are more akin to a quickly learned (and useful) trick than to a skill that requires practice.

Stanovich, K. E., & Cunningham, A. E. (1993). Where does knowledge come from? Specific associations between print exposure and information acquisition. *Journal of Educational Psychology, 85,* 211–229. Over the last twenty years, Cunningham and Stanovich have amassed a great deal of evidence showing that reading brings enormous cognitive benefits that are not available through other means.

3

Why Do Students Remember Everything That's on Television and Forget Everything I Say?

Question: Memory is mysterious. You may lose a memory created fifteen seconds earlier, such as when you find yourself standing in your kitchen trying to remember what you came there to fetch. Other seemingly trivial memories (for example, advertisements) may last a lifetime. What makes something stick in memory, and what is likely to slip away?

Answer: We can't store everything we experience in memory. Too much happens. So what should the memory system tuck away? Things that are repeated again and again? But what about a really important one-time event such as a wedding? Things that cause emotion? But then you wouldn't remember important yet neutral things (for example, most schoolwork). How can the memory system know what you'll need to remember later? Your memory system lays its bets this way: if you think about something carefully, you'll probably have to think about it again, so it should be stored. Thus your memory is not a product of what you want to remember or what you try to remember; it's a product of what you think about. A teacher once told me that for a fourth-grade unit on the Underground Railroad he had his students bake biscuits, because this was a staple food for runaway slaves. He asked what I thought about the assignment. I pointed out that his students probably thought for forty seconds about the relationship of biscuits to the Underground Railroad, and for forty minutes about measuring flour, mixing shortening, and so on. Whatever students think about is what they will remember. The cognitive principle that guides this chapter is:

> Memory is the residue of thought.

To teach well, you should pay careful attention to what an assignment will actually make students think about (not what you hope they will think about), because that is what they will remember.

The Importance of Memory

Every teacher has had the following experience: you teach what you think is a terrific lesson, full of lively examples, deep content, engaging problems to solve, and a clear message, but the next day students remember nothing of it except a joke you told and an off-the-subject aside about your family[1]—or worse, when you say, struggling to keep your voice calm, "The point of yesterday's lesson was that one plus one equals two," they look at you incredulously and say, "One plus one equals *two?*" Obviously, if the message of Chapter Two is "background knowledge matters," then we must closely consider how we can make sure that students acquire this background knowledge. So why do students remember some things and forget other things?

Let's start by considering why you fail to remember something. Suppose I said to you, "Can you summarize the last professional development seminar you attended?" Let's further suppose that you brightly answer, "Nope, I sure can't." Why don't you remember?

One of four things has happened, all of which are illustrated in Figure 1, a slightly elaborated version of the diagram of the mind that we've used before. You will recall that working memory is where you keep things "in mind," the location of consciousness. There is lots of information in the environment, most of which we are not aware of. For example, as I write this, the refrigerator is humming, birds are chirping outside, and there is pressure on my backside from the chair I'm sitting on—but none of

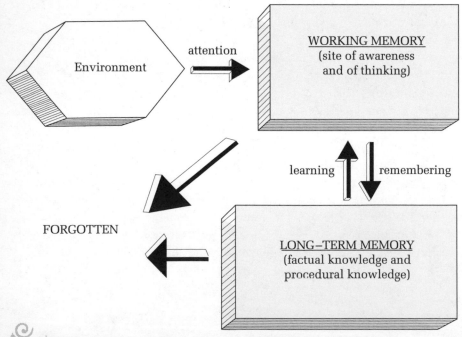

FIGURE 1: A slightly modified version of our simple diagram of the mind.

that was in my working memory (that is, my awareness) until I paid attention to it. As you can see in Figure 1, things can't get into long-term memory unless they have first been in working memory. So this is a somewhat complex way of explaining the familiar phenomenon: *If you don't pay attention to something, you can't learn it!* You won't remember much of the seminar if you were thinking about something else.

Information can enter working memory not only from the environment but also from long-term memory; that's what I mean when I refer to remembering, as shown by the labeled arrow. So another possible reason you don't remember is that the process by which things are drawn from long-term memory has failed. I discuss why that happens in Chapter Four.

A third possibility is that the information no longer resides in long-term memory— that it has been forgotten. I'm not going to discuss forgetting, but it's worth taking a moment to dispel a common myth. You sometimes hear that the mind records in exquisite detail everything that happens to you, like a video camera, but you just can't get at most of it—that is, memory failures are a problem of access. If you were given the right cue, the theory goes, anything that ever happened to you would be recoverable. For example, you may think you remember almost nothing of your childhood home, but when you revisit it the smell of the camellia blooms in the yard wipes away the years, and the memories that you thought were lost can be pulled out, like charms on a fine chain. Such experiences raise the possibility that *any* memory that you believe is lost can in principle be recovered again. Successful memory under hypnosis is often raised as evidence to support this theory. If the right cue (camellia blossoms or whatever it might be) can't be found, hypnosis allows you to probe the vault directly.

Although this idea is appealing, it's wrong. We know that hypnosis doesn't aid memory. That's easy to test in the laboratory. Simply give people some stuff to remember, then later hypnotize half of them and compare their recall to that of the people who were not hypnotized. This sort of experiment has been done dozens of times, and typical results are shown in Figure 2.[2] Hypnosis doesn't help. It does make you more confident that your memory is right, but it doesn't actually make your memory more accurate.

The other bit of evidence—that a good cue such as the odor of camellia can bring back long-lost memories—is much more difficult to test in a laboratory experiment, although most memory researchers believe that such recoveries are possible. But even if we allow that lost memories can be recovered in this way, it doesn't mean that *all* seemingly forgotten memories are recoverable—it just means that a few are. In sum, memory researchers see no reason to believe that all memories are recorded forever.

Now, let's return to our discussion of forgetting. Sometimes you *do* pay attention, so the material rattles around working memory for a while, but it never makes it to long-term memory. An example of a few such bits of information from my own experience are shown in Figure 3. *Lateral line* is a term I have looked up more than once, but I couldn't tell you now what it means. You doubtless have your own examples of things you are certain you *ought* to know, because you've looked them up or heard them (and thus they have been in working memory), yet they have never stuck in long-term memory.

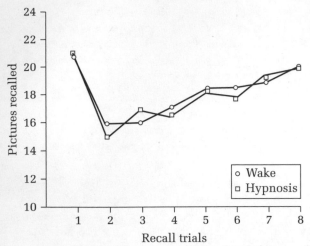

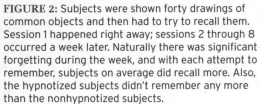

FIGURE 2: Subjects were shown forty drawings of common objects and then had to try to recall them. Session 1 happened right away; sessions 2 through 8 occurred a week later. Naturally there was significant forgetting during the week, and with each attempt to remember, subjects on average did recall more. Also, the hypnotized subjects didn't remember any more than the nonhypnotized subjects.

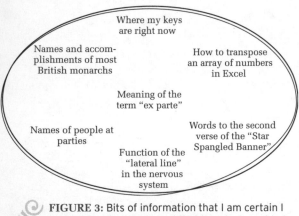

FIGURE 3: Bits of information that I am certain I have paid attention to and that thus have resided in my working memory but that have never made it into my long-term memory.

Just as odd is that some things have remained in your long-term memory for years although you had no intention of learning them; indeed, they held no special interest for you. For example, why do I know the jingle from the 1970s Bumble Bee tuna advertisement (Figure 4)?

You could make a good argument that understanding the difference between Figure 3 and Figure 4 is one of the core problems in education. We all know that students won't learn if they aren't paying attention. What's more mysterious is why, when they *are* paying attention, they sometimes learn and sometimes don't. What else is needed besides attention?

A reasonable guess is that we remember things that bring about some emotional reaction. Aren't you likely to remember really happy moments, such as a wedding, or really sad ones, such as hearing the news of the attacks on 9/11? You are, and in fact if you ask people to name their most vivid memories, they often relate events that probably had some emotional content, such as a first date or a birthday celebration (Figure 5).

Naturally we pay more attention to emotional events, and we are likely to talk about them later, so scientists have had to conduct very careful studies to show that it's really the emotion and not the repeated thought about these events that provides the boost to memory. The effect of emotion on memory is indeed real, and researchers have actually worked out some of the biochemistry behind it, but the emotion needs to be reasonably strong to have much impact on memory. If memory *depended* on emotion, we would remember little of what we encounter in school. So the answer *Things go into long-term memory if they create an emotional reaction* is not quite right. It's more accurate to say, *Things that create an emotional reaction will be better remembered, but emotion is not necessary for learning.*

Repetition is another obvious candidate for what makes learning work. Maybe the reason I remember the Bumble Bee tuna jingle (Figure 4) from thirty years

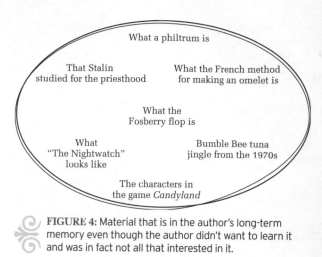

What a philtrum is

That Stalin studied for the priesthood

What the French method for making an omelet is

What the Fosberry flop is

What "The Nightwatch" looks like

Bumble Bee tuna jingle from the 1970s

The characters in the game *Candyland*

FIGURE 4: Material that is in the author's long-term memory even though the author didn't want to learn it and was in fact not all that interested in it.

ago is that I heard it a lot. Repetition is very important, and I discuss it in Chapter Five, but it turns out that not just any repetition will do. Material may be repeated

FIGURE 5: Emotional events tend to be well remembered, whether they are happy, such as a birthday party, or sad, such as a visit to the Holocaust Memorial in Berlin.

almost indefinitely and still not stick in your memory. For example, have a look at Figure 6. Can you spot the real penny among the counterfeits?

You have seen thousands of pennies in your lifetime—a huge number of repetitions. Yet, if you're like most people, you don't know much about what a penny looks like.[3] (The real penny is choice *A,* by the way.)

So repetition alone won't do it. It's equally clear that *wanting* to remember something is not the magic ingredient. How marvelous it would be if memory did work that way. Students would sit down with a book, say to themselves, "I want to remember this," and they would! You'd remember the names of people you've met, and you'd always know where your car keys are. Sadly, memory doesn't work that way, as demonstrated in a classic laboratory experiment.[4] Subjects were shown words on a screen one at a time and were asked to make a simple judgment about each word. (Some subjects had to say whether the word contained either an *A* or a *Q;* others had to say whether the word made them think of pleasant things or unpleasant things.) An important part of the experiment was that half of the subjects were told that their memory for the words would be tested later, after they had seen the whole list. The other subjects were not warned about the test. One of the remarkable findings was that knowing about the future test didn't improve subjects' memories. Other experiments have shown that telling subjects they'll be paid for each remembered word doesn't help much. So *wanting* to remember has little or no effect.

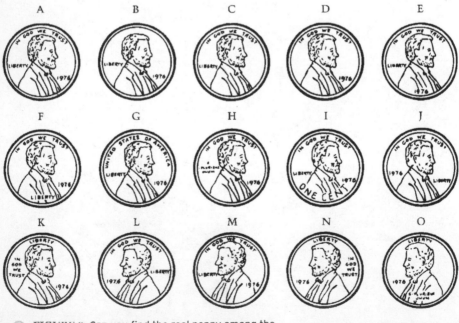

FIGURE 6: Can you find the real penny among the counterfeits? People are terrible at this task even though they have seen a penny thousands of times.

But there's another finding from this experiment that's still more important. Remember that when subjects saw each word they had to make a judgment about it—either about whether it contained an *A* or a *Q*, or about whether it made them think of pleasant or unpleasant things. The people who made the second type of judgment remembered nearly twice as many words as the people who made the first judgment. Now we seem to be getting somewhere. We've found a situation in which memory gets a big boost. But why would it help to think about whether a word is pleasant or not?

In this case it matters because judging pleasantness makes you think about what the word *means* and about other words that are related to that meaning. Thus, if you saw the word *oven,* you might think about cakes and roasts and about your kitchen oven, which doesn't work well, and so on. But if you were asked to judge whether *oven* contained an *A* or a *Q*, you wouldn't have to think about the meaning at all.

So it seems we're poised to say that *thinking about meaning is good for memory.* That's close, but not quite right. The penny example doesn't fit that generalization. In fact, the penny example shows just the opposite. I said that you've been exposed to a penny thousands of times (at least), and most of those times you were thinking about the penny's meaning—that is, you were thinking about its function, about the fact that it has monetary value, even if that value is modest. But having thought about the meaning of a penny doesn't help when you're trying to remember what the penny looks like, which is what the test in Figure 6 requires.

Here's another way to think about it. Suppose you are walking the halls of your school and you see a student muttering to himself in front of his open locker. You can't hear what he's saying, but you can tell from his tone that he's angry. There are several things you could focus on. You could think about the *sound* of the student's voice, you could focus on how he *looks,* or you could think about the *meaning* of the incident (why the student might be angry, whether you should speak to him, and so on). These thoughts will lead to different memories of the event the next day. If you thought only about the sound of the student's voice, the next day you'd probably remember that sound quite well but not his appearance. If you focused on visual details, then that's what you'd remember the next day, not what the student's voice sounded like. In the same way, if you think about the meaning of a penny but never about the visual details, you won't remember the visual details, even if they have been in front of your eyes ten thousand times.

Whatever you think about, that's what you remember. *Memory is the residue of thought.* Once stated, this conclusion seems impossibly obvious. Indeed, it's a very sensible way to set up a memory system. Given that you can't store everything away, how should you pick what to store and what to drop? Your brain lays its bets this way: If you don't think about something very much, then you probably won't want to think about it again, so it need not be stored. If you do think about something, then it's likely that you'll want to think about it *in the same way* in the future. If I think about what the student looks like when I see him, then his appearance is probably what I'll want to know about when I think about that student later.

There are a couple of subtleties to this obvious conclusion that we need to draw out. First, when we're talking about school, we usually want students to remember what things mean. Sometimes what things look like is important—for example, the beautiful facade of the Parthenon, or the shape of Benin—but much more often we want students to think about meaning. Ninety-five percent of what students learn in school concerns meaning, not what things look like or what they sound like.★ Therefore, a teacher's goal should almost always be to get students to think about meaning.

The second subtlety (again, obvious once it's made explicit) is that there can be different aspects of meaning for the same material. For example, the word *piano* has lots of meaning-based characteristics (Figure 7). You could think about the fact that it makes music, or about the fact that it's expensive, or that it's really heavy, or that it's made from fine-quality wood, and so on. In one of my all-time favorite experiments, the researchers led subjects to think of one or another characteristic of words by placing them in sentences—for example, "The moving men lugged the PIANO up the flight of stairs" or "The professional played the PIANO with a lush, rich sound."[5] The subjects knew that they needed to remember only the word in capitals. Later, experimenters administered a memory test for the words, with some hints. For *piano,* the hint was either "something heavy" or "something that makes music." The results showed that the subjects' memories were really good if the hint matched the way they had thought about *piano,* but poor if it didn't. That is, if the subjects read the moving men version of the sentence, hearing the cue "something that makes music" didn't help them remember *piano.* So it's not even enough to say, "You should think about meaning." You have to think about the right aspect of meaning.

FIGURE 7: Two pictures of a piano, each emphasizing a different characteristic.

Let me summarize what I've said about learning so far. For material to be learned (that is, to end up in long-term memory), it must reside for some period in working memory—that is, a student must pay attention to it. Further, *how* the student thinks of the experience completely determines what will end up in long-term memory.

The obvious implication for teachers is that they must design lessons that will ensure that students are thinking about the meaning of the material. A striking example of an assignment that didn't work for this reason came from my nephew's sixth-grade teacher. He was to draw a plot diagram of a book he had recently finished. The point of the plot diagram was to get him to think about the story elements and how they related to one another. The teacher's goal, I believe, was to encourage her students to think of novels as having *structure,* but the teacher thought that it would be useful to integrate art into this project, so she asked her students to draw pictures to represent the plot elements. That meant that my nephew thought very little about the relation between different plot elements and a great deal about how to draw a good castle. My daughter had completed a similar assignment some years earlier, but her teacher had asked students to use words or phrases rather than pictures. I think that assignment more effectively fulfilled the intended goal because my daughter thought more about how ideas in the book were related.

Now you may be thinking, "OK, so cognitive psychologists can explain why students have to think about what material means—but I really already knew they should think about that. Can you tell me *how* to make sure that students think about meaning?" Glad you asked.

What Good Teachers Have in Common

If you read Chapter One, you can easily guess a common technique that I would *not* recommend for getting students to think about meaning: trying to make the subject matter relevant to the students' interests. I know that sounds odd, so let me elaborate.

Trying to make the material relevant to students' interests doesn't work. As I noted in Chapter One, content is seldom the decisive factor in whether or not our interest is maintained. For example, I love cognitive psychology, so you might think, "Well, to get Willingham to pay attention to this math problem, we'll wrap it up in a cognitive psychology example." But Willingham is quite capable of being bored by cognitive psychology, as has been proved repeatedly at professional conferences I've attended. Another problem with trying to use content to engage students is that it's sometimes very difficult to do and the whole enterprise comes off as artificial. How would a math instructor make algebra relevant to my sixteen-year-old daughter? With a "real-world" example using cell phone minutes? I just finished pointing out that any material has different aspects of meaning. If the instructor used a math problem with cell phone minutes, isn't there some chance that my daughter would think about cell phones rather than about the problem? And that thoughts about cell phones would lead to thoughts about the text message she received earlier, which would remind her to change her picture on her Facebook profile, which would make her think about the zit she has on her nose . . . ?

So if content won't do it, how about style? Students often refer to good teachers as those who "make the stuff interesting." It's not that the teacher relates the material to students' interests—rather, the teacher has a way of interacting with students that they find engaging. Let me give a few examples from my own experience with fellow college-level teachers who are consistently able to get students to think about meaning.

Teacher A is the comedian. She tells jokes frequently. She never misses an opportunity to use a silly example.

Teacher B is the den mother. She is very caring, very directive, and almost patronizing, but so warm that she gets away with it. Students call her "Mom" behind her back.

Teacher C is the storyteller. He illustrates almost everything with a story from his life. Class is slow paced and low key, and he is personally quiet and unassuming.

Teacher D is the showman. If he could set off fireworks inside, he would do it. The material he teaches does not lend itself easily to demonstrations, but he puts a good deal of time and energy into thinking up interesting applications, many of them involving devices he's made at home.

Each of these teachers is one to whom students refer as making boring material interesting, and each is able to get students to think about meaning. Each style works well for the person using it, although obviously not everyone would feel comfortable taking on some of these styles. It's a question of personality.

Style is what the students notice, but it is only a part of what makes these teachers so effective. College professors typically get written student evaluations of their teaching at the end of every course. Most schools have a form for students to fill out that includes such items as "The professor was respectful of student opinions," "The professor was an effective discussion leader," and so on, and students indicate whether or not they agree with each statement. Researchers have examined these sorts of surveys to figure out which professors get good ratings and why. One of the interesting findings is that most of the items are redundant. A two-item survey would be almost as useful as a thirty-item survey, because all of the questions really boil down to two: Does the professor seem like a nice person, and is the class well organized? (See Figure 8.) Although they don't realize they are doing so, students treat each of the thirty items as variants of one of these two questions.

Although K–12 students don't complete questionnaires about their teachers, we know that more or less the same thing is true for them. The emotional bond between

FIGURE 8: How would each of these men be as a teacher? Dick Cheney is smart but seems rather cold and forbidding. The character Joey Tribbiani from *Friends* (played by actor Matt LeBlanc) is warm and friendly but not terribly smart. Teachers need to be both well organized and approachable.

students and teacher—for better or worse—accounts for whether students learn. The brilliantly well-organized teacher whom fourth graders see as mean will not be very effective. But the funny teacher, or the gentle storytelling teacher, whose lessons are poorly organized won't be much good either. Effective teachers have both qualities. They are able to connect personally with students, and they organize the material in a way that makes it interesting and easy to understand.

That's my real point in presenting these different types of teachers. When we think of a good teacher, we tend to focus on personality and on the way the teacher presents himself or herself. But that's only half of good teaching. The jokes, the stories, and the warm manner all generate goodwill and get students to pay attention. But then how do we make sure they think about meaning? That is where the second property of being a good teacher comes in—organizing the ideas in a lesson plan in a coherent way so that students will understand and remember. Cognitive psychology cannot tell us how to be personable and likable to our students, but I can tell you about one set of principles that cognitive psychologists know about to help students think about the meaning of a lesson.

The Power of Stories

The human mind seems exquisitely tuned to understand and remember stories—so much so that psychologists sometimes refer to stories as "psychologically privileged," meaning that they are treated differently in memory than other types of material. I'm going to suggest that organizing a lesson plan like a story is an effective way to help students comprehend and remember. It also happens to be the organizing principle used by the four teachers I described. The way in which each of them related emotionally to their students was very different, but the way they got their students to think about the meaning of material was identical.

Before we can talk about how a story structure could apply to a classroom, we must go over what a story structure is. There is not universal agreement over what makes a story, but most sources point to the following four principles, often summarized as *the four Cs*. The first C is *causality,* which means that events are causally related to one another. For example, "I saw Jane; I left the house" is just a chronological telling of events. But if you read, "I saw Jane, my hopeless old love; I left the house," you would understand that the two events are linked causally. The second C is *conflict*. A story has a main character pursuing a goal, but he or she is unable to reach that goal. In *Star Wars* the main character is Luke Skywalker, and his goal is to deliver the stolen plans and help destroy the Death Star. Conflict occurs because there is an obstacle to the goal. If Luke didn't have a worthy adversary—Darth Vader—it would make for a rather short movie. In any story the protagonist must struggle to meet his goal. The third C is *complications*. If Luke simply hammered away for ninety minutes at his goal of delivering the plans, that would be rather dull. Complications are subproblems that arise from the main goal. Thus, if Luke wants to deliver the plans, he must first get off his home planet, Tatooine—but he has no transportation. That's a complication that leads to his meeting another major character, Han Solo, and leaving the planet amid a hail of gunfire—always a movie bonus. The final C is *character*. A good story is built around strong, interesting characters, and the key to those qualities is *action*. A skillful storyteller shows rather than tells the audience what a character is like. For example, the first time the *Star Wars* audience sees Princess Leia she is shooting at storm troopers. Hence we don't need to be told that she is brave and ready to take action.

If we're trying to communicate with others, using a story structure brings several important advantages. First, stories are easy to comprehend, because the audience knows the structure, which helps to interpret the action. For example, the audience knows that events don't happen randomly in stories. There must be a causal connection, so if the cause is not immediately apparent, the audience will think carefully about the previous action to try to connect it to present events. For example, at one point in *Star Wars* Luke, Chewbacca, and Han are hiding on an Empire ship. They need to get to another part of the ship, and Luke suggests putting handcuffs on Chewbacca. That suggestion is mildly puzzling because Luke and Chewbacca are allies. The audience must figure out that Luke intends to pretend that Chewbacca is a prisoner and that he and Han are guards. The audience will do that bit of mental work because they know there must be a reason for this puzzling action.

Second, stories are interesting. Reading researchers have conducted experiments in which people read lots of different types of material and rate each for how interesting it is. Stories are consistently rated as more interesting than other formats (for example, expository prose), even if the same information is presented. Stories may be interesting because they demand the kind of inferences I discussed in Chapter One. Recall that problems (such as crossword puzzles) are interesting if they are neither too difficult nor too easy. Stories demand these medium-difficulty inferences, as in the handcuff example just presented.

Formal work in laboratory settings has shown that people rate stories as less interesting if they include too much information, thus leaving no inferences for the listener to make. But formal research is hardly necessary to confirm this phenomenon. We all have one or two friends who kill every story they tell with too much information. (See Figure 9.) An acquaintance of mine recently spent ten minutes relating that the owner of her favorite Chinese restaurant, which she hadn't visited in a year because they no longer took checks, informed her that he would make an exception for her. Delivered in fifteen seconds with cheeky pride, this story would have been cute. But with the details packed in (and no inferences for me to make) over the course of ten full minutes, it was all I could do not to scream.

Third, stories are easy to remember. There are at least two contributing factors here. Because comprehending stories requires lots of medium-difficulty inferences, you must think about the story's meaning throughout. As described earlier in the chapter, thinking about meaning is excellent for memory because it is usually meaning that you want to remember. Your memory for stories is also aided by their causal structure. If you remember one part of the plot, it's a good guess that the next thing that happened was caused by what you remember. For example, if you're trying to remember what happened after Luke put handcuffs on Chewbacca, you'll be helped by remembering that they were on an Empire ship (hence the ruse), which might help you remember that they went to rescue Princess Leia from the detention area.

FIGURE 9: Former head of state of the Soviet Union Mikhail Gorbachev was well known to reporters for giving answers that were boring because they were exhaustive. At a 1990 question-and-answer session with a dozen members of the U.S. Congress, Gorbachev answered the first question (about the Soviet economy) with a twenty-eight-minute monologue that covered all aspects of property rights while senators looked "glazed" or "weary." Senator Robert Dole later remarked, "He does have long answers."[6]

Putting Story Structure to Work

Now, all this about movies has been a diverting interlude (at least I hope it has), but what does it have to do with the classroom? My intention here is not to suggest that you simply tell stories, although there's nothing wrong with doing so. Rather, I'm suggesting something one step removed from that. Structure your lessons the way stories are structured, using the four Cs: causality, conflict, complications, and character. This doesn't mean you must do most of the talking. Small group work or projects or any other method may be used. The story structure applies to the way you *organize* the material that you encourage your students to think about, not to the methods you use to teach the material.

In some cases, the way to structure a lesson plan as a story is rather obvious. For example, history can be viewed as a set of stories. Events are caused by other events; there is often conflict involved; and so on. Still, thinking carefully about the four Cs as you consider a lesson plan can be helpful. It might encourage you to think about a different perspective from which to tell the story. For example, suppose you are planning a lesson on Pearl Harbor. You might first think of the organization shown in Figure 10. It's chronological and it makes the United States the main character—that is, events are taken from the U.S. point of view. Your goal is to get students to think about three points: U.S. isolationism before Pearl Harbor, the attack, and the subsequent "Germany first" decision and the putting of the United States on a war footing.

Suppose, however, you thought of the four Cs when you were telling this story. From that perspective, the United States is not the strong character. Japan is, because she had the goal that propelled events forward—regional domination—and she had significant obstacles to this goal—she lacked natural resources and she was embroiled in a protracted war with China. This situation set up a subgoal: to sweep up the European colonies in the South Pacific. Meeting that goal would raise Japan's standing as a world power and

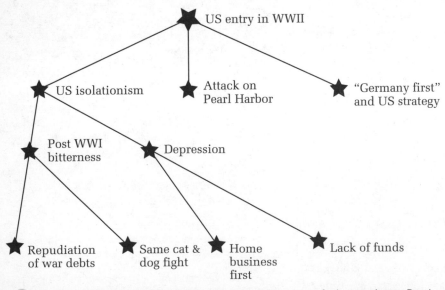

FIGURE 10: A tree diagram showing the typical structure of a lesson plan on Pearl Harbor. The organization is chronological.

Goal – become
a regional power

Finish war
with China

Get European
colonies

Deal with
US threat

Japan poor

European
countries
can't defend

US a
threat

Attack
the US

Dare US
to attack

Few raw
materials

US
embargo

Busy
fighting
Germany

Soviet
non-aggression
pact

Philippine
base

Battleships
at Pearl
Harbor

Long supply
lines

Not on
war footing

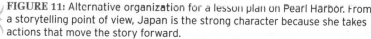

FIGURE 11: Alternative organization for a lesson plan on Pearl Harbor. From a storytelling point of view, Japan is the strong character because she takes actions that move the story forward.

help her obtain crucial raw materials for finishing the war with China. But that subgoal brought with it another complication. The United States was the other major naval power in the Pacific. How was Japan to deal with that problem? Rather than plundering the European colonies and daring the United States to intervene across five thousand miles of ocean (which the United States probably would not have done), Japan chose to try to eliminate the threat in one surprise attack. If one seeks to organize a lesson plan as a story, the one in Figure 10 is less compelling than the one in Figure 11.

My suggestion to use the Japanese point of view of Pearl Harbor doesn't mean that the American point of view should be ignored or deemed less important. Indeed, I could imagine a teacher in the United States electing not to use this story structure precisely because it takes a Japanese point of view in a U.S. history class. My point here is that using a story structure may lead you to organize a lesson in ways that you hadn't considered before. And the story structure does bring cognitive advantages.

Using storytelling to teach history seems easy, but can you really use a story structure in a math class? Absolutely. Here's an example of how I introduced the concept of a Z-score—a common way to transform data—when I taught introductory statistics. Begin with the simplest and most familiar example of probability—the coin flip. Suppose I have a coin that I claim is loaded—it always comes up heads. To prove it to you, I flip the coin and it does indeed come up heads. Are you convinced? College students understand that the answer should be no because there is a fifty-fifty chance that a fair coin would have come up heads. How about one hundred heads in a row? Clearly the odds are really small that a fair coin will come up heads one hundred times in a row, so you'd conclude that the coin isn't fair.

That logic—how we decide whether a coin is fishy or fair—is used to evaluate the outcome of many, if not most, scientific experiments. When we see headlines in the newspaper saying "New drug for Alzheimer's found effective" or "Older drivers less safe than younger" or "Babies who watch videos have smaller vocabularies," these conclusions rest on the same logic as the coin flip. How?

Suppose we want to know whether an advertisement is effective. We ask two hundred people, "Does Pepsodent give you sex appeal?" One hundred of these people have seen an advertisement for Pepsodent and one hundred have not. We want to know if the percentage of people in the saw-the-ad group who say it gives you sex appeal is higher than the percentage in the didn't-see-the-ad group who say it gives you sex appeal. The problem here is just like the problem with the coin-flip example. The odds of the saw-the-ad group being higher are around 50 percent. One of the two groups *has* to be higher. (If they happened to tie, we'd assume that the ad didn't work.)

The logic for getting around this problem is the same as it was for the coin-flip example. For the coin flip, we judged one hundred heads in a row as a highly improbable event *assuming that the coin was fair.* The odds of a fair coin coming up heads one hundred times in a row are very small. So if we observe that event—one hundred heads in a row—we conclude that our assumption must have been wrong. It's *not* a fair coin. So the saw-the-ad group being higher than the other group may also not be improbable—but what if that group was *much* more likely to answer yes? Just as we judged that there was something funny about the coin, so too we should judge that there is something funny about people who have seen the ad—at least funny when it comes to answering our question.

Of course *funny* in this context means "improbable." In the case of the coin, we knew how to calculate the "funniness," or improbability, of events because we knew the number of possible outcomes (two) and the probability of each individual outcome (.5), so it was easy to calculate the odds of successive events, as shown in Table 1. But here's our next problem: How do we calculate the "funniness," or probability, of other types of events? How much worse does the vocabulary of kids who watched videos have to be compared to that of kids who didn't watch videos before we're prompted to say, "Hey, these two groups of kids are not equal. If they were equal, their vocabularies would be equal. But their vocabularies are *very* unequal."

All of this description of coins, advertisements, and experiments is really a prelude to the lesson. I'm trying to get students to understand and care about the goal of the lesson, which is to explain how we can determine the probability of an event occurring by

TABLE 1: The odds, out of ten tosses, of tossing a successively greater number of heads.

Number of Tosses	Approximate Probability of All Heads
1	.5
2	.25
3	.125
4	.063
5	.031
6	.016
7	.008
8	.004
9	.002
10	.001

chance. That is the conflict for this lesson. Our worthy adversary in pursuit of this goal is not Darth Vader but the fact that most events we care about are not like coin flips—they don't have a limited number of outcomes (heads or tails) for which we know the probabilities (50 percent). That's a complication, which we address with a particular type of graph called a histogram; but implementing this approach leads to a further complication: we need to calculate the area under the curve of the histogram, which is a complex computation. The problem is solved by the Z-score, which is the point of the lesson (Figure 12).

A couple of things are worth noticing. A good deal of time—often ten or fifteen minutes of a seventy-five-minute class—is spent setting up the goal, or to put it another way, persuading students that it's important to know how to determine the probability of a chance event. The material covered during this setup is only peripherally related to the lesson. Talking about coin flips and advertising campaigns doesn't have much to do with Z-scores. It's all about elucidating the central conflict of the story.

Spending a lot of time clarifying the conflict follows a formula for storytelling from, of all places, Hollywood. The central conflict in a Hollywood film starts about twenty minutes into the standard one-hundred-minute movie. The screenwriter uses that twenty minutes to acquaint you with the characters and their situation so that when the main conflict arises, you're already involved and you care what happens to the characters. A film may start with an action sequence, but that sequence is seldom related to what will be the main story line of the movie. James Bond movies often start with a chase scene, but it's always part of some other case, not the case that Bond will work on for the bulk of the movie. The conflict for that case is introduced about twenty minutes into the film.

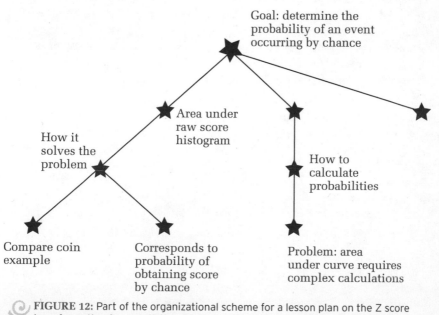

FIGURE 12: Part of the organizational scheme for a lesson plan on the Z score transformation for a statistics class.

When it comes to teaching, I think of it this way: The material I want students to learn is actually the answer to a question. *On its own, the answer is almost never interesting.* But if you know the question, the answer may be quite interesting. That's why making the question clear is so important. But I sometimes feel that we, as teachers, are so focused on getting to the answer, we spend insufficient time making sure that students understand the question and appreciate its significance.

Let me close this section by emphasizing again that there are many ways in which one can be a good teacher. I don't mean to imply that, according to cognitive science, every teacher should be using a story structure to shape his or her lesson plans. It's just one way that we can help ensure that students think about meaning. I am implying—well, no, I'm stating—that every teacher should get his or her students to think about the meaning of material—except sometimes, which is the subject of the next section.

But What If There Is No Meaning?

This chapter began by posing the question, *How can we get students to remember something?* The answer from cognitive science is straightforward: get them to think about what it means. In the previous section I suggested one method—story structure—for getting students to think about meaning.

It's fair to ask, however, whether there is material that students must learn that is pretty darn close to meaningless. For example, how can you emphasize meaning when students are learning the odd spelling of *Wednesday,* or that *enfranchise* means to give voting rights, or that *travailler* is the French verb for *work?* Some material just doesn't seem to have much meaning. Such material seems especially prevalent when one is entering a new field or domain of knowledge. A chemistry teacher might want students to learn in order the symbols for a few elements of the periodic table—but how can students think of the symbols H, He, Li, Be, B, C, N, O, and F in a deep, meaningful way when they don't know any chemistry?

Memorizing meaningless material is commonly called *rote memorization.* I will say more about what rote memory really is in Chapter Four, but for the moment let's just acknowledge that a student who has memorized the first nine elements of the periodic table has little or no idea why she has done so or what the ordering might mean. There are times when a teacher may deem it important for a student to have such knowledge ready in long-term memory as a stepping-stone to understanding something deeper. How can a teacher help the student get that material into long-term memory?

There is a group of memory tricks, commonly called *mnemonics,* that help people memorize material when it is not meaningful. Some examples are listed in Table 2.

I'm not a big fan of the peg-word and method-of-loci methods because they are hard to use for different sets of material. If I use my mental walk (back porch, dying pear tree, gravel driveway, and so on) to learn some elements of the periodic table, can I use the same walk to learn the conjugations for some French verbs? The problem is

TABLE 2: Common mnemonic methods. Mnemonics help you to memorize meaningless material.

Mnemonic	How It Works	Example
Peg word	Memorize a series of *peg words* by using a rhyme—for example, one is a bun, two is a shoe, three is a tree, and so on. Then memorize new material by associating it via visual imagery with the pegs.	To learn the list *radio, shell, nurse* you might imagine a radio sandwiched in a bun, a shoe on a beach with a conch in it, and a tree growing nurses' hats like fruit.
Method of loci	Memorize a series of locations on a familiar walk—for example, the back porch of your house, a dying pear tree, your gravel driveway, and so on. Then visualize new material at each "station" of the walk.	To learn the list *radio, shell, nurse* you might visualize a radio hanging by its cord on the banister of your back porch, someone grinding shells to use as fertilizer to revitalize the dying tree, and a nurse shoveling fresh gravel onto your driveway.
Link method	Visualize each of the items connected to one another in some way.	To learn the list *radio, shell, nurse* you might imagine a nurse listening intently to a radio while wearing large conch shells on her feet instead of shoes.
Acronym method	Create an acronym for the to-be-remembered words, then remember the acronym.	To learn the list *radio, shell, nurse* you might memorize the word RAiSiN using the capitalized letters as cues for the first letter of each word you are to remember.
First letter method	Similar to the acronym method, this method has you think of a phrase, the first letter of which corresponds to the first letter of the to-be-remembered material.	To learn the list *radio, shell,* nurse you could memorize the phrase "Roses smell nasty," then use the first letter of each word as a cue for the words on the list.
Songs	Think of a familiar tune to which you can sing the words.	To learn the list *radio, shell, nurse* you could sing the words to the tune of "Happy Birthday to You."

that there might be interference between the two lists; when I get to the gravel drive-way, I get confused about what's there because I've associated two things with it.

The other methods are more flexible because students can create a unique mnemonic for each thing they learn. The acronym method and the first-letter method are effec-tive, but students do need to have some familiarity with the material to be learned. I always think of the acronym HOMES when I'm trying to remember the names of the great lakes. If I didn't already know the names, these first-letter cues wouldn't do me much good, but the first letter of each lake's name pushes me over the edge from tip-of-the-tongue to ready recall. The first-letter method works in much the same way, and has the same limitation.

Setting to-be-learned information to music or chanting it to a rhythm also works quite well. Most of us learned the letters of the alphabet by singing the ABC song, and I've seen the state capitals set to the music of the "Battle Hymn of the Republic." Music and rhythm do make words remarkably memorable, and the song doesn't have to be particularly melodic. I can still remember the character Coach from the televi-sion show *Cheers* studying for a geography exam by singing (to the tune of "When the Saints Go Marching In"),

> Albania! Albania! You border on the Adriatic.
> Your land is mostly mountainous, and your main export is chrome.

The difficulty with songs is that they are more difficult to generate than the other mnemonic devices.

Why do mnemonics work? Primarily by giving you cues. The acronym ROY G. BIV gives you the first letter of each color in the spectrum of visible light. The first letter is quite a good cue to memory. As I discuss in the next chapter, memory works on the basis of cues. If you don't know anything about a topic, or if the things you're trying to remember are confusing because they are arbitrary (there's nothing about red that makes it obvious that its wavelength is longer than green), mnemonics help because they impose some order on the material.

Let me summarize what I've said in this chapter. If we agree that background knowl-edge is important, then we must think carefully about how students can acquire that background knowledge—that is, how learning works. Learning is influenced by many factors, but one factor trumps the others: students remember what they think about. That principle highlights the importance of getting students to think about the right thing at the right time. We usually want students to understand what things *mean*, which sets the agenda for a lesson plan. How can we ensure that students think about meaning? I offered one suggestion, which is to use the structure of a story. Stories are easily comprehended and remembered, and they are interesting; but one can't get students to *think* about meaning if the material *has* no meaning. In that case, it may be appropriate to use a mnemonic device.

Implications for the Classroom

Thinking about meaning helps memory. How can teachers ensure that students think about meaning in the classroom? Here are some practical suggestions.

Review Each Lesson Plan in Terms of What the Student Is Likely to Think About

This sentence may represent the most general and useful idea that cognitive psychology can offer teachers. The most important thing about schooling is what students will remember after the school day is over, and there is a direct relationship between what they think during the day and their later memory. So it's a useful double-check for every lesson plan to try to anticipate what the lesson will *actually* make students think about (rather than what you hope it will make them think about). Doing so may make it clear that students are unlikely to get what the teacher intended out of the lesson.

For example, I once observed a high school social studies class work in groups of three on projects about the Spanish Civil War. Each group was to examine a different aspect of the conflict (for example, compare it to the U.S. Civil War, or consider its impact on today's Spain) and then teach the remainder of the class what they had learned, using the method of their choice. The teacher took students to a computer laboratory to do research on the Internet. (They also used the library.) The students in one group noticed that PowerPoint was loaded on the computers, and they were very enthusiastic about using it to teach their bit to the other groups. The teacher was impressed by their initiative and gave his permission. Soon all of the groups were using PowerPoint. Many students had some familiarity with the basics of the program, so it could have been used effectively. The problem was that the students changed the assignment from "learn about the Spanish Civil War" to "learn esoteric features of PowerPoint." There was still a lot of enthusiasm in the room, but it was directed toward using animations, integrating videos, finding unusual fonts, and so on. At that point the teacher felt it was far too late to ask all of the groups to switch, so he spent much of the rest of the week badgering students to be sure their presentation had content, not just flash.

This story illustrates one of the reasons that experienced teachers are so good. This teacher clearly didn't let students use PowerPoint the next year, or possibly he thought of a way to keep them on task. Before you have accumulated these experiences, the next best thing is to think carefully about how your students will react to an assignment, and what it will make them think about.

Think Carefully About Attention Grabbers

Almost every teacher I have met likes, at least on occasion, to start class with an attention grabber. If you hook students early in the lesson, they should be curious to know what is behind whatever surprised or awed them. But attention grabbers may not always work. Here's a conversation I had with my oldest daughter when she was in sixth grade.

Dad: What did you do in school today?

Rebecca: We had a guest in science. He taught us about chemicals.

Dad: Oh yeah? What did you learn about chemicals?

Rebecca: He had this glass? That looked like water? But when he put this little metal thingy in it, it boiled. It was so cool. We all screamed.

Dad: Uh-huh. Why did he show you that?

Rebecca: I don't know.

The guest surely planned this demonstration to pique the class's interest, and that goal was met. I'm willing to bet that the guest followed the demonstration with an age-appropriate explanation of the phenomenon but that information was not retained. Rebecca didn't remember it because she was still thinking about how cool the demonstration was. You remember what you think about.

Another teacher once told me she wore a toga to class on the first day she began a unit on ancient Rome. I am sure that got her students' attention. I am also sure it continued to get their attention—that is, to distract them—once the teacher was ready for them to think about something else.

Here's one more example. A guest in a biology class asked the students to think of the very first thing they had ever seen. The students mulled that question over and generated such guesses as "the doctor who pulled me out," "Mom," and so forth. The guest then said, "Actually, the first thing each of you saw was the same. It was pinkish, diffuse light coming through your mother's belly. Today we're going to talk about how that first experience affected how your visual system developed, and how it continues to influence the way you see today." I love that example because it grabbed the students' attention and left them eager to hear more about the subject of the lesson.

As I alluded to earlier in the chapter, I think it is very useful to use the beginning of class to build student interest in the material, or as I put it, to develop the conflict. You might consider, however, whether the beginning of the class is really when they need an attention grabber. In my experience, the transition from one subject to another (or for older students, from one classroom and teacher to another) is enough to buy at least a few minutes of attention from students. It's usually the middle of the lesson that needs a little drama to draw students back from whatever reverie they might be in. But regardless of when it's used, think hard about how you will draw a connection between the attention grabber and the point it's designed to make. Will students understand the connection, and will they be able to set aside the excitement of the attention grabber and move on? If not, is there a way to change the attention grabber to help students make that transition? Perhaps the toga could be worn over street clothes and removed after the first few minutes of class. Perhaps the "metal thingy" demonstration would have been better *after* the basic principle was explained and students were prompted to predict what might happen.

Use Discovery Learning with Care

In discovery learning students learn by exploring objects, discussing problems with classmates, designing experiments, or any of a number of other techniques that use student inquiry rather than have the teacher tell students things. Indeed, the teacher ideally serves more as a resource than as the director of the class. Discovery learning has much to recommend it, especially when it comes to the level of student engagement. If students have a strong voice in deciding which problems they want to work on, they will likely be engaged in the problems they select, and will likely think deeply about the material, with attendant benefits. An important downside, however, is that what students will think about is less predictable. If students are left to explore ideas on their own, they may well explore mental paths that are not profitable. If memory is the residue of thought, then students will remember incorrect "discoveries" as much as they will remember the correct ones.

Now this doesn't mean that discovery learning should never be used, but it does suggest a principle for when to use it. Discovery learning is probably most useful when the environment gives prompt feedback about whether the student is thinking about a problem in the right way. One of the best examples of discovery learning is when kids learn to use a computer, whether they are learning an operating system, a complex game, or a Web application. Kids show wonderful ingenuity and daring under these circumstances. They are not afraid to try new things, and they shrug off failure. They learn by discovery! Note, however, that computer applications have an important property: when you make a mistake, it is immediately obvious. The computer does something other than what you intended. This immediate feedback makes for a wonderful environment in which "messing around" can pay off. (Other environments aren't like that. Imagine a student left to "mess around" with frog dissection in a biology class.) If the teacher does not direct a lesson to provide constraints on the mental paths that students will explore, the environment itself can do so effectively in a discovery learning context, and that will help memory.

Design Assignments So That Students Will Unavoidably Think About Meaning

If the goal of a lesson plan is to get students to think about the meaning of some material, then it's pretty clear that the best approach is one in which thinking about meaning is unavoidable. One of the things that has always amazed me as a memory researcher is the degree to which people do not know how their own memory system works. It doesn't do any good to tell people, "Hey, I'm going to test your memory for this list of words later," because people don't know what to do to make the words memorable. But if you give people a simple task in which they *must* think of the meaning—for example, rating how much they like each word—they will remember the words quite well.

This idea can be used in the classroom as well as in the laboratory. At the start of this chapter I said that asking fourth graders to bake biscuits was not a good way to get them to appreciate what life on the Underground Railroad was like because they spend too much time thinking about measuring flour and milk. The goal was to get students thinking about the experience of runaway slaves. So a more effective lesson would be to lead students to consider that experience by, for example, asking them where they supposed runaway slaves obtained food, how they were able to prepare it, how they were able to pay for it, and so forth.

Don't Be Afraid to Use Mnemonics

Many teachers I have met shudder at the use of mnemonics. They conjure up images of nineteenth-century schoolrooms with children chanting rhymes of the state capitals. But as bad as a classroom would be if a teacher used *only* mnemonics, they do have their time and place, and I don't think teachers should have this instructional technique taken away from them.

When is it appropriate to ask students to memorize something before it has much meaning? Probably not often, but there will be times when a teacher feels that some material—meaningless though it may be now—must be learned for the student to move forward. Typical examples would be learning letter-sound associations prior to reading, and learning vocabulary in both their native language and foreign languages.

It might also be appropriate to memorize some material using mnemonics in parallel with other work that emphasizes meaning. When I was in elementary school, I was not required to memorize the multiplication table. Instead I practiced using different materials and techniques that emphasized what multiplication actually means. These techniques were effective, and I readily grasped the concept. But by about fifth grade, not knowing the multiplication table by heart really slowed me down because the new things I was trying to learn had multiplication embedded in them. So every time I saw 8×7 within a problem I had to stop and figure out the product. In the sixth grade I moved to a new school, where my teacher quickly figured out what was going on and made me memorize the multiplication table. It made math a lot easier for me, although it took a few weeks before I would admit it.

Try Organizing a Lesson Plan Around the Conflict

There is a conflict in almost any lesson plan, if you look for it. This is another way of saying that the material we want students to know is the answer to a question—and the question is the conflict. The advantage of being very clear about the conflict is that it yields a natural progression for topics. In a movie, trying to resolve a conflict leads to new complications. That's often true of school material too.

Start with the material you want your students to learn, and think backward to the intellectual question it poses. For example, in a science class you might want sixth graders to know the models of the atom that were competing at the turn of the twentieth century. These are the answers. What is the question? In this story, the goal is to understand the nature of matter. The obstacle is that the results of different experiments appear to conflict with one another. Each new model that is proposed (Rutherford, cloud, Bohr) seems to resolve the conflict but then generates a new complication—that is, experiments to test the model seem to conflict with other experiments. If this organization seems useful to you, you might spend a good bit of time thinking about how to illustrate and explain to students the question, "What is the nature of matter?" Why should that question interest sixth graders?

As I've emphasized, structuring a lesson plan around conflict can be a real aid to student learning. Another feature I like is that, if you succeed, you are engaging students with the actual substance of the discipline. I've always been bothered by the advice "make it relevant to the students," for two reasons. First, it often feels to me that it doesn't apply. Is the Epic of Gilgamesh relevant to students in a way they can understand right now? Is trigonometry? Making these topics relevant to students' lives will be a strain, and students will probably think it's phony. Second, if I can't convince students that some material is relevant, does that mean I shouldn't teach it? If I'm continually trying to build bridges between students' daily lives and their school subjects, the students may get the message that school is always about them, whereas I think there is value, interest, and beauty in learning about things that don't have much to do with me. I'm not saying it never makes sense to talk about things students are interested in. What I'm suggesting is that student interests should not be the main driving force of lesson planning. Rather, they might be used as initial points of contact that help students understand the main ideas you want them to consider, rather than as the reason or motivation for them to consider these ideas.

In the previous chapter I argued that students must have background knowledge in order to think critically. In this chapter I discussed how memory works, in the hope that by understanding this we can maximize the likelihood that students will learn this background knowledge; much of the answer to how we can do this was concerned with thinking about meaning. But what if students don't understand the meaning? In the next chapter I discuss why it is hard for students to comprehend the meaning of complex material, and what you can do to help.

Note
* I made up this statistic.

Bibliography

Less Technical

Druxman, M. B. (1997). The art of storytelling: How to write a story . . . any story. Westlake Village, CA: Center Press. If you are interested in learning more about how stories are structured, this is a readable instruction manual.

Schacter, D. L. (2002). The seven sins of memory: How the mind forgets and remembers. Boston: Houghton Mifflin. A very readable account of why we remember and forget, with lots of examples that the reader can relate to, as well as descriptive studies of people with brain damage.

More Technical

Britton, B. K., Graesser, A. C., Glynn, S. M., Hamilton, T., & Penland, M. (1983). Use of cognitive capacity in reading: Effects of some content features of text. *Discourse Processes, 6,*

39–57. A study showing that people find stories more interesting than other types of text, even when they contain similar information.

Kim, S-i. (1999). Causal bridging inference: A cause of story interestingness. *British Journal of Psychology, 90*, 57–71. In this study the experimenter varied the difficulty of the inference that readers had to make to understand the text, and found that texts were rated as most interesting when the inferences were of medium-level difficulty.

Markman, A. B. (2002). Knowledge representation. In H. D. Pashler & D. L. Medin (Eds.), *Steven's handbook of experimental psychology*, Vol. 2: *Memory and cognitive processes*. (3rd ed., pp. 165–208). Hoboken, NJ: Wiley. A thorough treatment of how memories are represented in the mind, and of what representation actually means.

Meredith, G. M. (1969). Dimensions of faculty-course evaluation. *Journal of Psychology: Interdisciplinary and Applied, 73*, 27–32. An article showing that college students' attitudes toward professors are determined mostly by whether the professor is organized and seems nice. Not every study on this topic breaks it down in exactly this way, but this is the typical result.

4

Why Is It So Hard for Students to Understand Abstract Ideas?

Question: I once observed a teacher helping a student with geometry problems on the calculation of area. After a few false starts, the student accurately solved a word problem calling for the calculation of the area of a tabletop. A problem came up shortly thereafter that required the student to calculate the area of a soccer field. He looked blank and, even with prompting, did not see how this problem was related to the one he had just solved. In his mind, he had solved a problem about tabletops, and this problem was about soccer fields—completely different. Why are abstract ideas—for example, the calculation of area—so difficult to comprehend in the first place and, once comprehended, so difficult to apply when they are expressed in new ways?

Answer: Abstraction is the goal of schooling. The teacher wants students to be able to apply classroom learning in new contexts, including those outside of school. The challenge is that the mind does not care for abstractions. The mind prefers the concrete. That's why, when we encounter an abstract principle—for example, a law in physics such as, force = mass × acceleration—we ask for a concrete example to help us understand. The cognitive principle that guides this chapter is

> We understand new things in the context of things we already know, and most of what we know is concrete.

Thus it is difficult to comprehend abstract ideas, and difficult to apply them in new situations. The surest way to help students understand an abstraction is to expose them to many different versions of the abstraction—that is, to have them solve area calculation problems about tabletops, soccer fields, envelopes, doors, and so on. There are some promising new techniques to hurry this process.

Understanding Is Remembering in Disguise

In Chapter Two I emphasized that factual knowledge is important to schooling. In Chapter Three I described how to make sure that students acquire those facts—that is, I described how things get into memory But the assumption so far has been that students understand what we're trying to teach them. As you know, we can't bank on that. It's often difficult for students to understand new ideas, especially ones that are *really* novel, meaning they aren't related to other things they have already learned. What do cognitive scientists know about how students understand things?

The answer is that they understand new ideas (things they don't know) by relating them to old ideas (things they do know). That sounds fairly straightforward. It's a little like the process you go through when you encounter an unfamiliar word. If you don't know, for example, what *ab ovo* means, you look it up in a dictionary. There you see the definition "from the beginning." You know those words, so now you have a good idea of what *ab ovo* means.★

The fact that we understand new ideas by relating them to things we already know helps us understand some principles that are familiar to every teacher. One principle is the usefulness of analogies; they help us understand something new by relating it to something we already know about. For example, suppose I'm trying to explain Ohm's law to a student who knows nothing about electricity. I tell her that electricity is power created by the flow of electrons and that Ohm's law describes some influences on that flow. I tell her that Ohm's law is defined this way:

$$I = V/R$$

I is a measure of electrical current, that is, how fast the electrons are moving. *V*, or voltage, is the potential difference, which causes electrons to move. Potential will "even out," so if you have a difference in electrical potential at two points, that difference causes movement of electrons. *R* is a measure of resistance. Some materials are very effective conduits for electron movement (low resistance) whereas others are poor conduits (high resistance).

Although it's accurate, this description is hard to understand, and textbooks usually offer an analogy to the movement of water. Electrons moving along a wire are like water moving through a pipe. If there is high pressure at one end of the pipe (for example,

FIGURE 1: "force = mass X acceleration" is difficult to understand because it is abstract. It's easier to understand with a concrete example. Use the same force (a man swinging a bat) to hit different masses–a baseball or an automobile. We understand that the acceleration of the ball and the acceleration of the car will be quite different.

created by a pump) and lower pressure at the other end, the water will move, right? But the movement is slowed by friction from the inside of the pipe, and it can be slowed even more if we partially block the pipe. We can describe how fast the water moves with a measure such as gallons per minute. So, in terms of the water analogy, Ohm's law says that how fast water flows depends on the amount of water pressure and the amount of resistance in the pipes. That analogy is helpful because we are used to thinking about water moving in pipes. We call on this prior knowledge to help us understand new information, just as we call on our knowledge of the word *beginning* to help us understand *ab ovo*.

So new things are understood by relating them to things we already understand. That's why analogies help (Figure 1). Another consequence of our dependence on prior knowledge is our need for concrete examples. As you know, abstractions—for example, force = mass × acceleration, or a description of the poetical meter iambic pentameter—are hard for students to understand, even if all of the terms are defined. They need concrete examples to illustrate what abstractions mean. They need to hear:

> Is *this* the *face* that *launched* a *thous*and *ships?*
> And *burnt* the *top*less *towers* of *Illium?*

and

> Rough *winds* do *shake* the *darling buds* of *May*
> And *summer's lease* hath *all* too *short* a *date*

and other examples before they can feel they understand iambic pentameter.

Examples help not only because they make abstractions concrete. Concrete examples don't help much if they're not familiar. Suppose you and I had the following conversation:

ME: Different scales of measurement provide different types of information. Ordinal scales provide ranks, whereas on an interval scale the differences between measurements are meaningful.

YOU: That was utter gobbledygook.

ME: OK, here are some concrete examples. The Mohs scale of mineral hardness is an ordinal scale, whereas a successful Rasch model provides an interval measurement. See?

YOU: I think I'll go get a coffee now.

So it's not simply that giving concrete examples helps. (A better explanation of scales of measurement appears in Figure 2.) They must also be *familiar* examples, and the Mohs scale and the Rasch model are not familiar to most people. It's not the concreteness, it's the familiarity that's important; but most of what students are familiar with is concrete, because abstract ideas are so hard to understand.

FIGURE 2: There are four, and only four, ways that numbers on a scale relate to one another. In a *nominal* scale, each number refers to one thing but the numbers are arbitrary—for example, the number on a football jersey tells you nothing about the quality of the player. On an *ordinal* scale, the numbers are meaningful, but they tell you nothing about the distance between them. In a horse race, for example, you know that the first place horse was ahead of the second place finisher, but you don't know by how much. On an *interval* scale, not only are the numbers ordered, but also the intervals are meaningful—for example, the difference between 10 and 20 degrees is the same as the interval between 80 and 90 degrees. "Zero" on an interval scale is arbitrary; that is, zero degrees Celsius doesn't mean there is no temperature. A *ratio* scale, such as age, has a true zero point: that is, zero years means the absence of any years.

So, understanding *new* ideas is mostly a matter of getting the right *old* ideas into working memory and then rearranging them—making comparisons we hadn't made before, or thinking about a feature we had previously ignored. Have a look at the explanation of force in Figure 1. You know what happens when you hit a ball with a bat, and you know what happens when you hit a car with a bat, but have you ever before held those two ideas in mind at the same time and considered that the different outcome is due to the difference in mass?

Now you see why I claim that understanding is remembering in disguise. No one can pour new ideas into a student's head directly. Every new idea must build on ideas that the student already knows. To get a student to understand, a teacher (or a parent or book or television program) must ensure that the right ideas from the student's long-term memory are pulled up and put into working memory. In addition, the right features of these memories must be attended to, that is, compared or combined or somehow manipulated. For me to help you understand the difference between ordinal and interval measurement, it's not enough for me to say, "Think of a thermometer and think of a horse race." Doing so will get those concepts into working memory, but I also have to make sure they are compared in the right way (Figure 2).

FIGURE 3: Here are three other examples of scales of measurement: centimeters (as measured by a ruler), ratings from 1 to 7 of how much people like Shredded Wheat, and the numbered tracks on a CD. Which scale of measurement does each of these examples use?

We all know, however, that it's not really this simple. When we give students one explanation and one set of examples, do they understand? Usually not. Now that you have looked at Figure 2, would you say you "understand" scales of measurement? You know more than you did before, but your knowledge probably doesn't feel very deep, and you may not feel confident that you could identify the scale of measurement for a new example, say, centimeters on a ruler (Figure 3).

To dig deeper into what helps students understand, we need to address these two issues. First, even when students "understand," there are really degrees of comprehension. One student's understanding can be shallow while another's is deep. Second, even if students understand in the classroom, this knowledge may not transfer well to the world outside the classroom. That is, when students see a new version of what is at heart an old problem, they may think they are stumped, even though they recently solved the same problem. They don't know that they know the answer! In the next two sections I elaborate on each issue, that is, on shallow knowledge and on lack of transfer.

Why Is Knowledge Shallow?

Every teacher has had the following experience: You ask a student a question (in class or perhaps on a test), and the student responds using the exact words you used when you explained the idea or with the exact words from the textbook. Although his answer is certainly correct, you can't help but wonder whether the student has simply memorized the definition by rote and doesn't understand what he's saying.

This scenario brings to mind a famous problem posed by the philosopher John Searle.[1] Searle wanted to argue that a computer might display intelligent behavior without really *understanding* what it is doing. He posed this thought problem: Suppose a person is alone in a room. We can slip pieces of paper with Chinese writing on them under the door. The person in the room speaks no Chinese but responds to each message. He has an enormous book, each page of which is divided into two columns. There are strings of Chinese characters on the left and on the right. He scans the book until he matches the character string on the slip of paper to a string in the left-hand column. Then he carefully copies the characters in the right-hand column onto the piece of paper and slips it back under the door. We have posed a question in Chinese and the person in the room has responded in Chinese. Does the person in the room understand Chinese?

Almost everyone says no. He's giving sensible responses, but he's just copying them from a book. Searle provided this example to argue that computers, even if they display sophisticated behavior such as comprehending Chinese, aren't thinking in the way in which we understand the term. We might say the same thing about students. Rote knowledge might lead to giving the right response, but it doesn't mean the student is thinking.[†]

We can see examples of "sophisticated answers" that don't have understanding behind them in "student bloopers," which get forwarded with regularity via e-mail. Some of them are good examples of rote knowledge; for example, "Three kinds of blood vessels are arteries, vanes, and caterpillars," and "I would always read the works of the Cavalier poets, whose works always reflected the sentiment 'Cease the day!'" In addition to giving us a chuckle, these examples show that the student has simply memorized the "answer" without comprehension.

The fear that students will end up with no more than rote knowledge has been almost a phobia in the United States, but the truth is that rote knowledge is probably relatively rare. *Rote knowledge* (as I'm using the term) means you have *no* understanding of the material. You've just memorized words, so it doesn't seem odd to you that Cavalier poets, best known for light lyrics of love and their romantic view of life,

would have the philosophy "Cease the day!" (Figure 4).

Much more common than rote knowledge is what I call *shallow knowledge,* meaning that students have some understanding of the material but their understanding is limited. We've said that students come to understand new ideas by relating them to old ideas. If their knowledge is shallow, the process stops there. Their knowledge is tied to the analogy or explanation that has been provided. They can understand the concept only in the context that was provided. For example, you know that "Seize the day!" means "Enjoy the moment without worrying about the future," and you remember that the teacher said that "Gather ye rosebuds while ye may" (from Herrick's *To the Virgins, to Make Much of*

FIGURE 4: Seventeenth-century poet Robert Herrick, one of the best-known Cavalier poets.

Time) is an example of this sentiment. But you don't know much more. If the teacher provided a new poem, you would be hard put to say whether it was in the style of a Cavalier poet.

We can contrast shallow knowledge with deep knowledge. A student with deep knowledge knows more about the subject, and the pieces of knowledge are more richly interconnected. The student understands not just the parts but also the *whole*. This understanding allows the student to apply the knowledge in many different contexts, to talk about it in different ways, to imagine how the system as a whole would change if one part of it changed, and so forth. A student with deep knowledge of Cavalier poetry would be able to recognize elements of Cavalier ideals in other literatures, such as ancient Chinese poetry, even though the two forms seem very different on the surface. In addition, the student would be able to consider what-if questions, such as "What might Cavalier poetry have been like if the political situation in England had changed?" They can think through this sort of question because the pieces of their knowledge are so densely interconnected. They are interrelated like the parts of a machine, and the what-if question suggests the replacement of one part with another. Students with deep knowledge can predict how the machine would operate if one part were to be changed.

Obviously teachers want their students to have deep knowledge, and most teachers try to instill it. Why then would students end up with shallow knowledge? One obvious reason is that a student just might not be paying attention to the lesson. The mention of "rosebuds" makes a student think about the time she fell off her Razor Scooter into the neighbor's rose bush, and the rest of the poem is lost on her. There are other, less obvious reasons that students might end up with shallow knowledge.

Here's one way to think about it. Suppose you plan to introduce the idea of government to a first-grade class. The main point you want students to understand is that people living or working together set up rules to make things easier for everyone. You will use two familiar examples—the classroom and students' homes—and then introduce the idea that there are other rules that larger groups of people agree to live by. Your plan is to ask your students to list some of the rules of the classroom and consider why each rule exists. Then you'll ask them to list some rules their families have at home and consider why those rules exist. Finally, you'll ask them to name some rules that exist outside of their families and classroom, which you know will take a lot more prompting. You hope your students will see that the rules for each group of people— family, classroom, and larger community—serve similar functions. (See Figure 5.)

A student with rote knowledge might later report, "Government is like a classroom because both have rules." The student has no understanding of what properties the two groups have in common. The student with shallow knowledge understands that a government is like a classroom because both groups are a community of people who need to agree on a set of rules in order for things to run smoothly and to be safe. The student understands the parallel but can't go beyond it. So for example, if asked, "How is government *different* from our school?" the student would be stumped. A student with deep knowledge would be able to answer that question, and might successfully extend the analogy to consider other groups of people who might need to form rules, for example, his group of friends playing pickup basketball.

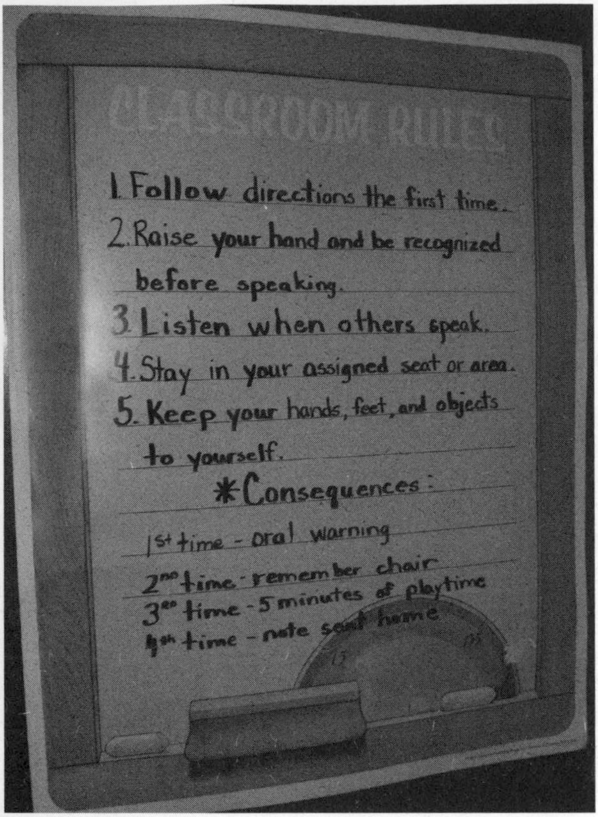

FIGURE 5: Most classrooms have rules, sometimes made public in a list like this one. Understanding the need for rules in a classroom may be a stepping-stone to understanding why a group of people working or playing together benefits from a set of rules.

This example can help us understand why all students might not get deep knowledge. The target knowledge—that groups of people need rules—is pretty abstract. It would appear, then, that the right strategy would be to teach that concept directly. But I said before that students don't understand abstractions easily or quickly. They need examples. That's why it would be useful to use the example of the classroom rules. In fact, a student might be able to say, "When people come together in a group, they usually need some rules," but if the student doesn't understand how a classroom, a family, and a community all exemplify that principle, he doesn't really get it. Thus deep knowledge means understanding *everything*—both the abstraction and the examples, and how they fit together. So, it is much easier to understand why most students have shallow knowledge, at least when they begin to study a new topic. Deep knowledge is harder to obtain than shallow.

Why Doesn't Knowledge Transfer?

This chapter is about students' understanding of abstractions. If someone understands an abstract principle, we expect they will show *transfer*. When knowledge transfers, that means they have successfully applied old knowledge to a new problem. Now, in some sense *every* problem is new; even if we see the same problem twice, we might see it in a different setting, and because some time has passed, we could say we have changed, even if only a little bit. Most often when psychologists talk about transfer they mean the new problem looks different from the old one, but we do have applicable knowledge to help us solve it. For example, consider the following two problems:

Jayne is reseeding her lawn. The lawn is 20 feet wide and 100 feet long. She knows that lawn seed costs $10 per bag, and that each bag will seed 1,000 square feet. How much money does Jayne need to seed her whole lawn?

Jon is varnishing his tabletop, which is 72 inches long and 36 inches wide. The varnish he needs costs $8 per can, and each can will cover 2,300 square inches. How much money does he need to buy the varnish?

Each problem requires calculating the area of a rectangle, dividing the result by the quantity offered in the purchasable unit (bags of seed or cans of varnish), rounding up to the nearest whole number, and then multiplying that result by the cost of each unit. The two problems differ in what psychologists call their *surface structure*—that is, the first problem is framed in terms of reseeding a lawn and the second in terms of varnishing a table. The problems have the same *deep structure* because they require the same steps for solution. The surface structure of each problem is a way to make the abstraction concrete.

Obviously the surface structure of a problem is unimportant to its solution. We would expect that a student who can solve the first problem should be able to solve the second problem, because it's the deep structure that matters. Nevertheless, people seem to be much more influenced by surface structure than they ought to be. In a classic experiment showing this influence,[2] the experimenters asked college students to solve the following problem:

Suppose you are a doctor faced with a patient who has a malignant tumor in his stomach. It is impossible to operate on the patient, but unless the tumor is destroyed, the patient will die. There is a kind of ray that can be used to destroy the tumor. If the rays reach the tumor all at once at a sufficiently high intensity, the tumor will be destroyed. Unfortunately, at this intensity the healthy tissue the rays pass through on the way to the tumor will also be destroyed. At lower intensities the rays are harmless to healthy tissue, but they will not affect the tumor either. What type of procedure might be used to destroy the tumor with the rays and at the same time avoid destroying the healthy tissue?

If a subject didn't solve it—and most couldn't—the experimenter told him or her the solution: send a number of rays of low intensity from different directions and have them all converge on the tumor; that way each weak ray can safely pass through the healthy tissue, but all of the rays will meet at the tumor, so it will be destroyed. The experimenter made sure the subjects understood the solution, then presented them with the following problem:

A dictator ruled a small country from a fortress. The fortress was situated in the middle of the country, and many roads radiated outward from it, like spokes on a wheel. A great general vowed to capture the fortress and free the country of the dictator. The general knew that if his entire army could attack the fortress at once, it could be captured. But a spy reported that the dictator had planted mines on each of the roads. The mines were set so that small bodies of men could pass over them safely, because the dictator needed to be able to move troops and workers about; however, any large force would detonate the mines.

Not only would this activity blow up the road, but the dictator would destroy many villages in retaliation. How could the general attack the fortress?

The two problems have the same deep structure: when combined forces will cause collateral damage, scatter your forces and have them converge from different directions on the point of attack. That solution may seem obvious, but it wasn't obvious to the subjects. Only 30 percent solved the second problem, even though they had *just heard* the conceptually identical problem and its solution.

Why was transfer so poor? The answer goes back to how we understand things. When we read or when we listen to someone talking, we are interpreting what is written or said in light of what we already know about similar topics. For example, suppose you read this passage: "Felix, the second named storm of the season to become a hurricane, gained strength with astonishing speed overnight, with wind speeds of 150 miles per hour and stronger gusts. Forecasters predict that the storm's path may take it to the coast of Belize within the next twelve hours." In Chapter Two I emphasized that prior knowledge is necessary to comprehend this sort of text. If you don't know what sort of storms are named and where Belize is, you don't fully understand these sentences. In addition, your background knowledge will also shape how you interpret *what comes next*. The interpretation of these sentences drastically narrows how you will interpret new text. For example, when you see the word *eye* you won't think of the organ that sees, nor of the loop at the top of a needle, nor of a bud on a potato, nor of a round spot on a peacock's feather, and so on. You'll think of the center of a hurricane. And if you see the word *pressure* you'll immediately think of atmospheric pressure, not peer-group pressure or economic pressure.

So our minds assume that new things we read (or hear) will be related to what we've just read (or heard). This fact makes understanding faster and smoother. Unfortunately, it also makes it harder to see the deep structure of problems. That's because our cognitive system is always struggling to make sense of what we're reading or hearing, to find relevant background knowledge that will help us interpret the words, phrases, and sentences. But the background knowledge that seems applicable almost always concerns the surface structure. When people read the tumor-and-rays problem, their cognitive system narrows the interpretation of it (just as it does for the hurricane sentences) according to what sort of background knowledge the reader has, and that's likely to be some knowledge of tumors, rays, doctors, and so forth. When the person later reads the other version of the problem, the background knowledge that seems relevant concerns dictators, armies, and fortresses. That's why transfer is so poor. The first problem is taken to be one about tumors, and the second problem is interpreted as being about armies.

The solution to this problem seems self-evident. Why not tell people to think about the deep structure as they read? The problem with this advice is that the deep structure of a problem is not obvious. Even worse, an almost limitless number of deep structures *might* be applicable. As you're reading about the dictator and the castle, it's hard to think simultaneously, Is the deep structure the logical form *modus tollens*? Is the deep structure one of finding the least common multiple? Is the deep structure Newton's third law of motion? To see the deep structure, you must understand how all parts of the problem relate to one another, and you must know which parts are important and which are not. The surface structure, on the other hand, is perfectly obvious: this problem is about armies and fortresses.

The researchers who did the tumor-and-rays experiment also tried telling the subjects, "Hey, that problem about the tumor and the rays might help you in solving this problem about armies and a fortress." When they told them that, almost everyone could solve the problem. The analogy was easy to see. The fortress is like the tumor, the armies are like the rays, and so on. So the problem was that people simply didn't realize that the two problems were analogous.

Other times we get poor transfer even when students know that a new problem shares deep structure with another problem they've solved. Picture a student who knows that the algebra word problem he's working on is an illustration of solving simultaneous equations with two unknowns, and there are examples in his textbook outlining the process. The surface structures of the solved textbook problem and the new problem are different—one is about a hardware store's inventory and the other is about cell phone plans—but the student knows he should disregard the surface structure and focus on the deep structure. To use the textbook example to help himself, however, he must figure out how the surface structure of each problem maps onto the deep structure. It's as though he understands the tumor problem and its solution, but when presented with the fortress problem he can't figure out whether the armies are playing the role of the rays, the tumor, or the healthy tissue. As you might guess, when a problem has lots of components and lots of steps in its solution, it more often happens that transfer is hampered by difficulty in mapping from a solved problem to the new one (Figure 6).

This discussion makes it sound as though it's virtually impossible for knowledge to transfer, as though we are powerless to look beyond the surface structure of what we read or hear. Obviously that's not true. *Some* of the subjects in the experiments I described did think of using the problem they had seen before, although the percentage who did so is surprisingly small. In addition, when faced with a novel situation, an adult will usually approach it in a more fruitful way than a child will. Somehow the adult is making use of his or her experience so that knowledge is transferring. In other words, it's a mistake to think of our old knowledge transferring

FIGURE 6: Students know that when they come across a math or science problem they can't solve, it's useful to look in their textbook for an analogous problem that is already solved. But finding an analogous problem doesn't guarantee a solution; the student may not be able to map the problem posed to the problem in the book.

to a new problem only when the source of that background knowledge is obvious to us. When we see the tumor-and-rays problem for the first time, we don't simply say, "I've never seen that problem or one like it before, so I give up." We have strategies for coming up with solutions, even though they may ultimately not work. Those strategies must be based on our experience—on other problems we've solved, things we know about tumors and rays, and so on. In that sense, we're *always* transferring knowledge of facts and knowledge of problem solutions, even when we feel like we've never seen this sort of problem before. Not very much is known about this type of transfer, however, precisely because it's so hard to trace where it comes from.

In the next chapter I discuss, among other things, how to maximize the chances that knowledge will transfer.

Implications for the Classroom

The message of this chapter seems rather depressing: it's hard to understand stuff, and when at last we do, it won't transfer to new situations. It's not quite that grim, but the difficulty of deep understanding shouldn't be underestimated. After all, if understanding were easy for students, teaching would be easy for you! Here are a few ideas on how to meet this challenge in the classroom.

To Help Student Comprehension, Provide Examples and Ask Students to Compare Them

As noted earlier, experience helps students to see deep structure, so provide that experience via lots of examples. Another strategy that might help (although it has not been tested extensively) is to ask students to compare different examples. Thus an English teacher trying to help her students understand the concept of *irony* might provide the following examples:

- In *Oedipus Rex,* the Delphic Oracle predicts that Oedipus will kill his father and marry his mother. Oedipus leaves his home in an effort to protect those he believes to be his parents, but thus sets in motion events that eventually make the prediction come true.

- In *Romeo and Juliet*, Romeo kills himself because he believes that Juliet is dead. When Juliet awakens, she is so distraught over Romeo's death that she commits suicide.

- In *Othello*, the noble Othello implicitly trusts his advisor Iago when he tells him that his wife is unfaithful, whereas it is Iago who plots against him.

The students (with some prompting) might come to see what each example has in common with the others. A character does something expecting one result, but the opposite happens because the character is missing a crucial piece of information: Oedipus is adopted, Juliet is alive, Iago is a deceiver. The audience knows that missing piece of information and therefore recognizes what the outcome will be. The outcome of each play is even more tragic because as the audience watch the events unfold, they know that the unhappy ending could be avoided if the character knew what they know.

Dramatic irony is an abstract idea that is difficult to understand, but comparing diverse examples of it may help students by forcing them to think about deep structure. Students know that the point of the exercise is not shallow comparisons such as, "Each play has men and women in it." As discussed in Chapter Two, we remember what we think about. This method of getting students to think about deep structure may help.

Make Deep Knowledge the Spoken and Unspoken Emphasis

You very likely let your students know that you expect them to learn what things mean—that is, the deep structure. You should also ask yourself whether you send unspoken messages that match that emphasis. What kind of questions do you pose in class? Some teachers pose mostly factual questions, often in a rapid-fire manner: "What does b stand for in this formula?" or "What happens when Huck and Jim get back on the raft?" The low-level facts are important, as I've discussed, but if that's all you ask about, it sends a message to students that that's all there is.

Assignments and assessments are another source of implicit messages about what is important. When a project is assigned, does it demand deep understanding or is it possible to complete it with just a surface knowledge of the material? If your students are old enough that they take quizzes and tests, be sure these test deep knowledge. Students draw a strong implicit message from the content of tests: if it's on the test, it's important.

Make Your Expectations for Deep Knowledge Realistic

Although deep knowledge is your goal, you should be clear-eyed about what students can achieve, and about how quickly they can achieve it. Deep knowledge is hard-won and is the product of much practice. Don't despair if your students don't yet have a deep understanding of a complex topic. Shallow knowledge is much better than no knowledge at all, and shallow knowledge is a natural step on the way to deeper knowledge. It may be years before your students develop a truly deep understanding, and the best that any teacher can do is to start them down that road, or continue their progress at a good pace.

In this chapter I've described why abstract ideas are so difficult to understand, and why they are so difficult to apply in unfamiliar situations. I said that practice in thinking about and using an abstract idea is critical to being able to apply it. In the next chapter I talk at greater length about the importance of practice.

Notes

*You may have noticed a problem. If we understand things by relating them to what we already know, how do we understand the *first* thing we ever learn? To put it another way, how do we know what *beginning* means? If we look that word up we see that it means "a start." And if we look up the word *start* we see it defined as "a beginning." It seems, then, that defining words with other words won't really work, because we quickly run into circular definitions.

This is a fascinating issue, but it's not central to the discussion in this chapter. A short answer is that some meanings are directly understandable from our senses. For example, you know what *red* means without resorting to a dictionary. These meanings can serve as anchors for other meanings, and help us avoid the circularity problem that we saw in the *ab ovo* example.

† Not everyone is persuaded by Searle's argument. Different objections have been raised, but the most common is that the example of the man alone in a room doesn't capture what computers might be capable of.

Bibliography

More Technical

Gentner, D., Loewenstein, J., & Thompson, L. (2003). Learning and transfer: A general role for analogical reasoning. *Journal of Educational Psychology, 95,* 393–405. Dedre Gentner has been champion of the idea of improving transfer by asking students to compare different examples.

Holyoak, K. J. (2005). Analogy. In K. J. Holyoak & R. G. Morrison (Eds.), *The Cambridge handbook of thinking and reasoning* (pp. 117–142). Cambridge, UK: Cambridge University Press. An overview of the uses of analogy in understanding new concepts and reasoning.

Mayer, R. E. (2004). Teaching of subject matter. *Annual Review of Psychology, 55,* 715–744. A comprehensive overview of specific subject matter domains, with special attention to transfer.

5

Is Drilling Worth It?

Question: Drilling has been given a bad name. The very use of the military term *drill* in place of the more neutral term *practice* implies something mindless and unpleasant that is performed in the name of discipline rather than for the student's profit. Then too, the phrase "drill and kill" has been used as a criticism of some types of instruction; the teacher drills the students, which is said to kill their innate motivation to learn. On the other side of this debate are educational traditionalists who argue that students *must* practice in order to learn some facts and skills they need at their fingertips—for example, math facts such as $5 + 7 = 12$. Few teachers would argue that drilling boosts students' motivation and sense of fun. Does the cognitive benefit make it worth the potential cost to motivation?

Answer: The bottleneck in our cognitive system is the extent to which we can juggle several ideas in our mind simultaneously. For example, it's easy to multiply 19×6 in your head, but nearly impossible to multiply $184,930 \times 34,004$. The processes are the same, but in the latter case you "run out of room" in your head to keep track of the numbers. The mind has a few tricks for working around this problem. One of the most effective is practice, because it reduces the amount of "room" that mental work requires. The cognitive principle that guides this chapter is

> It is virtually impossible to become proficient at a mental task without extended practice.

You cannot become a good soccer player if as you're dribbling, you still focus on how hard to hit the ball, which surface of your foot to use, and so on. Low-level processes like this must become automatic, leaving room for more high-level concerns, such as game strategy. Similarly, you cannot become good at algebra without knowing math facts by heart. Students must practice some things. But not all material needs to be practiced. In this chapter I elaborate on why practice is so important, and I discuss which material is important enough to merit practice, and how to implement practice in a way that students find maximally useful and interesting.

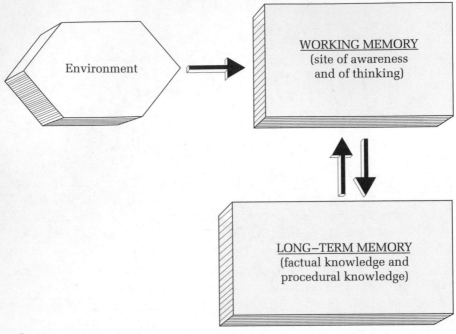

FIGURE 1: Our simple model of the mind.

Why practice? One reason is to gain a minimum level of competence. A child practices tying her shoelaces with a parent or teacher's help until she can reliably tie them without supervision. We also practice tasks that we can perform but that we'd like to improve. A professional tennis player can hit a serve into his opponent's court every time, but he nevertheless practices serving in an effort to improve the speed and placement of the ball. In an educational setting, both reasons—mastery and skill development—seem sensible. Students might practice long division until they master the process, that is, until they can reliably work long-division problems. Other skills, such as writing a persuasive essay, might be performed adequately, but even after students have the rudiments down, they should continue to practice the skill in an effort to refine and improve their abilities.

These two reasons to practice—to gain competence and to improve—are self-evident and probably are not very controversial. Less obvious are the reasons to practice skills when it appears you have mastered something and it's not obvious that practice is making you any better. Odd as it may seem, that sort of practice is essential to schooling. It yields three important benefits: it reinforces the basic skills that are required for the learning of more advanced skills, it protects against forgetting, and it improves transfer.

Practice Enables Further Learning

To understand why practice is so important to students' progress, let me remind you of two facts about how thinking works.

Figure 1 (which you also saw in Chapter One) shows that working memory is the site of thinking. Thinking occurs when you combine information in new ways. That information might be drawn from the environment or from your long-term memory or from both. For example, when you're trying to answer a question like "How are a butterfly and a dragonfly alike?" your thoughts about the characteristics of each insect reside in working memory as you try to find points of comparison that seem important to the question.

A critical feature of working memory, however, is that it has limited space. If you try to juggle too many facts or to compare them in too many ways, you lose track of what you're doing. Suppose I said, "What do a butterfly, a dragonfly, a chopstick, a pillbox, and a scarecrow have in common?"* These are simply too many items to compare simultaneously. As you're thinking about how to relate a pillbox to a chopstick, you've already forgotten what the other items are.

This lack of space in working memory is a fundamental bottleneck of human cognition. You could dream up lots of ways that your cognitive system could be improved—more accurate memory, more focused attention, sharper vision, and so on—but if a genie comes out of a lamp and offers you one way to improve your mind, ask for more working memory capacity. People with more capacity are better thinkers, at least for the type of thinking that's done in school. There is a great deal of evidence that this conclusion is true, and most of it follows a very simple logic: Take one hundred people, measure their working memory capacity, then measure their reasoning ability,† and see whether their scores on each test tend to be the same. To a surprising degree, scoring well on a working-memory test predicts scoring well on a reasoning test, and a poor working-memory score predicts a poor reasoning score (although working memory is not everything—recall that in Chapter Two I emphasized the importance of background knowledge).

Well, you're not going to get more working-memory capacity from a genie. And because this chapter is about practice, you might think I'm going to suggest that students do exercises that will improve their working memory. Sadly, such exercises don't exist. As far as anyone knows, working memory is more or less fixed—you get what you get, and practice does not change it.

There are, however, ways to cheat this limitation. In Chapter Two I discussed at length how to keep more information in working memory by compressing the information. In a process called *chunking,* you treat several separate things as a single unit. Instead of maintaining the letters *c, o, g, n, i, t, i, o,* and *n* in working memory, you chunk them into a single unit, the word *cognition.* A whole word takes up about the same amount of room in working memory that a single letter does. But chunking letters into a word requires that you know the word. If the letters were *p, a, z, z, e, s, c,* and *o,* you could chunk them effectively if you happened to know that *pazzesco* is an Italian word meaning "crazy." But if you didn't have the word in your long-term memory, you could not chunk the letters.

Thus, the first way to cheat the limited size of your working memory is through factual knowledge. There is a second way: you can make the processes that manipulate information in working memory more efficient. In fact, you can make them so efficient that they are virtually cost free. Think about learning to tie your shoes.

FIGURE 2: This fellow has recently learned to tie his shoes. He can tie them every time, but it consumes all of his working memory to do so. With practice, however, the process will become automatic.

Initially it requires your full attention and thus absorbs all of working memory, but with practice you can tie your shoes *automatically* (Figure 2).

What used to take all of the room in working memory now takes almost no room. As an adult you can tie your shoes while holding a conversation or even while working math problems in your head (in the unlikely event that the need arises). Another standard example, as I've already mentioned, is driving a car. When you first learn to drive, doing so takes all of your working-memory capacity. As with tying your shoes, it's the stuff you're *doing* that takes up the mental space—processes like checking the mirrors, monitoring how hard you're pressing the accelerator or brake to adjust your speed, looking at the speedometer, judging how close other cars are. Note that you're not trying to keep a lot of things (like letters) in mind simultaneously; when you do that, you can gain mental space by chunking. In this example, you're trying to do a lot of things in rapid succession. Of course, an experienced driver seems to have no problem in doing all of these things, and can even do other things, such as talk to a passenger.

Mental processes can become automatized. Automatic processes require little or no working memory capacity. They also tend to be quite rapid in that you seem to know just what to do without even making a conscious decision to do it. An experienced driver glances in the mirror and checks his blind spot before switching lanes, without thinking to himself "OK, I'm about to switch lanes, so what I need to do is check my mirrors and glance at the blind spot."

For an example of an automatic process, take a look at Figure 3 and name what each of the line drawings represents. Ignore the words and name the pictures.

As you doubtless noticed, sometimes the words matched the pictures and sometimes they didn't. It probably felt more difficult to name the pictures when there was a mismatch. That's because when an experienced reader sees a printed word, it's quite difficult not to read it. Reading is automatic. Thus the printed word *pants* conflicts with the word you are trying to retrieve, *shirt*. The conflict slows your response. A child just learning to read wouldn't show this interference, because reading is not automatic for him. When faced with the letters *p, a, n, t,* and *s*, the child would need to painstakingly (and thus slowly) retrieve the sounds associated with each letter, knit them together, and recognize that the resulting combination of sounds forms the word *pants*. For the experienced reader, those processes happen in a flash and are a good example of the properties of automatic processes: (1) They happen very quickly. Experienced readers read common words in less than a quarter of a second. (2) They are prompted by a stimulus in the environment, and if that stimulus is present, the process may occur even if you wish it wouldn't. Thus you know it would be easier not to read the words in Figure 3, but you can't seem to avoid doing so. (3) You are not aware of the components of the automatic

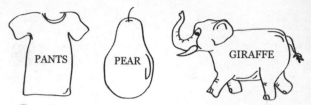

FIGURE 3: Name each picture, ignoring the text. It's hard to ignore when the text doesn't match the picture, because reading is an automatic process.

process. That is, the component processes of reading (for example, identifying letters) are never conscious. The word *pants* ends up in consciousness, but the mental processes necessary to arrive at the conclusion that the word is *pants* do not. The process is very different for a beginning reader, who is aware of each constituent step ("that's a *p*, which makes a 'puh' sound . . .").

The example in Figure 3 gives a feel for how an automatic process operates, but it's an unusual example because the automatic process interferes with what you're trying to do. Most of the time automatic processes help rather than hinder. They help because they make room in working memory. Processes that formerly occupied working memory now take up very little space, so there is space for *other* processes. In the case of reading, those "other" processes would include thinking about what the words actually mean. Beginning readers slowly and painstakingly sound out each letter and then combine the sounds into words, so there is no room left in working memory to think about meaning (Figure 4). The same thing can happen even to experienced readers. A high school teacher asked a friend of mine to read a poem out loud. When he had finished reading, she asked what he thought the poem meant. He looked blank for a moment and then admitted he had been so focused on reading without mistakes that he hadn't really noticed what the poem was about. Like a first grader, his mind had focused on word pronunciation, not on meaning. Predictably, the class laughed, but what happened was understandable, if unfortunate.

The same considerations are at play in mathematics. When students are first introduced to arithmetic, they often solve problems by using counting strategies. For example, they solve 5 + 4 by beginning with 5 and counting up four more numbers to yield the answer 9. This strategy suffices to solve simple problems, but you can see what happens as problems become more complex. For example, in a multidigit problem like 97 + 89, a counting strategy becomes much less effective. The problem is that this more complex problem demands that more processes be carried out in working memory. The student might add 7 and 9 by counting and get 16 as the result. Now the student must remember to write down the 6, then solve 9 + 8 by counting, while remembering to add the carried 1 to the result.

The problem is much simpler if the student has memorized the fact that 7 + 9 = 16, because she arrives at the correct answer for that subcomponent of the problem at a much lower cost to working memory. Finding a fact in long-term memory and putting it into working memory places almost no demands on working memory. It

FIGURE 4: This sentence is written in a simple code: 1 = A, 2 = B, 3 = C, and so on, with a new line denoting a new word. The efforts of a beginning reader are a bit like your efforts to decode this sentence, because the value of each letter must be figured out. If you make the effort to decode the sentence, try doing it without writing down the solution; like the beginning reader, you will likely forget the beginning of the sentence by the time you are decoding the end of the sentence.‡

1

12 15 14 7 19 20 1 14 4 9 14 7

7 15 1 12

15 6

8 21 13 1 14

5 21 13 1 14

5 14 17 21 9 18 25

9 19

20 15

21 14 4 5 18 19 20 1 14 4
15 21 18 19 5 12 22 5 19

is no wonder that students who have memorized math facts do better in all sorts of math tasks than students whose knowledge of math facts is absent or uncertain. And it's been shown that practicing math facts helps low-achieving students do better on more advanced mathematics.

I've given two examples of facts that students often need to retrieve: which sounds go with which letters when reading, and math facts such as $9 + 7 = 16$. In both cases, the automatization comes about through memory retrieval—that is, given the right stimulus in the environment, a useful fact pops into working memory. There are other sorts of automatization that entail other processes. Notable examples are handwriting and keyboarding. Initially, forming or keyboarding letters is laborious and consumes all of working memory. It's hard to think of the content of what you're trying to write because you have to focus on getting the letters right; but with practice, you are able to focus on the content. In fact, it's likely that other processes in writing become automatized as well. For more advanced students, rules of grammar and usage are second nature. They don't need to think about the agreement of a sentence's subject and verb, or about refraining from ending a sentence with a preposition.

To review, I've said that working memory is the place in the mind where thinking happens—where we bring together ideas and transform them into something new. The difficulty is that there is only so much room in working memory, and if we try to put too much stuff in there, we get mixed up and lose the thread of the problem we were trying to solve, or the story we were trying to follow, or the factors we were trying to weigh in making a complex decision. People with larger working-memory capacities are better at these thinking tasks. Although we can't make our working memory larger, we *can*, as I have said, make the contents of working memory smaller in two ways: by making facts take up less room through chunking, which requires knowledge in long-term memory and is discussed in Chapter Two; and by shrinking the processes we use to bring information into working memory or to manipulate it once it is there.

So now we get to the payoff: What is required to make these processes shrink, that is, to get them to become automatized? You know the answer: practice. There may be a workaround, a cheat, whereby you can reap the benefits of automaticity without paying the price of practicing. There may be one, but if there is, neither science nor the collected wisdom of the world's cultures has revealed it. As far as anyone knows, the only way to develop mental facility is to repeat the target process again and again and again.

You can see why I said that practice enables further learning. You may have "mastered" reading in the sense that you know which sounds go with which letters, and you can reliably string together sounds into words. So why keep practicing if you know the letters? You practice not just to get faster. What's important is getting so good at recognizing letters that retrieving the sound becomes automatic. If it's automatic, you have freed working-memory space that used to be devoted to retrieving the sounds from long-term memory—space that can now be devoted to thinking about meaning.

What's true of reading is true of most or all school subjects, and of the skills we want our students to have. They are hierarchical. There are basic processes (like retrieving math facts or using deductive logic in science) that initially are demanding of working memory but with practice become automatic. Those processes must become automatic in order for students to advance their thinking to the next level. The great philosopher Alfred North Whitehead captured this phenomenon in this comment: "It is a profoundly erroneous truism, repeated by all copybooks and by eminent people when they are making speeches, that we should cultivate the habit of thinking of what we are doing. The precise opposite is the case. Civilization advances by extending the number of important operations which we can perform without thinking about them."[1]

Practice Makes Memory Long Lasting

Several years ago I had an experience that I'll bet you've had. I happened on some papers from my high school geometry class. I don't think I could tell you three things about geometry today, yet here were problem sets, quizzes, and tests, all in my handwriting, and all showing detailed problem solutions and evidence of factual knowledge.

This sort of experience can make a teacher despair. The knowledge and skills that my high school geometry teacher painstakingly helped me gain have vanished, which lends credence to the occasional student complaint, "We're never gonna *use* this stuff." So if what we teach students is simply going to vanish, what in the heck are we teachers doing?

Well, the truth is that I remember a *little* geometry. Certainly I know much less now than I did right after I finished the class—but I do know more than I did before I took it. Researchers have examined student memory more formally and have drawn the same conclusion: we forget much (but not all) of what we have learned, and the forgetting is rapid.

In one study, researchers tracked down students who had taken a one-semester, college-level course in developmental psychology between three and sixteen years earlier.[2] The students took a test on the course material. Figure 5 shows the results, graphed separately for students who initially got an A in the course and students who got a B or lower. Overall, retention was not terrific. Just three years after the course, students remembered half or less of what they learned, and that percentage dropped until year seven, when it leveled off. The A students remembered more overall, which is not that surprising—they knew more to start with. But they forgot just like the other students did, and at the same rate.

So, apparently, studying hard doesn't protect against forgetting. If we assume that A students studied hard, we have to acknowledge that they forget at the same rate as everyone else. But something else does protect against forgetting: *continued* practice. In another study, researchers located people of varying ages and administered a test of basic algebra.[3] More than one thousand subjects participated in the experiment, so there were lots of people with varied backgrounds. Most important was that they varied in how much math they had taken.

Have a look at Figure 6, which shows scores on an algebra test.[§] Everyone took the test at the same time, for the purpose of the experiment. The scores are separated into four groups on the basis of how many math courses people took in high school and college. Focus first on the bottommost curve. It shows the scores of people who

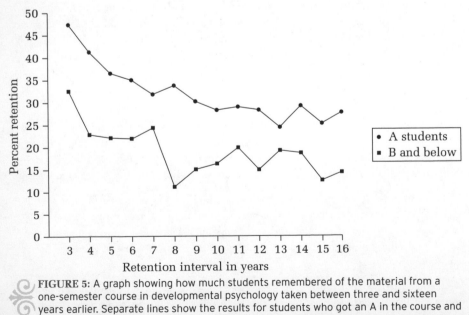

FIGURE 5: A graph showing how much students remembered of the material from a one-semester course in developmental psychology taken between three and sixteen years earlier. Separate lines show the results for students who got an A in the course and those who got a B or lower.

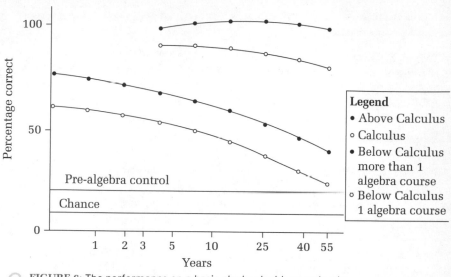

FIGURE 6: The performance on a basic algebra test by people who took the course between one month and fifty-five years earlier. The four lines of data correspond to four groups, separated by how much math they took *after* basic algebra.

took one algebra course. As you move from left to right, the time since they took the course increases, so the leftmost dot (around 60 percent correct) comes from people who *just* finished taking an algebra course, and the rightmost dot represents people who took algebra fifty-five years ago! The bottommost curve looks as you would expect it to; the longer it was since they took an algebra course, the worse they did on the algebra test.

The next curve up shows the scores of people who took more than one algebra course. As you might hope, they did better on the test but showed evidence of forgetting, just like the other group. Now look at the topmost line. These are the scores of people who took math courses beyond calculus. What's interesting about this line is that it's flat! People who took their last math course more than fifty years ago still know their algebra as well as people who took it five years ago!

What's going on here? This effect is *not* due to people who go on to take more math courses being smarter, or better at math. It's not shown in the graph, but just as in the previous study of developmental psychology, separating out students who got A's, B's, or C's in their first algebra course makes no difference—they all forget at the same rate. To put it another way, a student who gets a C in his first algebra course but goes on to take several more math courses will remember his algebra, whereas a student who gets an A in his algebra course but doesn't take more math will forget it. That's because taking more math courses guarantees that you will continue to think about and *practice* basic algebra. If you practice algebra enough, you will effectively never forget it. Other studies have shown exactly the same results with different subject matter, such as Spanish studied as a foreign language.

One thing these studies don't make clear is whether you get longer-lasting memory because you practice *more* or because your practice is stretched out over time.

Researchers have also investigated the importance of *when* you study. The *when* refers not to time of day but to how you space your studying. Let me put it this way: The previous section emphasizes that studying for two hours is better than studying for one. OK. Suppose you decide to study something for two hours. How should you distribute those 120 minutes? Should you study for 120 minutes in a row? Or for 60 minutes one day, then 60 minutes the next? How about 30 minutes each week for four weeks?

Doing a lot of studying right before a test is commonly known as *cramming*. I remember that when I was in school, students would brag that they had crammed for a test and done well but couldn't remember any of the material a week later. (An odd thing to brag about, I know.) Research bears out their boasts. If you pack lots of studying into a short period, you'll do okay on an immediate test, but you will forget the material quickly. If, on the other hand, you study in several sessions with delays between them, you may not do quite as well on the immediate test but, unlike the crammer, you'll remember the material longer after the test (Figure 7).

The spacing effect probably does not surprise teachers all that much; certainly we all know that cramming doesn't lead to long-lasting memory. In contrast, then, it makes sense that spreading out your studying would be better for memory than cramming. It's important, however, to make explicit two important implications of the spacing effect. We've been talking about the importance of practice, and we've just said that practice works better if it's spaced out. So you can get away with *less practice* if you space it out than if you bunch it together. Spacing practice has another benefit. *Practice,* as we've been using the term, means continuing to work at something that you've already mastered. By definition, that sounds kind of boring, even though it

Sunday	Monday	Tuesday	Wednesday	Thursday	Friday	Saturday
		1	2	3	4	5
6	7 study	8 study	9 study	10 study STUDY STUDY STUDY STUDY	11 test TEST	12
13	14	15	16	17	18 test TEST	19
20	21	22	23	24	25	26
27	28	29	30	31		

FIGURE 7: This simple figure illustrates what cognitive scientists call the spacing effect in memory. Student 1 (all capitals) studied four hours the day before the first test, whereas Student 2 (lowercase) studied for one hour on each of four days prior to the test. Student 1 will probably do a bit better on this test than Student 2, but Student 2 will do much better on the second test, administered a week later.

brings cognitive benefits. It will be somewhat easier for a teacher to make such tasks interesting for students if they are spaced out in time.

Practice Improves Transfer

In Chapter Four I discussed at length the challenges of transferring what you already know to new situations. Remember the problem of attacking the tumor with the rays? Even when subjects had just heard an analogous story that contained the problem solution (attacking a castle with small groups of soldiers), they didn't transfer the knowledge to the tumor-rays problem. As I mentioned then, transfer *does* occur, even when there is no obvious surface similarity between the situations. It occurs, but it's rare. What can we do to increase the odds? What factors make a student more likely to say, "Hey, I've seen problems like this before and I remember how to solve them!"?

It turns out that many factors contribute to successful transfer, but a few of them are especially important. As I've said, transfer is more likely when the surface structure of the new problem is similar to the surface structure of problems seen before. That is, the coin collector will more likely recognize that she can work a problem involving fractions if the problem is framed in terms of exchanging money rather than if a mathematically equivalent problem is framed as one of calculating the efficiency of an engine.

Practice is another significant contributor to good transfer. Working lots of problems of a particular type makes it more likely that you will recognize the underlying structure of the problem, even if you haven't seen this particular version of the problem before. Thus, reading the soldiers-and-fort story makes it just a little more likely that you'll know what to do when you encounter the tumor-and-rays problem; but if you've read *several* stories in which a force is dispersed and converges at a target point, it is much more likely that you'll recognize the deep structure of the problem.

To put it another way, suppose you read the following problem:

> You are planning a trip to Mexico. You learn that you will save a significant charge if you bring American dollars, exchange them for Mexican pesos once there, and pay for your hotel in cash. You're staying four nights and the hotel costs one hundred Mexican pesos per night. What other information do you need in order to calculate how many dollars to bring, and what calculations will you make?

Why does an adult immediately see the deep structure of this problem but a fourth grader does not?

FIGURE 8: You can immediately understand this as a permission rule: If you are not wearing both shoes and a shirt, you will not be served. This rule is easy to understand, not only because it is familiar but also because its deep structure is one you've encountered many times before.

Researchers think there are a couple of reasons that this is so. The first reason is that practice makes it more likely that you will really understand the problem in the first place and that you will remember it later. If you don't understand and remember the necessary principle, there's not much hope of it transferring to a new situation. That's pretty obvious. But suppose a fourth grader does understand division. Why doesn't he see that it would be useful in solving the problem? And how come you do?

Remember that in Chapter Four I said that as you read, the possible interpretations of what comes next are drastically narrowed. I used the example of a brief description of a hurricane and said that if you later saw the word *eye,* it wouldn't make you think of the eye with which you see, nor of the bud on a potato, and so on. The point is that as you're reading (or listening to someone talk), you are interpreting what is written, based on your associations with similar topics. You know about a lot of things that are associated with the word *eye,* and your mind picks out the right associates on the basis of the context of what you're reading. You don't have to make that selection consciously, thinking to yourself, "Hmm . . . now, I wonder which meaning of *eye* is appropriate here?" The right meaning just pops into mind.

Contextual information can be used not only for understanding individual words with several possible meanings, but also for understanding the *relationships* of different things in what you read. For example, suppose I start to tell you a story: "My wife and I vacationed on a small island, and there is a peculiar law there. If two or more people are walking together after dark, they must each have a pen with them. The hotel had a reminder on the door and pens everywhere, but when we went out to dinner the first night, I forgot to bring mine."

As you read this story, you effortlessly understand the point: I violated a rule. Note that you don't have relevant background knowledge about the surface structure—you've never heard a rule like this before and it doesn't make much sense. But you have lots of experience with the functional relationship of the story elements, that is, the story centers on a *permission.* In a permission relationship, you must fulfill a precondition before you are permitted to do something (Figure 8). For example, in order to drink alcohol, you must be at least twenty-one years old. In order to be out at night on a small island with another person, you must each have a pen. You also know that when there is a rule about permissions, there is usually a consequence for breaking the rule. Thus, when I start telling you my odd story, you can likely predict where the story will go next: it's going to center on whether I get caught without my pen, and if I do get caught, what the consequences are. A sympathetic listener would humor me by saying, "Oh no! Did you get caught without your pen?" If instead a listener said, "Really? What kind of pens did the hotel give you?" I would think he didn't understand the point of the story.

When I tell you the story about the pen, the idea of a "permission rule" pops into your mind as automatically as the meaning of "center of a hurricane" does when you read the word *eye* in the hurricane story. You understand *eye* in context because you have seen the word *eye* used to refer to the center of a hurricane many times before. In the same way, the deep structure of a permission rule pops into mind when you hear the story about the pens—and for the same reason you have lots of practice thinking about permission rules. The only difference between a permission rule and an eye is that the latter is a single word and the former is an idea shaped by the relationship of a few concepts. Your mind stores functional relationships between concepts (such as the idea of a permission) just as it stores the meaning of individual words.

The first time someone tells you that *eye* can refer to the center of a hurricane, you don't have any trouble understanding it; but that doesn't mean that the next time you encounter *eye* the correct meaning will pop into mind. It's more likely that you'll be a little puzzled and need to work out from the context what it means. For *eye* to be interpreted automatically the right way, you will need to see it a few times—in short, you will need to practice it. The same is true of deep structures. You might understand a deep structure the first time you see it, but that doesn't mean you're going to recognize it automatically when you encounter it again. In sum, practice helps transfer because practice makes deep structure more obvious.

In the next chapter I talk about what happens when we have had a great deal of practice with something. I compare experts and beginners, and describe the radical differences between them.

Implications for the Classroom

I began this chapter by pointing out that there are two obvious reasons to practice: to gain minimum competence (as when a teenager practices driving with a manual shift until he can reliably use it) and to gain proficiency (as when a golfer practices putts to improve her accuracy). I then suggested a third reason to continue practicing mental skills, even when there are not obvious improvements in our abilities. Such practice yields three benefits: (1) it can help the mental process become automatic and thereby enable further learning; (2) it makes memory long lasting; and (3) it increases the likelihood that learning will transfer to new situations.

The downside of this sort of practice is probably obvious: It is pretty boring to practice something if we're not getting any better at it! Here are some ideas about how we can reap some of the benefits of practice while minimizing the costs.

What Should Be Practiced?

Not everything can be practiced extensively. There simply isn't time, but fortunately not everything needs to be practiced. The benefits that I've said will accrue from practice provide some direction as to what sorts of things should be practiced. If practice makes mental processes automatic, we can then ask, *Which processes need to become automatic?* Retrieving number facts from memory seems to be a good candidate, as does retrieving letter sounds from memory. A science teacher may decide that his students need to have at their fingertips basic facts about elements. In general, the processes that need to become automatic are probably the building blocks of skills that will provide the most benefit if they are automatized. Building blocks are the things one does again and again in a subject area, and they are the prerequisites for more advanced work.

Space Out the Practice

There is no reason that all of the practice with a particular concept needs to occur within a short span of time or even within a particular unit. In fact, there is good reason to space out practice. As noted earlier, memory is more enduring when practice is spaced out, and practicing the same skills again and again is bound to be boring. It is better to offer some change. An additional benefit of spacing may be that students will get more practice in thinking through how to apply what they know. If all of the practice of a skill is bunched together, students will know that every problem they encounter must be a variant of the skill they are practicing. But if material from a week or a month or three months ago is sometimes included, students must think more carefully about how to tackle the problem, and about what knowledge and skills they have that might apply. Then too, remember that you are not the only teacher your students will encounter. An English teacher might think it's very important for her students to understand the use of imagery in poetry, but the knowledge and skills necessary to appreciate imagery will be acquired over years of instruction.

Fold Practice into More Advanced Skills

You may target a basic skill as one that needs to be practiced to the point of mastery, *but that doesn't mean that students can't also practice it in the context of more advanced skills.* For example, students may need to practice retrieving sounds in response to printed letters, but why not put that practice into the context of interesting reading, insofar as possible? A competent bridge player needs to be able to count the points in a hand as a guide to bidding, but if I were a bridge instructor I wouldn't have my students do nothing but count points until they could do so automatically. Automaticity takes *lots of practice.* The smart way to go is to distribute practice not only across time but also across activities. Think of as many creative ways as you can to practice the really crucial skills, but remember that students can still get practice in the basics while they are working on more advanced skills.

Notes

* These items may have other features in common, but I selected them because they are all compound words.

† Working memory capacity is usually tested by having people do some simple mental work while they simultaneously try to maintain some information in working memory. For example, one measure requires the subject to listen to a mixture of letters and digits (for example, 3T41P8) and then recite back the digits followed by the letters, in order (that is, 1348PT). This task requires that the subject remember which digits and letters were said while simultaneously comparing them to get the order right. The experimenter administers multiple trials, varying the number of digits and letters to get an estimate of the maximum number the subject can get right. There are lots of ways to measure reasoning; standard IQ tests are sometimes used, or tests more specifically focused on reasoning, with problems like "If P is true, then Q is true. Q is not true. What, if anything, follows?" There is also a reliable relationship between working memory and reading comprehension.

‡ This exercise could be taken as another example of how background knowledge can help you to learn. The sentence translates to "A long-standing goal of human inquiry is to understand ourselves," which is the first sentence from another book I wrote, *Cognition,* which I expect is unfamiliar to you. Think how much easier the decoding would have been, and how much easier the translation would be to remember, if the coded sentence were something in your long-term memory, such as, "In the beginning, God created the heavens and the earth."

§ You'll notice that the curves in this graph seem remarkably smooth and consistent. There are actually many factors that contribute to students' retention of algebra. This graph shows performance after these other factors have been statistically removed, so the graph is an idealization that makes it easier to visualize the effect of the number of math courses taken. You're not seeing the raw scores on this graph, but it is a statistically accurate representation of the data.

Bibliography

Less Technical

Rohrer, D., & Pashler, H. (2007). Increasing retention without increasing study time. *Current Directions in Psychological Science, 16,* 183–186. A fairly readable short review of the studies showing that distributed practice leads to more enduring memories, and therefore requires less time than practice that is lumped together.

More Technical

Ackerman, P. L., Beier, M. E., & Boyle, M. O. (2005). Working memory and intelligence: The same or different constructs? *Psychological Bulletin, 131,* 30–60. In this comprehensive review the authors argue that the relationship between working memory and intelligence is lower than everyone thinks it is—but the "lower" estimate the authors offer is still quite high! It's followed by responses from three other research teams.

Cepeda, N. J., Pashler, H., & Vul, E. (2006). Distributed practice in verbal recall tasks: A review and quantitative synthesis. *Psychological Bulletin, 132,* 354–380. A comprehensive review of the effect of distributed practice on memory.

Cumming, J., & Elkins, J. (1999). Lack of automaticity in the basic addition facts as a characteristic of arithmetic learning problems and instructional needs. *Mathematical Cognition, 5,* 149–180. This is one of many articles verifying that students who do not know their basic math facts to the point of automaticity have problems with higher-level math.

6

What's the Secret to Getting Students to Think Like Real Scientists, Mathematicians, and Historians?

Question: Educators and policymakers sometimes express frustration that curricula seem so far removed from the subjects they purport to cover. For example, history curricula emphasize facts and dates. The good curricula try to give students some sense of the debates within history. (I once heard an educator rail at the idea of a textbook summing up "*the* causes of the U.S. Civil War" as though they were a settled matter.) But very few curricula encourage students to think as historians do—that is, to analyze documents and evidence and build a case for an interpretation of history. Similarly, science curricula have students memorize facts and conduct lab experiments in which predictable phenomena are observed, but students do not practice actual scientific thinking, the exploration and problem solving that *are* science. What can be done to get students to think like scientists, historians, and mathematicians?

Answer: This protest against school curricula has a surface plausibility: How can we expect to train the next generation of scientists if we are not training them to do what scientists actually do? But a flawed assumption underlies the logic, namely that students are cognitively capable of doing what scientists or historians do. The cognitive principle that guides this chapter is:

> Cognition early in training is fundamentally different from cognition late in training.

It's not just that students know less than experts; it's also that what they know is organized differently in their memory. Expert scientists did not think like experts-in-training when they started out. They thought like novices. In truth, no one thinks like a scientist or a historian without a great deal of training. This conclusion doesn't mean that students should never try to write a poem or conduct a scientific experiment; but teachers and administrators should have a clear idea of what such assignments will do for students.

Think back to your science classes in middle and high school. If you're like me, they were structured as follows: (1) at home you read a textbook that explained some principle of biology, chemistry, or physics; (2) the next day the teacher explained the principle; (3) with a partner you conducted a laboratory exercise meant to illustrate the principles; and (4) that night you completed a problem set in order to practice the application of the principle.

These activities don't seem to give students any practice in what scientists actually *do*. For example, scientists don't know the outcome of an experiment before they do it—they do the experiment to find out what will happen, and they must interpret the results, which are often surprising or even self-contradictory. In fact, high schoolers know that laboratory exercises have predictable outcomes, so their focus is probably not on what the lab is meant to illustrate but more on whether they "did it right." Likewise, historians don't read and memorize textbooks—they work with original sources (birth certificates, diaries, contemporary newspaper accounts, and the like) to construct sensible narrative interpretations of historical events. If we're not giving students practice in doing the things that historians and scientists actually do, in what sense are we teaching them history and science?

Real scientists are experts. They have worked at science for forty hours (likely many more) each week for years. It turns out that those years of practice make a qualitative, not quantitative, difference in the way they think compared to how a well-informed amateur thinks. Thinking like a historian, a scientist, or a mathematician turns out to be a very tall order indeed. I'll start this discussion by giving you a sense of what expert thinkers do and how they do it.

What Do Scientists, Mathematicians, and Other Experts Do?

Obviously what experts do depends on their field of expertise. Still, there are important similarities among experts, not only in scholarly fields such as history, math, literature, and science, but also in applied fields such as medicine and banking, and in recreational pursuits such as chess, bridge, and tennis.

The abilities of experts are often well illustrated in the television show *House,* in which the grumpy, brilliant Dr. House (Figure 1) solves mysterious medical cases that leave other physicians stumped.

Following is a synopsis of one of House's cases that will help us understand how experts think.[1]

1. House sees a sixteen-year-old boy who complains of double vision and night terrors. House notes that if there's been no trauma to the brain, night terrors in teens are most commonly associated with terrible stress such as witnessing a murder or being sexually abused. *Tentative diagnosis: sexual abuse.*

2. House finds out that the boy's brain *was* subject to trauma; he was hit in the head during a lacrosse game. Irritated to learn this fact so late in the interview, House concludes that the boy has a concussion and snappishly says that the emergency room doctor who examined him after the game obviously "screwed up." *Tentative diagnosis: concussion.*

3. The boy is sitting on a counter swinging his leg as House leaves. House notices the boy's leg jerk and identifies it as the sort of movement our bodies makes when we're falling asleep—but the boy isn't falling asleep. This observation changes everything. House suspects a degenerative disease. He orders the boy admitted.

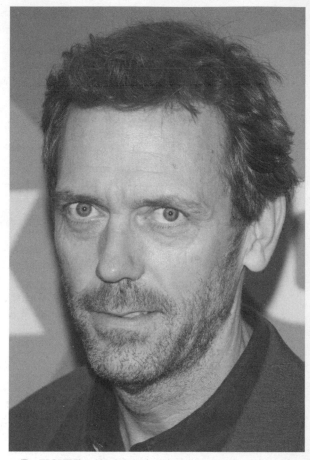

FIGURE 1: Hugh Laurie, who plays expert diagnostician Gregory House.

4. House orders a sleep test (which appears to confirm the night terrors), blood work, and a brain scan, on which other doctors see nothing but on which House sees that one brain structure is slightly misshapen, which he guesses is due to fluid pressure. *Tentative diagnosis: a blockage in the system that bathes the brain in protective fluid. The blockage causes pressure on the brain, which causes the observed symptoms.*

5. House orders a procedure to test whether the fluid around the brain is moving normally. The test reveals blockages, so surgery is ordered.

6. During surgery, chemical markers in the fluid around the brain that are associated with multiple sclerosis are discovered—but the damage to the brain that is associated with the disease is not observed. *Tentative diagnosis: multiple sclerosis.*

7. The patient has a hallucination. House realizes that the boy has been having hallucinations, not night terrors. That makes it unlikely that he has multiple sclerosis, but likely that he has an infection in his brain. Tests showed

no evidence of an infection, but House comments that false negatives for neurosyphilis occur about 30 percent of the time. *Tentative diagnosis: neurosyphilis.*

8. The patient has another hallucination, which leads House to believe that the boy doesn't have neurosyphilis; if he did, he would be getting better from the treatment. House learns that the patient was adopted—the parents hid this fact, even from the boy. House speculates that the boy's biological mother was not vaccinated for measles and that the boy contracted measles sometime before age six months. Although the boy recovered, the virus mutated, traveled to the brain, and went dormant for sixteen years. *Final diagnosis: subacute sclerosing panencephalitis.*

Naturally I've skipped a great deal of the information in this episode—which is a lot more entertaining than this recap—but even this summary shows some of the behaviors that are typical of experts.

House, like any other physician, is bombarded with information: data from his own examination, results from multiple laboratory tests, the facts of the medical history, and so forth. We normally think that having more information is good, but that's not really true—just think of your reaction when you use Google and get five million results. Medical students have a hard time separating the wheat from the chaff, but experienced doctors seem to have a sixth sense about what is important and what should be ignored. For example, House shows little concern for the patient's double vision. (He initially says, "get glasses.") He focuses his attention on the night terrors. Experience also makes House more sensitive to subtle cues that others miss; he alone notices the odd jerk in the boy's leg.

As you would expect from the discussion in Chapter Two, experts have a lot of background knowledge about their fields. But it takes more than knowledge to be an expert. Experts-in-training often know as much (or nearly as much) as experts. The doctors who train under House seldom look blank when he makes a diagnosis or calls their attention to a symptom. But House can access the *right* information from memory with great speed and accuracy. It's information that the more junior doctors have in their memories but just don't think of.

Expertise extends even to the types of mistakes that are made. When experts fail, they do so gracefully. That is, when an expert doesn't get the right answer, the wrong answer is usually a pretty good guess. House is frequently wrong on his way to the correct diagnosis (the show would last just five minutes if he never made mistakes), but his guesses are portrayed as making sense, whereas the tentative assessments of his junior associates often do not. House will point out (usually with withering sarcasm) that an important symptom (or lack of symptom) makes the proposed diagnosis impossible.

A final feature of expert performance is not illustrated in the preceding example, but it is quite important. Experts show better transfer to similar domains than novices do. For example, a historian can analyze documents outside her area of expertise and still come up with a reasonable analysis. The analysis will take longer and will not be quite as detailed as it would be for material in her own area, but it will be much more like an expert's analysis than a novice's. You can imagine what might happen if someone who had reviewed movies for *Newsweek* for the last ten years were asked to write a financial advice column for the *Wall Street Journal.* A lot of his expertise would be bound to writing about movies, but many of his writing skills (such as clarity and sentence structure) *would* transfer, and the resulting columns would certainly be more professional than those undertaken by a random amateur.

Compared to novices, experts are better able to single out important details, produce sensible solutions, and transfer their knowledge to similar domains. These abilities are seen not only in doctors but also in writers, mathematicians, chess players—and teachers. For example, novice teachers often fail to notice misbehaviors whereas experts rarely miss them. (No wonder students often wonder at an experienced teacher seeming to have "eyes in the back of her head"!) Like House, expert teachers can also access information rapidly. Compared to novices, they can think of more ways to explain a concept, and they can think of these alternatives more quickly.

What Is in an Expert's Mental Toolbox?

I've described what experts are able to do. So how are they able to do it? What problem-solving abilities or specialized knowledge is required? And how can we make sure that students have whatever it takes?

The mechanisms that experts rely on are a bit like the ones I've talked about before. In Chapter One I identified working memory as a significant bottleneck to effective thinking. Working memory is the workspace in which thought occurs, but the space is limited, and if it gets crowded, we lose track of what we're doing and thinking fails. I identified two ways of getting around the limitation of working memory: background knowledge (Chapter Two) and practice (Chapter Five). Novices can get an edge on thinking through either mechanism. Experts use both too, but their extensive experience makes these strategies even more effective.

Remember, background knowledge helps us overcome the working-memory limitation because it allows us to group, or "chunk," pieces of information—such as treating the letters *C, B,* and *S* as the single unit *CBS*. It will surely not surprise you to learn that experts have lots of background knowledge in their area of expertise. But the expert mind has another edge over the minds of the rest of us. It's not just that there is a lot of information in an expert's long-term memory; it's also that the information in that memory is organized differently from the information in a novice's long-term memory.

Experts don't think in terms of surface features, as novices do; they think in terms of *functions*, or deep structure. For example, one experiment compared chess experts and novices.[2] Subjects were briefly shown a chess board with the pieces in a midgame position. They were then given an empty chess board and told to try to recreate the position they had just seen. The experimenters paid particular attention to the order in which subjects placed the pieces. What they observed was that people put the pieces back in clusters, meaning they put back four or five pieces rapidly, then paused, then put down another three or four pieces, then paused, and so forth. They paused as they took a moment to remember the next cluster of pieces. The experimenters found that novices' clusters were based on position; for example, a novice might first place all of the pieces that were in one corner of the board, then the pieces that were in another corner of the board, and so on. The experts, in contrast,

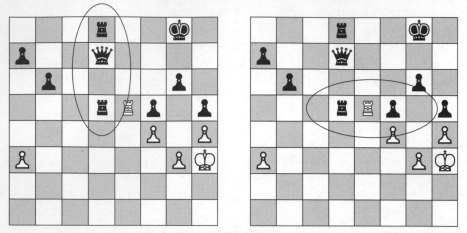

FIGURE 2: In this experiment, people get a brief look at a chess board and then must replicate the configuration of pieces on a blank board. Experts and novices both do so in chunks—they put a few pieces on the board, then pause as they recall the next cluster from memory, then place the next few pieces, and so on. Novices tend to group pieces based on proximity—nearby pieces go in the same chunk, as shown on the right board whereas experts group pieces by function—pieces that are strategically related in the game go in the same chunk, as shown on the left board.

used clusters based on *functional* units; that is, pieces were in the same cluster not because they were next to each other but because one piece threatened the other, or because one piece supported the other in defense (Figure 2).

We can generalize by saying that experts think abstractly. Remember that in Chapter Four I said that people find abstract ideas hard to understand because they focus on the surface structure, not on the deep structure. Experts don't have trouble understanding abstract ideas, because they see the deep structure of problems. In a classic demonstration of this idea, physics novices (undergraduates who had taken one course) and physics experts (advanced graduate students and professors) were given twenty-four physics problems and asked to put them into categories.[3] The novices created categories based on the objects in the problems; problems using springs went into one category, problems using inclined planes went into another, and so on. The experts, in contrast, sorted the problems on the basis of the physical principles that were important to their solution; for example, all of the problems that relied on conservation of energy were put into the same group whether they used springs or planes (Figure 3).

This generalization—that experts have abstract knowledge of problem types but novices do not—seems to be true of teachers too. When confronted with a classroom management problem, novice teachers typically jump right into trying to solve the problem, but experts first seek to define the problem, gathering more information if necessary. Thus expert teachers have knowledge of different *types* of classroom management problems. Not surprisingly, expert teachers more often solve these problems in ways that address root causes and not just the behavioral incident. For example, an expert is more likely than a novice to make a permanent change in seating assignments.

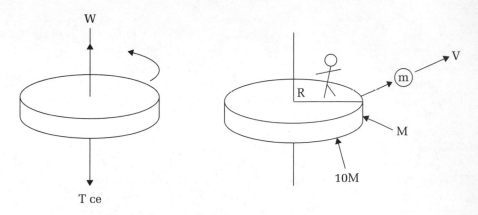

Novice 2: *"Angular velocity, momentum,
circular things"*

Novice 3: *"Rotational kinematics, angular
speeds, angular velocities"*

Novice 6: *"Problems that have something
rotating: angular speed"*

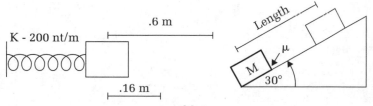

Expert 2: *"Conservation of Energy"*

Expert 3: *"Work-Energy Theorem.
They are all straightforward
problems"*

Expert 4: *"These can be done from energy
considerations. Either you should
know the principle of Conservation
of Energy, or work is lost somewhere."*

FIGURE 3: Novices tended to put the top two figures in the same category
because both figures involve a rotating disk. Experts tended to put the two
figures on the bottom in the same category because both figures use the
conservation-of-energy principle in their solution.

In Chapter Four I said that transfer is so difficult because novices tend to focus on surface features and are not very good at seeing the abstract, functional relationships among problems that are key to solving them. Well, *that* is what experts are great at. They have representations of problems and situations in their long-term memories, and those representations are abstract. That's why experts are able to ignore unimportant details and home in on useful information; thinking functionally makes it obvious what's important. That's also why they show good transfer to new problems. New problems differ in surface structure, but experts recognize the deep, abstract structure. That's also why their judgments usually are sensible, even if they are not quite right. For example, experienced doctors think in terms of the body's underlying physiology. They know the systems of the body well enough that they can intuit how these systems are behaving on the basis of the outward symptoms, and their knowledge of the systems is rich enough that they will seldom, if ever, say something about them that is self-contradictory or absurd. In contrast, beginning medical students can recognize patterns of symptoms that they've memorized, but they don't think functionally, so when they encounter an unfamiliar pattern, they aren't sure how to interpret it.

The second way to get around the limited size of working memory is to practice procedures so many times that they become automatic. That way the procedures don't take space in working memory. Tie your shoes a few hundred times and you no longer need to think about it; your fingers just fly through the routine without any direction from thought processes that would crowd working memory. Experts have automatized many of the routine, frequently used procedures that early in their training required careful thought. Expert bridge players can count the points in a hand without thinking about it. Expert surgeons can tie sutures automatically. Expert teachers have routines with which they begin and end class, call for attention, deal with typical disruptions, and so on. It's interesting to note that novice teachers often script their lessons, planning exactly what they will say. Expert teachers typically do not. They plan different ways that they will discuss or demonstrate a concept, but they don't write out scripts, which suggests that the process of translating abstract ideas into words that their students can understand has become automatic.

So, experts save room in working memory through acquiring extensive, functional background knowledge, and by making mental procedures automatic. What do they do with that extra space in working memory? Well, one thing they do is talk to themselves. What sort of conversation does an expert have with herself? Often she talks about a problem she is working on, and does so at that abstract level I just described. The physics expert says things like "This is probably going to be a conservation of energy problem, and we're going to convert potential energy into kinetic energy."[4]

What's interesting about this self-talk is that the expert can draw implications from it. The physics expert just mentioned has already drawn a hypothesis about the nature of the problem, and as she continues reading, she will evaluate whether her hypothesis is right. Indeed, this expert next said, "Now I'm really sure, because we're going to squash the spring and that is going to be more potential energy." Thus experts do not just narrate what they are doing. They also generate hypotheses, and so test their own understanding and think through the implications of possible solutions in progress. Talking to yourself demands working memory, however, so novices are much less likely to do it. If they do talk to themselves, what they say is predictably more shallow than what experts say. They restate the problem, or they try to map the problem to a familiar formula. When novices talk to themselves they narrate what they are doing, and what they say does not have the beneficial self-testing properties that expert talk has.

How Can We Get Students to Think Like Experts?

I've discussed the capabilities of scientists, historians, mathematicians, and experts in general. They see problems and situations in their chosen field functionally rather than at the surface level. Seeing things that way enables them to home in on important details among a flood of information, to produce solutions that are always sensible and consistent (even if they are not always right), and to show some transfer of their knowledge to related fields. In addition, many of the routine tasks that experts perform have become automatic through practice.

Sounds great. How can we teach students to do that? Unfortunately, the answer to this question is not exactly cheering. It should be obvious that offering novices advice such as "talk to yourself" or "think functionally" won't work. Experts do those things, but only because their mental toolbox enables them to do so. The only path to expertise, as far as anyone knows, is practice (Figure 4).

A number of researchers have tried to understand expertise by examining the lives of experts and comparing them to what we might call near-experts. For example, one group of researchers asked violin players to estimate the number of hours they had practiced the violin at different ages.[6] Some of the subjects (professionals) were already associated with internationally known symphony orchestras. The others were music students in their early twenties. Some of the students (the best violinists) had been nominated by their professors as having the potential for careers as international soloists; others (the "good" violinists) were studying with the same goal, but their professors thought they had less potential. Subjects in the fourth group

FIGURE 4: New York City's Carnegie Hall is a renowned concert venue. An old joke has a young man stopping an older woman on the street in Manhattan and asking, "Pardon me, ma'am. How do I get to Carnegie Hall?" The woman soberly replies, "Practice, practice, practice." The directions page of the Carnegie Hall website refers to this joke, and psychological research indicates that it's true.[5] Expertise does require extensive practice.

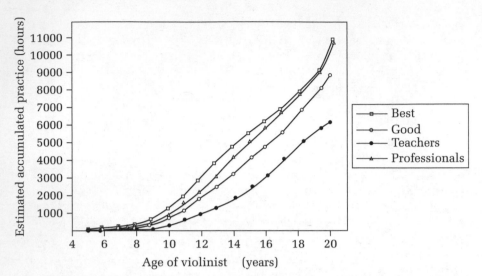

FIGURE 5: Experimenters asked violinists how many hours per week (on average) they practiced at different ages. This graph shows the total number of hours accumulated over the years, making it easier to see trends. The best students reported practicing about as much as the middle-aged professionals (up to the age of twenty), which is more than the good violinists say they practiced; indeed, by age twenty the best violinists had accumulated almost 50 percent more time than the good violinists. Not surprisingly, the future music teachers had practiced much less (although they are of course quite competent violinists by most standards).

were studying not to be professional performers but rather to be music teachers. Figure 5 shows the average cumulative number of hours that each of the four groups of violinists practiced between the ages of five and twenty. Even though the good violinists and the best violinists were all studying at the same music academy, there was a significant difference in the amount of practice since childhood reported by the two groups.

Other studies have taken a more detailed biographical approach. Over the last fifty years there have been a few instances in which a researcher has gained access to a good number (ten or more) of prominent scientists, who have agreed to be interviewed at length, take personality and intelligence tests, and so forth. The researcher has then looked for similarities in the backgrounds, interests, and abilities of these great men and women of science. The results of these studies are fairly consistent in one surprising finding. The great minds of science were not distinguished as being exceptionally brilliant, as measured by standard IQ tests; they were very smart, to be sure, but not the standouts that their stature in their fields might suggest. What *was* singular was their capacity for sustained work. Great scientists are almost always workaholics. Each of us knows his or her limit; at some point we need to stop working and watch a stupid television program, read *People* magazine, or something similar. Great scientists have incredible persistence, and their threshold for mental exhaustion is very high (Figure 6).

Another implication of the importance of practice is that we can't be experts until we put in our hours. A number of researchers have endorsed what has become known as the "ten-year rule": one can't become an expert in any field in less than ten years, be it physics, chess, golf, or mathematics.[7] This rule has been applied to fields as diverse as musical composition, mathematics, poetry, competitive swimming, and car sales. It has been argued that prodigies such as Mozart, who began composing at age five, are not exceptions to the ten-year rule, because their early output is usually imitative and is not recognized by their peers as exceptional. Even if we were to allow for a few prodigies every century, the ten-year rule holds up pretty well.

FIGURE 6: Thomas Alva Edison, who is famous for inventing or greatly improving the light bulb, the fluoroscope (an early version of the X-ray machine), the phonograph, and motion pictures. Edison is also famous for his work habits; one-hundred-hour work weeks were not uncommon, and he often took cat naps in his laboratory rather than sleeping at home. It is small wonder he said that "genius is 1 percent inspiration, 99 percent perspiration."

There's nothing magical about a decade; it just seems to take that long to learn the background knowledge and to develop the automaticity that I've been talking about in this chapter. Indeed, it's been shown that those who have less time to practice take longer than a decade, and in fields where there is less to learn—short-distance sprinting or weightlifting, for example—one can achieve greatness with only a few years of practice. In most fields, however, ten years is a good rule of thumb. And study and practice do not end once one achieves expert status. The work must continue if the status is to be maintained (Figure 7).

Implications for the Classroom

Experts are not simply better at thinking in their chosen field than novices are; experts actually think in ways that are qualitatively different. Your students are not experts, they are novices. How should that impact your teaching?

Students Are Ready to Comprehend but Not to Create Knowledge

After reading this chapter you should have a good idea of how mathematicians, scientists, and historians differ from novices. They have worked in their field for years,

FIGURE 7: In 1989, Jazz great Hank Jones received the National Endowment for the Arts Jazz Master award. In 2005, at age eighty-seven, Jones was asked in an interview if he still practiced. His response: "Oh, of course, of course, yes. I don't see how anybody can do without practicing, you know. I do scales, exercises . . ."[8]

and the knowledge and experience they have accumulated enables them to think in ways that are not open to the rest of us. Thus, trying to get your students to think like them is not a realistic goal. Your reaction may well be, "Well, sure. I never really expected that my students are going to win the Nobel Prize! I just want them to understand some science." That's a worthy goal, *and it is very different from the goal of students thinking like scientists.*

Drawing a distinction between *knowledge understanding* and *knowledge creation* may help. Experts create. For example, scientists create and test theories of natural phenomena, historians create narrative interpretations of historical events, and mathematicians create proofs and descriptions of complex patterns. Experts not only understand their field, they also add new knowledge to it.

A more modest and realistic goal for students is *knowledge comprehension.* A student may not be able to develop his own scientific theory, but he can develop a deep understanding of existing theory. A student may not be able to write a new narrative of historical fact, but she can follow and understand a narrative that someone else has written.

Student learning need not stop there. Students can also understand how science works and progresses, *even if they are not yet capable of using that process very well or at all.* For example, students could learn about landmark findings in science as a way of understanding science as a method of continual refinement of theory rather than as the "discovery" of immutable laws. Students might read different accounts of the Constitutional Convention as a way of learning how historians develop narratives.

Again, the goal is to provide students with some understanding of how others create knowledge rather than to ask students to engage in activities of knowledge creation.

Activities That Are Appropriate for Experts May at Times Be Appropriate for Students, but Not Because They Will Do Much for Students Cognitively

I've said that a key difference between the expert and the well-informed amateur lies in the expert's ability to create new knowledge versus the amateur's ability to understand concepts that others have created. Well, what happens if you ask students to create new knowledge? What will be the result if you ask them to design a scientific experiment or analyze a historical document? Nothing terrible is going to happen, obviously. The mostly likely outcome will be that they won't do it very well; for reasons I've described in this chapter and in Chapter Two, a lot of background knowledge and experience are required.

But a teacher might have other reasons for asking students to do these things. For example, a teacher might ask her students to interpret the results of a laboratory experiment not with the expectation that she is teaching them to think like scientists but instead to highlight a particular phenomenon or to draw their attention to the need for close observation of an experiment's outcome.

Assignments that demand creativity may also be motivating. A music class may well emphasize practice and proper technique, but it may also encourage students to compose their own works simply because the students would find it fun and interesting. Is such practice necessary or useful in order for students to think like musicians? Probably not. Beginning students do not yet have the cognitive equipment in place to compose, but that doesn't mean they won't have a great time doing so, and that may well be reason enough.

The same is true of science fairs. I've judged a lot of science fairs, and the projects are mostly—not to put too fine a point on it—terrible. The questions that students try to answer are usually lousy, because they aren't really fundamental to the field; and students don't appear to have learned much about the scientific method, because their experiments are poorly designed and they haven't analyzed their data sensibly. But some of the students are really proud of what they have done, and their interest in science or engineering has gotten a big boost. So although the *creative* aspect of the project is usually a flop, science fairs seem to be good bets for motivation.

The bottom line is that posing to students challenges that demand the creation of something new is a task beyond their reach—but that doesn't mean you should never pose such tasks. Just keep in mind what the student is or is not getting out of it.

Don't Expect Novices to Learn by Doing What Experts Do

When considering how to help students gain a skill, it seems only natural to encourage them to emulate someone who already knows how to do what you want

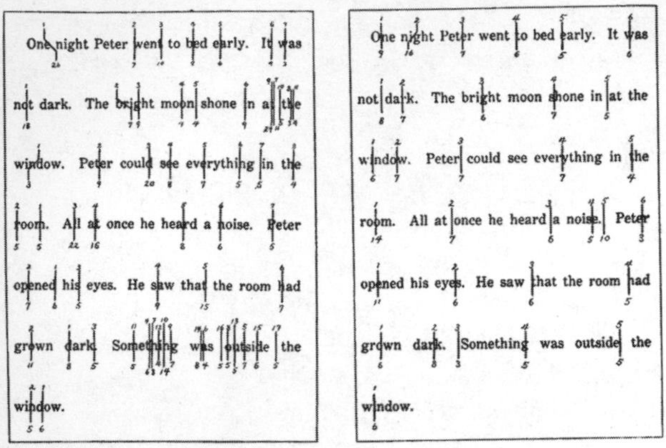

FIGURE 8: Each line shows where the reader's eyes paused when reading a paragraph. At left are typical results for a beginning reader, and at right are results for an expert reader. It's true that experts' eyes stop less often compared to the eyes of beginners (if you've never done so before, watch someone's eyes as they read—it's interesting), but that doesn't mean an expert's strategy is one that beginners can use.

them to do. Thus, if you want students to know how to read a map, find someone who is a good map reader and start training them in the methods this person uses. As logical as this technique sounds, it can be a mistake because, as I've emphasized, there are significant differences between how experts and novices think.

Consider this example: How should we teach reading? Well, if you look at expert readers, when they read they make fewer eye movements than unskilled readers do. So it could be said that the better way to read is by recognizing entire words, and that students should be taught that method from the start, because that's how good readers read. Indeed, an older educational psychology textbook on my shelf cites the eye movement data shown in Figure 8 and makes exactly this argument.[9]

Such arguments should be viewed with suspicion. In this case we know from other data that expert readers can take in whole words at a time, but they didn't necessarily start off reading that way. In the same way expert tennis players spend most of their time during a match thinking about strategy and trying to anticipate what their opponent will do. But we shouldn't tell novices to think about strategy; novices need to think about footwork and about the basics of their strokes.

Whenever you see an expert doing something differently from the way a nonexpert does it, it may well be that the expert used to do it the way the novice does it, and that doing so was a necessary step on the way to expertise. Ralph Waldo Emerson put it more artfully: "Every artist was first an amateur."[10]

Bibliography

Less Technical

Bloom, B. S. (1985). *Developing talent in young people.* New York: Ballantine Books. This book is the product of a survey of one hundred world-class experts in their fields: athletes, scientists, musicians, and so on. The book's message is that experts are not born but made, and it describes the methods by which experts train.

Feltovich, P. J., Prietula, M. J., & Ericsson, K. A. (2006). Studies of expertise from psychological perspectives. In K. A. Ericsson, N. Charness, P. J. Feltovich, & R. R. Hoffman (Eds.),

The Cambridge handbook of expertise and expert performance (pp. 41–68). Cambridge, UK: Cambridge University Press. Although this chapter appears in an academic volume, it is a quite readable overview of the psychological characteristics of experts.

More Technical

Glaser, R., & Chi, M. T.H. (1988). Overview. In M.T.H. Chi, R. Glaser, & M. J. Farr (Eds.), *The nature of expertise* (pp. xv–xxviii). Hillsdale, NJ: Erlbaum. This chapter lists the principle cognitive differences between experts and novices. Twenty years after its publication, the list holds up quite well.

Hogan, T., Rabinowitz, M., & Craven, J. A. (2003). Representation in teaching: Inferences from research of expert and novice teachers. *Educational Psychologist, 38,* 235–247. This article reviews research on the differences between novice and expert teachers from a cognitive perspective of expertise.

Simon, H. A., & Chase, W. G. (1973). Skill in chess. *American Scientist, 61,* 394–403. A classic article on expertise that includes the proposal of the ten-year rule and the estimate that fifty thousand game positions are stored in the minds of chess masters.

Tittle, C. K. (2006). Assessment of teacher learning and development. In P. A. Alexander & P. H. Winne (Eds.), *Handbook of educational psychology* (2nd ed., pp. 953–984). Mahwah, NJ: Erlbaum. A broad review of what teachers know and of the impact that has on their practice.

7

How Should I Adjust My Teaching for Different Types of Learners?

Question: All children are different. Is it true that some students learn best visually (they have to see it to learn it) and some auditorily (they have to hear it to learn it)? How about linear thinkers versus holistic thinkers? It seems that tailoring instruction to each student's cognitive style is potentially of enormous significance; perhaps struggling students would do much better with other teaching methods. At the same time, analyzing and catering to multiple learning styles in the same classroom seems like an enormous burden on the teacher. Which differences are the important ones?

Answer: It's important to keep in mind what the hypothesis behind *learning styles* actually is. The prediction of any learning styles theory is that teaching method one might be good for Sam but bad for Donna, whereas teaching method two might be good for Donna but bad for Sam. Further, this difference between Sam and Donna persists; that is, Sam consistently prefers one type of teaching and Donna prefers another. An enormous amount of research exploring this idea has been conducted in the last fifty years, and finding the difference between Sam and Donna that would fit this pattern has been the holy grail of educational research, but no one has found consistent evidence supporting a theory describing such a difference. The cognitive principle guiding this chapter is:

> Children are more alike than different in terms of how they think and learn.

Note that the claim is not that all children are alike, nor that teachers should treat children as interchangeable. Naturally some kids like math whereas others are better at English. Some children are shy and some are outgoing. Teachers interact with each student differently, just as they interact with friends differently; but teachers should be aware that, as far as scientists have been able to determine, there are not categorically different types of learners.

Styles and Abilities

Let's start with a couple of questions. Suppose you're an eleventh-grade biology teacher. You have a student, Kathy, who is really struggling. She seems to be trying her best, and you've spent extra time with her, but she's still falling farther behind. You discuss the problem with some fellow teachers and learn, among other things, that Kathy is regarded as a gifted poet. Would you consider asking Kathy's English teacher to work with you to relate poetry to her biology lessons in the hope that she will better grasp the concepts?

Here's another case. Like Kathy, Lee is struggling in your biology class. He likes science, but he had a great deal of trouble understanding the unit on the Krebs citric acid cycle. His low score on a quiz prompts his parents to come in for a conference. They believe the problem lies in the way the material was presented; the Krebs cycle was presented in a linear fashion and Lee tends to think holistically. They politely ask whether there is a way to expose Lee to new material in a holistic manner rather than a sequential one, and they offer to help out in any way they can. What would you say to them?

It's obvious that students are different. The stories just presented exemplify the great hope inherent in this fact: that teachers can use these differences to reach students. For example, a teacher might take a student's strength and use it to remedy a weakness, such as using Kathy's knowledge of poetry to help her grasp science. A second possibility is that teachers might take advantage of students' different ways of learning; for example, if Lee doesn't understand a concept very well, it may be because of a poor match between how he learns best and how the material was taught. Relatively minor changes in the presentation may make difficult material easier to understand.

Now, it must be admitted that these exciting possibilities imply more work for the teacher. Playing to a student's strengths (as in Kathy's case) or changing how you present material (as in Lee's case) means changing your instruction and potentially doing something different for each student in the class. That sounds like a lot of extra work. Would it be worth it?

Research by cognitive scientists into the differences among students can shed light on this question, but before I get into that research, it is important to clarify whether I'm talking about differences in cognitive *abilities* or differences in cognitive *styles.** The definition of *cognitive ability* is straightforward: it means capacity for or success in certain types of thought. If I say that Sarah has a lot of ability in math, you know I mean she tends to learn new mathematical concepts quickly. In contrast to abilities, *cognitive styles* are biases or tendencies to think in a particular way, for example to think sequentially (of one thing at a time) or holistically (of all of the parts simultaneously).

Abilities and styles differ in a few important ways. Abilities are how we deal with content (for example, math or language arts) and they reflect the level (that is, the quantity) of what we know and can do. Styles are how we prefer to think and learn. We consider having more ability as being better than having less ability, but we do not consider one style as better than any other style. One style might be more effective for a particular problem, but all styles are equally useful overall, by definition. (If they weren't, we would be talking about abilities, not styles.) To use a sports analogy, we might say that two football players have equal ability even if they have very different styles on the field; for example, one might be a risk taker and the other might be a conservative player (Figure 1).

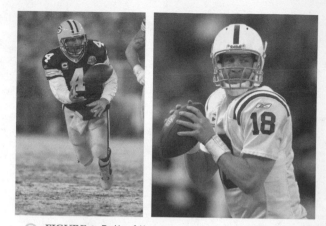

FIGURE 1: Both of these quarterbacks—Brett Favre on the left and Peyton Manning on the right—are considered among the best of the last twenty years. In terms of ability, most fans would say they are comparable; but in terms of style, they differ, with Favre being more of a risk taker and Manning favoring a more conservative game.

In the chapter's introductory paragraphs I said that students' ways of learning are more alike than different. How can that be true given that the differences among students seem so obvious and often so large? In the remainder of this chapter I consider styles and abilities in turn, and try to reconcile the differences among students with the conclusion that these differences don't mean much for teachers.

Cognitive Styles

Some people are impulsive, others take a long time to make decisions. Some people seem to enjoy making situations complex, others relish simplicity. Some people like to think about things concretely, others prefer abstractions. We all have intuitions about how people think, and beginning in the 1940s, experimental psychologists took a strong interest in testing these intuitions. The distinctions they tested were usually framed as opposites (for example, broad/narrow or sequential/holistic), with the understanding that the styles were really a continuum and that most people fall somewhere in the middle of the two extremes. Table 1 shows a few of the distinctions that psychologists evaluated.

As you read through the table, which shows just a fraction of the dozens of classification schemes that have been proposed, you'll probably think that many of the schemes sound at least plausible. How can we know which one is right, or if several of them are right?

TABLE 1: Some of the many distinctions among cognitive styles that have been proposed and tested by psychologists.

Cognitive Styles	Description
Broad/narrow	Preference for thinking in terms of a few categories with many items versus thinking in many categories with few items
Analytic/nonanalytic	Tendency to differentiate among many attributes of objects versus seeking themes and similarities among objects
Leveling/sharpening	Tendency to lose details versus tendency to attend to details and focus on differences
Field dependent/field independent	Interpreting something in light of the surrounding environment versus interpreting it independently of the influence of the environment
Impulsivity/reflectiveness	Tendency to respond quickly versus tendency to respond deliberately
Automatization/restructuring	Preference for simple repetitive tasks versus preference for tasks that require restructuring and new thinking
Converging/diverging	Logical, deductive thinking versus broad, associational thinking
Serialist/holist	Preference for working incrementally versus preference for thinking globally
Adaptor/innovator	Preference for established procedures versus preference for new perspectives
Reasoning/intuitive	Preference for learning by reasoning versus preference for learning by insight
Visualizer/verbalizer	Preference for visual imagery versus preference for talking to oneself when solving problems
Visual/auditory/kinesthetic	Preferred modality for perceiving and understanding information

Psychologists have a few ways to test these proposals. First, they try to show that cognitive style is stable within an individual. In other words, if I say you have a particular cognitive style, that style ought to be apparent in different situations and on different days; it should be a stable part of your cognitive makeup. Cognitive styles should also be consequential; that is, using one cognitive style or another ought to have implications for the important things we do. If I claim that some people think serially and other people think holistically, then these two types of people ought to differ in how they learn mathematics, for example, or history, or in how they understand literature. Finally, we have to be sure that a cognitive style is not really an ability measure. Remember, styles are supposed to represent biases in how we prefer to think; they are not supposed to be measures of how *well* we think.

This last point seems kind of obvious, but it has been an issue for some of the distinctions made in Table 1. For example, people who are more likely to evaluate something they see independently of the object's relationship to other objects are called *field independent*, whereas *field dependent* people tend to see an object in terms of its relationship to other things (Figure 2).

People are classified as field dependent or independent only on the basis of visual tests, which don't seem to be very cognitive. But it seems plausible that what's true of vision—that field-dependent people see relationships whereas field–independent people see individual details—may also be true for all sorts of cognitive tasks. That's a neat idea, but the problem is that field-independent people tend to outperform field-dependent people on most cognitive measures. Now, remember that field dependence is supposed to be a cognitive style, and that, on average, people with different styles are not supposed to differ in ability. The fact that they do implies that the tests shown in

Here is a simple form, which we have labeled "x":

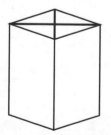

This simple form, named "x," is hidden within the more complex figure below:

FIGURE 2: Two methods of determining field dependence or independence. At left is the rod-and-frame test. The rod and frame are luminous and are viewed in a darkened room. The subject adjusts the rod so that it is vertical. If the subject's adjustment is strongly influenced by the surrounding frame, she is field dependent—if not, she is field independent. At right is one item from an embedded-figures test, in which the subject tries to find the simple figure hidden in the more complex one. Success on tasks like this indicates field independence. Like the rod-and-frame task, it seems to indicate an ability to separate a part of one's visual experience from everything else one is seeing.

Figure 2 actually measure ability in some way rather than style, although we may not be sure what the mechanism is.

I've mentioned that a cognitive styles theory must have the following three features: it should consistently attribute to a person the same style, it should show that people with different styles think and learn differently, and it should show that people with different styles do not, on average, differ in ability. At this point there is not a theory that has these characteristics. That doesn't mean that cognitive styles don't exist—they certainly might; but after decades of trying, psychologists have not been able to find them. To get a better sense of how this research has gone, let's examine one theory more closely: the theory of visual, auditory, and kinesthetic learners.

Visual, Auditory, And Kinesthetic Learners

The concept of visual, auditory, and kinesthetic learners is probably familiar to you. It states that each person has a preferred way of receiving new information, through one of three senses. Vision (seeing) and audition (hearing) are clear enough, but kinesthesia might require an explanation. Kinesthesia is the sensation that tells you where your body parts are. If you were to close your eyes and I moved your arm as though you were, say, waving, you would know where your arm was even though you couldn't see it. That information comes from special receptors in your joints, muscles, and skin. That's kinesthesia.

The visual–auditory–kinesthesia theory holds that everyone can take in new information through any of the three senses, but most of us have a preferred sense. When learning something new, visual types like to see diagrams, or even just to see in print the words that the teacher is saying. Auditory types prefer descriptions, usually verbal, to which they can listen. Kinesthetic learners like to manipulate objects physically; they move their bodies in order to learn (Figure 3).

FIGURE 3: Learners with different styles might benefit from different ways of presenting the same material. When learning addition, for example, a visual learner might view groupings of objects, an auditory learner might listen to sets of rhythms, and a kinesthetic learner might arrange objects into groups.

To give you a backdrop against which to evaluate this theory, I'll start with a few facts about memory that cognitive scientists have worked out. People do differ in their visual and auditory memory abilities.[†] That is, our memory system can store both what things look like and what they sound like. We use visual memory representations when we create a visual image in our mind's eye. For example, suppose I ask you, "What is the shape of a German shepherd's ears?" or "How many windows are there in your classroom?" Most people say they answer these questions by creating a visual image and inspecting it. A great deal of work by experimental psychologists during the 1970s showed that such images do have a lot of properties in common with vision—that is, there's a lot of overlap between your "mind's eye" and the parts of your brain that allow you to see. We also store some memories as sound, such as Katie Couric's voice, the roar of the MGM lion, or our mobile phone's ringtone. If I ask you, for example, "Who has a deeper voice: your principal or your superintendant?" you will likely try to imagine each person's voice and compare them. We can store both visual and auditory memories, and as with any other cognitive function, each of us varies in how effectively we do so. Some of us have very detailed and vivid visual and auditory memories; others of us do not.

Cognitive scientists have also shown, however, that we don't store all of our memories as sights or sounds. We also store memories in terms of what they mean to us. For example, if a friend tells you a bit of gossip about a coworker (who was seen coming out of an adult bookshop), you *might* retain the visual and auditory details of the story (for example, how the person telling the story looked and sounded), but you might remember only the content of the story (adult bookshop) without remembering any of the auditory or visual aspects of being told. *Meaning* has a life of its own, independent of sensory details (Figure 4).

Now we're getting to the heart of the visual–auditory -kinesthetic theory. It is true that some people have especially good visual or auditory memories. In that sense there are visual learners and auditory learners. But that's not the key prediction of the theory. The key prediction is that students will learn better when instruction matches their cognitive style. That is, suppose Anne is an auditory learner and Victor is a visual learner. Suppose further that

FIGURE 4: What does the word *footbath* mean? You know it means to soak one's feet, usually when they are sore but also, perhaps, as a way of pampering yourself. Your knowledge of the word *footbath* is stored as a *meaning*, independent of whether you first learned the word by seeing someone take a footbath, by hearing a description of it, or by actually soaking your own feet. Most of what teachers want students to know is stored as meaning.

I give Anne and Victor two lists of new vocabulary words to learn. To learn the first list, they listen to a tape of the words and definitions several times; to learn the second list, they view a slide show of pictures depicting the words. The theory predicts that Anne should learn more words on the first list than on the second whereas Victor should learn more words on the second list than on the first. Dozens of studies have been conducted along these general lines, including studies using materials more like those used in classrooms, and overall the theory is not supported. Matching the "preferred" modality of a student doesn't give that student any edge in learning.

How can that be? Why doesn't Anne learn better when the presentation is auditory, given that she's an auditory learner? *Because auditory information is not what's being tested!* Auditory information would be the particular sound of the voice on the tape. What's being tested is the meaning of the words. Anne's edge in auditory memory doesn't help her in situations where meaning is important. Similarly, Victor might be better at recognizing the visual details of the pictures used to depict the words on the slides, but again, that ability is not being tested.

The situation described in this experiment probably matches most school lessons. Most of the time students need to remember what things mean, not what they sound like or look like. Sure, sometimes that information counts; someone with a good visual memory will have an edge in memorizing the particular shapes of countries on a map, for example, and someone with a good auditory memory will be better at getting the accent right in a foreign language. But the vast majority of schooling is concerned with what things mean, not with what they look like or sound like.

So does that mean that the visual-auditory-kinesthetic theory is correct some small proportion of the time, such as when students are learning foreign language accents or countries on a map? Not really. Because the point of the theory is that the same material can be presented in different ways to match each student's strength. So what the teacher ought to do (according to the theory) is this: when learning countries on a map, the visual learners should view the shapes of the countries but the auditory learners should listen to a description of each country's shape; and when learning a foreign accent, the auditory learners should listen to a native speaker but the visual learners will learn more quickly if they view a written representation of the sounds. It seems obvious that this approach won't work.

If the visual-auditory-kinesthetic theory is wrong, why does it seem so right? About 90 percent of teachers believe there are people who are predominantly visual, auditory, or kinesthetic learners, and about the same proportion of undergraduates at the University of Virginia (where I teach) believe it too. There are probably a few factors that contribute to the theory's plausibility. First, it has become commonly accepted wisdom. It's one of those facts that everyone figures must be right because everyone believes it.

Another important factor is that something similar to the theory *is* true. Kids do differ in their visual and auditory memories. For example, maybe you've watched in wonder as a student has painted a vivid picture of an experience from a class field trip and thought, "Wow, Lacy is obviously a visual learner." As I've described, Lacy may well have a really good visual memory, but that doesn't mean she's a "visual learner" in the sense that the theory implies.

A final reason that the visual-auditory-kinesthetic theory seems right is a psychological phenomenon called the *confirmation bias.* Once we believe something, we unconsciously interpret ambiguous situations as being consistent with what we already believe. For example, suppose a student is having difficulty understanding Newton's first law. You try explaining it a few different ways, and then you give the example of a magician yanking a tablecloth off a table without disturbing the plates and cutlery that lie on top of the cloth. Suddenly the idea clicks for the student.

You think, "Aha. That visual image helped him understand. He must be a visual learner." But maybe the example was just a good one and it would have helped any student, or maybe the idea would have clicked for this student after hearing just one more example, visual or not. Why the student understood Newton's first law from the example is ambiguous, and it is only your tendency to interpret ambiguous situations in ways that confirm what you already believe that led you to identify the student as a visual learner (Figure 5). The great novelist Tolstoy put it this way: "I know that most men, including those at ease with problems of the greatest complexity, can seldom accept the simplest and most obvious truth if it be such as would oblige them to admit the falsity of conclusions which they have proudly taught to others, and which they have woven, thread by thread, into the fabrics of their life".[1]

I've gone into a lot of detail about the visual-auditory-kinesthetic theory because it is so widely believed, even though psychologists know that the theory is not right. What I have said about this theory goes for all of the other cognitive styles theories as well. The best you can say about any of them is that the evidence is mixed.

Earlier I drew an important distinction between styles and abilities. In this section I've addressed cognitive styles—biases or tendencies to think or learn in a particular way. In the next section I discuss abilities and how we should think about differences in them among students.

FIGURE 5: When my first daughter was born, one of the nurses told me, "Oh, it'll be crazy here in a few days. Full moon coming up, you know." Many people believe that all sorts of interesting things happen during a full moon: the murder rate goes up, emergency room admissions increase, as do calls to police and fire departments, and more babies are born, among other things. Actually, this hypothesis has been exhaustively examined, and it's wrong. Why do people believe it? One factor is the confirmation bias. When it's a full moon and the delivery room is busy, the nurse notices and remembers it. When the delivery room is busy and it's *not* a full moon, she doesn't take note of it.

Abilities and Multiple Intelligences

What is mental ability? How would you characterize someone who is mentally able? A moment of reflection tells us that there are lots of tasks for which we use our minds, and most of us are good at some of them and not so good at others. In other words, we have to talk about mental abilities, not mental ability. We've all known people who seemed gifted with words but could barely handle the math necessary to balance a checkbook, or who could pick out a tune on any musical instrument but seemed to fall all over themselves when attempting anything athletic.

The logic underlying the idea of mental ability is as follows: if there is a single ability—call it intelligence, if you like—underlying different mental activities, then someone who is good at one type of mental activity (for example, math) should be good at all mental activities. But if some people are good at one mental activity (math) and poor at another (reading comprehension), then those activities must be supported by different mental processes. For more than one hundred years, psychologists have been using this logic to investigate the structure of thought. In a typical study, an experimenter takes one hundred people and administers to each of them, say, an algebra test, a geometry test, a grammar test, a vocabulary test, and a reading comprehension test. What we would expect to happen is that each person's scores on the English tests (grammar, vocabulary, and reading comprehension) would hang together—that is, if a person scored well on one of the English tests it would mean he was good at English, so he would tend also to score well on the other English tests. Likewise, people who scored well on one math test would probably score well on the other math test, reflecting high math ability. But the scores on the math and English tests wouldn't be so highly related. If you did this experiment, that's more or less what you'd see.[‡]

This sounds like pretty obvious stuff. When I was in graduate school, one of my professors called commonsense findings "*bubbe* psychology." *Bubbe* is Yiddish for "grandmother," so *bubbe* psychology is giving fancy labels to stuff that your grandmother could have told you (Figure 6). As far as we've gone, it is pretty obvious stuff. It can get a lot more complicated when we try to get more detailed (and the statistical techniques are pretty complex). But roughly speaking, what you noticed in school is true: some kids are talented at math, some are musical, and some are athletic, and they are not necessarily the same kids.

Educators got much more interested in this type of research in the mid-1980s when Howard Gardner, a professor at Harvard, published his theory of multiple intelligences. Gardner proposed that there are seven intelligences, to which he later added an eighth. They are listed in Table 2 (on p. 124).

As I've mentioned, Gardner was certainly not the first to generate a list of human abilities, and his list does not look radically different from the ones others have described. In fact, most psychologists think Gardner didn't really get it right. He discounted a lot of the work that came before his, for reasons that researchers have thought were not justified, and he made some claims that were known at the time to be wrong—for example, that the intelligences were relatively independent of one another, which he later deemphasized.

Educators were (and are) interested not so much in the particulars of the theory but in three claims associated with the theory:

> *Claim 1:* The list in Table 2 is one of *intelligences,* not abilities or talents.
>
> *Claim 2:* All eight intelligences should be taught in school.
>
> *Claim 3:* Many or even all of the intelligences should be used as conduits when presenting new material. That way each student will experience the material via his or her best intelligence, and thus each student's understanding will be maximized.

Gardner made the first of these claims, and it is an interesting, debatable point. The other two points have been made by others on the basis of Gardner's work, and Gardner disagrees with them. I'll describe why each claim is interesting, and try to evaluate what it might mean for teachers.

Let's start with Claim 1, that the list shown in Table 2 represents intelligences, not abilities or talents. Gardner has written extensively on this point. He argues that some abilities—namely, logical-mathematical and linguistic—have been accorded greater status than they deserve. Why should those abilities get the special designation "intelligence" whereas the others get the apparently less glamorous title "talent"? Indeed, insisting that musical ability should be called musical intelligence, for example, carries a good share of the theory's appeal. Gardner himself has commented more than once that

FIGURE 6: The author's *bubbe,* who, like most grandmothers, knew a lot of psychology.

TABLE 2: Gardner's eight intelligences.

Intelligence	Description	Profession requiring high levels of given intelligence
Linguistic	Facility with words and language	Attorney, novelist
Logical-mathematical	Facility with logic, inductive and deductive reasoning, and numbers	Computer programmer, scientist
Bodily-kinesthetic	Facility with body movement, as in sports and dance	Athlete, dancer, mime
Interpersonal	Facility in understanding others' emotions, needs, and points of view	Salesperson, politician
Intrapersonal	Facility in understanding one's own motivations and emotions	Novelist
Musical	Facility in the creation, production, and appreciation of music	Performer, composer
Naturalist	Facility in identifying and classifying flora or fauna	Naturalist, chef
Spatial	Facility in the use and manipulation of space	Architect, sculptor

if he had referred to seven talents instead of seven intelligences, the theory would not have received much attention.

So? Are they intelligences or talents? On the one hand, the cognitive scientist in me agrees with Gardner. The mind has many abilities, and there is not an obvious reason to separate two of them and call them "intelligence" while referring to other mental processes by another label. On the other hand, the term *intelligence* has an entrenched meaning, at least in the West, and it's unwise to suppose that a sudden switch of the meaning will not have any fallout. I believe that confusion over Gardner's definition versus the old definitions of *intelligence* helps to explain why other people have made the other two claims—the ones with which Gardner disagrees.

Claim 2 is that all eight intelligences should be taught in school. The argument for this claim is that schools should be places where the intelligences of *all* children are celebrated. If a student is high in intrapersonal intelligence, that intelligence should be nourished and developed, and the student should not be made to feel inferior if he is lower in linguistic and logical-mathematical intelligences, the ones that are usually heavily weighted in school curricula. There is a surface plausibility to this claim. It appeals to our sense of fairness; all intelligences should be on the same footing.

Gardner disagrees, however, saying that curricular decisions should be made first on the basis of the values of the community, and that his multiple intelligences theory can help guide the implementation of the curricular goals.

The claim that all intelligences should be taught in school is, I believe, a reflection of relabeling *talents* as *intelligences*. Part of our understanding of intelligence is that intelligent people do well in school.[§] As a result of this assumption, some people's thinking, I believe, has gone this way:

> Children go to school to develop their native intelligence.
>
> A new intelligence has been discovered.
>
> Therefore, schools should develop the new intelligence.

Some educators do seem to think that Gardner "discovered" that people have musical intelligence, spatial intelligence, and so forth whereas musical intelligence is of course the same thing your *bubbe* would have recognized as musical talent. I personally believe that music should be part of school curricula, but the idea that cognitive scientists could tell you anything to support that position is wrong.

The third claim states that it is useful to introduce new ideas through multiple intelligence avenues; for example, when students are learning how to use commas, they might write a song about commas (musical intelligence), search the woods for creatures and plants in the shape of a comma (naturalist intelligence), and create sentences with their bodies, assuming different postures for different parts of speech (bodily-kinesthetic intelligence).[2] The expectation is that different children will come to understand the comma by different means, depending on their intelligence. The idea will click for the student who is high in naturalist intelligence during the search-the-woods exercise, and so on.

Gardner disavows this idea, and he's right to do so. The different abilities (or intelligences, if you like) are not interchangeable. Mathematical concepts have to be learned mathematically, and skill in music won't help.[¶] Writing a poem about the arc that a golf club should take will not help your swing. These abilities are not completely insulated from one another, but they are separate enough that you can't take one skill you're good at and leverage it to bolster a weakness.

Some people have suggested that we might at least be able to get students interested in subject matter by appealing to their strength. To get the science whiz reading for pleasure, don't hand him a book of Emily Dickinson's poetry; give him the memoirs of physicist Richard Feynman. I think that's a sensible idea, if not terribly startling. I also think it will only take you so far. It's a lot like trying to appeal to students' individual interests, a point I took up in Chapter One.

Conclusions

Let me summarize what I've said in this chapter. Everyone can appreciate that students differ from one another. What can (or should) teachers do about that? One would hope we could use those differences to improve instruction. Two basic methods have been suggested. One approach is based on differences in cognitive style—that is, if one matches the method of instruction to the preferred cognitive style of the child, learning will be easier. Unfortunately, no one has described a set of styles for which there is good evidence.

The second way that teachers might take advantage of differences among students is rooted in differences in abilities. If a student is lacking in one cognitive ability, the hope would be that she could use a cognitive strength to make up for, or at least bolster, the cognitive weakness. Unfortunately, there is good evidence that this sort of substitution is not possible. To be clear, it's the substitution idea that is wrong; students definitely do differ in their cognitive abilities (although the description in Gardner's multiple intelligences theory is widely regarded as less accurate than other descriptions).

Implications for the Classroom

I admit I felt like a bit of a Grinch as I wrote this chapter, as though I had a scowl on my face as I typed "wrong, wrong, wrong" about the optimistic ideas others have offered regarding student differences. As I stated at the start of the chapter, I am not saying that teachers should not differentiate instruction. I hope and expect that they will. But when they do so, they should know that scientists cannot offer any help. It would be wonderful if scientists had identified categories of students along with varieties of instruction best suited to each category, but after a great deal of effort, they have not found such types, and I, like many others, suspect they don't exist. I would advise teachers to treat students differently on the basis of the teacher's experience with each student and to remain alert for what works. When differentiating among students, craft knowledge trumps science.

That said, I do have some positive thoughts on what all of this means for your classroom.

Think in Terms of Content, Not in Terms of Students

Learning-style theories don't help much when applied to students, but I think they are useful when applied to content. Take the visual-auditory-kinesthetic distinction. You might want students to experience material in one or another modality depending on what you want them to get out of the lesson; a diagram of Fort Knox should be seen, the national anthem of Turkmenistan should be heard, and the *cheche* turban (used by Saharan tribes to protect themselves against sun and wind) should be worn. The distinctions in Table 1 provide a number of interesting ways to think about lesson plans: Do you want students to think deductively during a lesson, or to free-associate creatively? Should they focus on similarities among concepts they encounter, or should they focus on the details that differentiate those concepts? Table 1 may help you to focus on what you hope your students will learn from a lesson and how to help them get there.

Change Promotes Attention

Every teacher knows that change during a lesson invigorates students and refocuses their attention. If the teacher has been doing a lot of talking, something visual (a video or a map) offers a welcome change. Table 1 provides a number of ways to think about change during the course of a lesson. If the students' work has demanded a lot of logical, deductive thinking, perhaps an exercise that calls for broad, associative thinking is in order. If their work has required many rapid responses, perhaps they should do another task that calls for thoughtful, measured responses. Rather than individualizing the required mental processes for each student, give all of your students practice in all of these processes, and view the transitions as an opportunity for each student to start fresh and refocus his or her mental energies.

There Is Value in Every Child, Even If He or She Is Not "Smart in Some Way"

I am willing to bet you have heard someone say, "Every student is intelligent in some way," or ask students to identify "What kind of smart are you?" I think teachers say this in an effort to communicate an egalitarian attitude to students: everyone is good at something. But there are a couple of reasons to be leery of this attitude. First, this sort of statement rubs me the wrong way because it implies that intelligence brings value. Every child *is* unique and valuable, whether or not they are intelligent or have much in the way of mental ability. I admit that being the father of a severely mentally retarded child probably makes me sensitive on this issue. My daughter is not intelligent in any sense of the word, but she is a joyful child who brings a lot of happiness to a lot of people.

Second, it's not necessarily the case that every child is smart in some way. The exact percentage of children who are "smart" would depend on how many intelligences you define and whether "smart" means "top 10 percent" or "top 50 percent," and so on. It doesn't much matter—there will always be some kids who are in fact not especially gifted in any of the intelligences. In my experience, telling kids that they have a skill they don't possess seldom works. (If a child is briefly fooled, her peers are usually happy to bring reality crashing down on her head.)

Third, for reasons I describe in the next chapter, it is *never* smart to tell a child that she's smart. Believe it or not, doing so makes her less smart. Really.

Don't Worry—and Save Your Money

If you have felt nagging guilt that you have not evaluated each of your students to assess their cognitive style, or if you think you know what their styles are and have not adjusted your teaching to them—don't worry about it. There is no reason to think that doing so will help. And if you were thinking of buying a book or inviting someone in for a professional development session on one of these topics, I advise you to save your money.

If "cognitive styles" and "multiple intelligences" are not helpful ways to characterize how children differ, what's a better way? Why do some children seem to breeze through mathematics while others struggle? Why do some children love history, or geography? The importance of background knowledge has come up again and again in this book. In Chapter One I argued that background knowledge is an important determinant of what we find interesting; for example, problems or puzzles that seem difficult but not impossible pique our interest. In Chapter Two I explained that background knowledge is an important determinant of much of our success in school. Cognitive processes (such as analyzing, synthesizing, and critiquing) cannot operate alone. They need background knowledge to make them work.

Still, background knowledge is not the only difference between students. There is something to the idea that some students are simply really clever. In the next chapter I explore that idea, and I focus on what we can do to maximize the potential of all students, regardless of how clever they are.

Notes

* Some people differentiate between cognitive styles (how we think) and learning styles (how we learn). I don't think this distinction is very important, so I use the term *cognitive styles* throughout this chapter, even when I'm talking about learning.

† We differ in kinesthesia too, but the literature on this is more complicated to describe, so I'm going to stick to visual and auditory examples.

‡ Actually, the math and English scores are not completely unrelated. Good scores on one are predictive of good scores on the other, but the relationship is weaker than the relationship of one math score to another math score.

§ In fact, modern intelligence testing began in France in the late nineteenth century as a way of predicting who would excel in school and who would not.

¶ Although music and rhythm can help us to memorize things, including mathematical formulae, they won't help us gain a deep understanding of what the formulae do. The reasons that music helps us memorize things are fascinating, but a discussion of them would take us too far afield.

Bibliography

Less Technical

Deary, I. J. (2001). *Intelligence: A very short introduction.* London: Oxford University Press. As the title promises, a very short (152 pages) introduction and overview of what is known about intelligence.

Kosslyn, S. M. (1983). *Ghosts in the mind's machine.* New York: Norton. A highly readable account of how visual imagery works in the mind, and how it differs from meaning-based representations.

Willingham, D. T. (2004, Summer). Reframing the mind. *Education Next,* 19–24. This article covers the more technical problems in the multiple intelligences theory, namely why psychologists prefer other accounts of ability over Gardner's.

More Technical

Coffield, F., Moseley, D., Hall, E., & Ecclestone, K. (2004). *Should we be using learning styles? What research has to say about practice.* London: Learning and Skills Research Center. Available at http://www.lsda.org.uk/files/PDF/1540.pdf. A review of the literature on learning styles; focuses on adult education but is still useful.

Gardner, H. (2006). *Multiple intelligences: New horizons.* New York: Basic Books. The most up-to-date account of Gardner's views on intelligence.

Kavale, K. A., Hirshoren, A., & Forness, S. R. (1998). Meta-analytic validation of the Dunn and Dunn model of learning-style preferences: A critique of what was Dunn. *Learning Disabilities Research & Practice, 13*, 75–80. A review of multiple studies that examined the psychological reality of the visual-auditory-kinesthetic theory of learning.

Nickerson, R. S. (1998). Confirmation bias: A ubiquitous phenomenon in many guises. *Review of General Psychology, 2*, 175–220. A somewhat dated but still relevant review of the confirmation bias.

Rayner, S., & Riding, R. (1997). Towards a categorization of cognitive styles and learning styles. *Educational Psychology, 17*, 5–27. A comprehensive summary and categorization of different cognitive-style theories.

Rotton, J., & Kelly, I. W. (1985). Much ado about the full moon: A meta-analysis of lunar-lunacy research. *Psychological Bulletin, 97*, 296–306. This article reviews thirty-seven studies that sought a link between the lunar cycle and various behaviors (such as psychiatric disturbances, homicides, and crisis calls). No relationship is observed.

8

How Can I Help Slow Learners?

Question: It's a cruel fact that some children just don't seem to be cut out for schoolwork. That's not to say they don't have valuable skills. For example, we've all heard stories of business titans who fared poorly in school. But certainly we would like all students to get everything they can out of school. How can school be optimized for students who don't have the raw intelligence that other students have?

Answer: Americans, like other Westerners, view intelligence as a fixed attribute, like eye color. If you win the genetic lottery, you're smart; but if you lose, you're not. This notion of intelligence as fixed by genetics has implications for school and work. One implication is that smart people shouldn't need to work hard in order to get good grades—after all, they are smart. As a corollary, if you work hard, that must mean you're not smart. The destructive cycle is obvious: students want to get good grades so that they look smart, but they can't study to do so because that marks them as dumb. In China, Japan, and other Eastern countries, intelligence is more often viewed as malleable. If students fail a test or don't understand a concept, it's not that they're stupid—they just haven't worked hard enough yet. This attribution is helpful to students because it tells them that intelligence is under their control. If they are performing poorly, they can do something about it. So which view is correct, the Western or the Eastern? There is some truth in both. Our genetic inheritance does impact our intelligence, but it seems to do so mostly through the environment. There is no doubt that intelligence can be changed. The cognitive principle that guides this chapter is:

> Children do differ in intelligence, but intelligence can be changed through sustained hard work.

It is a good idea to model the belief in malleable intelligence for students. You can do so in how you administer praise and in how you talk to students about their successes and failures.

It would be nice if all of our students were equally capable—if the only differences in their performance at school were due to differences in how hard they worked. It would somehow make school seem fairer. Regardless of how desirable that might be, most teachers would say it's a pipe dream. Some students are simply smarter than others. Knowing what to do for the bright ones is not that tough—offer them more challenging material. But what about those who have difficulty keeping up? How can teachers ensure that they are getting all they can from school?

To start, we need to clarify what's meant by *intelligence.* If given a few minutes to write our own definition, we might say that intelligent people can understand complex ideas and use different forms of reasoning. They can also overcome obstacles by engaging thought, and they learn from their experiences. I think this definition is in line with common sense, and it happens to be a paraphrase of the definition created by a task force appointed by the American Psychological Association.* Although many finer distinctions could be made, the overall idea—that some people reason well and catch on to new ideas quickly—captures most of what we mean when we say "intelligence."

There are two things to note about this definition. First, it doesn't include abilities in music, athletics, or other fields that Gardner included in his theory of multiple intelligences. As described in Chapter Seven, most researchers consider those abilities just as important as those that are considered aspects of intelligence, but calling them intelligences rather than talents muddies the waters of communication and doesn't advance the science. Second, this definition actually seems to include just one intelligence. An implication is that if someone is intelligent, she should be equally good at both math and language arts. We all know people who are *not* equally gifted in these two fields. So how could this definition be right?

There is in fact overwhelming evidence that there is a general intelligence—that is, "if you're smart, you're smart." But it's not the whole story. Here's one way that psychologists research this topic. Suppose I hypothesize that there is a single type of intelligence. It's usually called *g*, short for general intelligence. You, on the other hand, argue that there are two types of intelligence—one verbal and one mathematical. Now suppose you and I find one hundred students, each of whom is willing to take four tests: two math tests (say, a calculation test and a word problem test) and two verbal tests (for example, a vocabulary test and a reading comprehension test). I think "if you're smart, you're smart," so anyone who does well on one of the tests ought to do well on the other three (and anyone who does poorly on one test will do poorly on the others). You, in contrast, think that verbal and mathematical intelligence are separate, so someone who does well on the reading comprehension test is likely to do well on the vocabulary test, but that success should predict nothing about how she will do on the math tests (Figure 1).

So which of these two models is right? Neither. Data from tens of thousands of people have been evaluated, and they show a pattern that has something in common with each model. The model on the left of Figure 1 predicts that verbal and math test scores

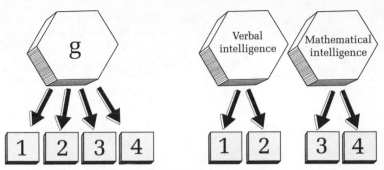

FIGURE 1: Two views of intelligence. According to the view on the left, a single type of intelligence underlies all intellectual tasks. So doing well on the vocabulary test implies that you have a lot of *g*, which implies that you should also do well on the other three tests. In the model on the right, doing well on the vocabulary test implies that you have high verbal intelligence but tells us nothing about how much mathematical intelligence you have, because the two are separate. Data from hundreds of studies show that neither of these models is correct. The model in Figure 2 is commonly accepted.

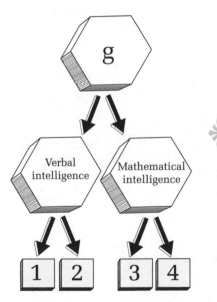

FIGURE 2: The dominant view of intelligence. There is a general intelligence that contributes to many different types of mental tasks, but there are also particular types of intelligence that are supported by the general intelligence processes. Almost everyone agrees that there are verbal and mathematical intelligences, although some people think these should be broken down further.

will be related to one another, whereas the model on the right predicts that they will be unrelated. The data show that the verbal test scores are in fact related to the math test scores—but the verbal test scores are more related to one another than they are to the math tests. That pattern fits the model shown in Figure 2. Separate cognitive processes contribute to verbal and mathematical intelligences, but *g* contributes something to each of them too.

What exactly is g? It's not known. People suggest it might be related to the speed or the capacity of working memory, or even that it's a reflection of how quickly the neurons in our brains can fire. Knowing what underlies g is not important to our purposes. What is important is that g is real. We know that having a lot of g predicts that we will do well in school and well in the workplace. Even though most researchers don't think that g is the whole story when it comes to intelligence (as should be obvious from

Figure 2), researchers often refer to g when considering why some people are quite intelligent and others less so. Now that we better understand what intelligence is, we can turn our attention to the next question: What makes people more or less intelligent?

What Makes People Intelligent?

In Chapters Five and Six I emphasized the importance of practice and hard work to expertise in cognitive tasks. Perhaps people who are intelligent are those who have had a lot of practice doing the sorts of tasks that are used to define intelligence; for whatever reason, they have been exposed to lots of complex ideas (and explanations of these ideas), have had many opportunities to reason in a supportive environment, and so on.

The other view is that intelligence is a matter not of work and practice but rather of carefully selecting one's parents. In other words, intelligence is mostly genetic.

Some people are born smart and although they might further develop this ability through practice, they will be pretty smart even if they do little or nothing to develop their intelligence (Figure 3).

I've proposed two answers to the question *Where does intelligence come from?* and both answers are rather extreme: all nature (that is, genetics) or all nurture (that is, experience). Whenever the question *Is it nature or is it nurture?* is asked, the answer is almost always *both*, and it's almost always difficult to specify how genes and experiences interact. The same answer applies

FIGURE 3: Two views of intelligence. On the left is Charles Darwin, commonly credited as the chief architect and promulgator of the theory of evolution. In a letter to Francis Galton, his half cousin and a brilliant polymath, Darwin said, "I have always maintained that, excepting fools, men [do] not differ much in intellect, only in zeal and hard work." Not everyone agrees. On the right is actor Keanu Reeves. "I'm a meathead. I can't help it, man. You've got smart people and you've got dumb people. I just happen to be dumb."

to the question about intelligence, but there has been a significant shift in researchers' points of view in the last twenty years, from thinking that the answer is "both, but probably mostly genetic" to thinking it's "both, but probably mostly environmental." Let me describe the evidence on both sides. Once we better understand why people are intelligent, we'll better understand how to help students who seem to lack intelligence.

I've just said that intelligence is very likely a product of genetic *and* environmental factors combining in complex ways. So how can we untangle them? The most common strategy is to examine whether pairs of people are similarly intelligent. For example, identical twins share 100 percent of their genes, and fraternal twins (like all siblings) share 50 percent of their genes. So, testing whether identical twins are close to each other in intelligence more often than fraternal twins are will help us determine the importance of genes (Figure 4). In addition, we can examine whether the intelligence of siblings raised in the same household is more similar than the intelligence of siblings who were raised in different households—that is, siblings who were separated at birth and adopted by different families. Siblings who were raised in the same household didn't have identical environments but they had the same parents, had similar exposure to literature, television, and other sources of culture, likely went to the same school, and so forth.

Table 1 compares several types of relationships and tells us a lot about the relative importance of genetics and how we are raised.

FIGURE 4: Identical twins James and Oliver Phelps (who played Fred and George Weasley in the Harry Potter movies) were raised in the same household and share 100 percent of their genes. Fraternal twins (although they look alike) Mary Kate and Ashley Olson were raised in the same household but, like all non-twin siblings, share just 50 percent of their genes. Comparing how similar the intelligence of identical twins is to how similar the intelligence of fraternal twins is helps researchers evaluate the importance of genetics to intelligence.

Relationship	Percentage of genes shared	Environment
Identical twins, raised together	100	Similar
Fraternal twins, raised together	50	Similar
Identical twins, raised apart	100	Different
Fraternal twins, raised apart	50	Different
Adoptive siblings	0	Similar

TABLE 1: This table shows different sibling relationships and the genetic and environmental similarities within each pair. Hundreds of sibling pairs in each category were tested and researchers evaluated how similar twins are in intelligence and other attributes. Identical and fraternal twins can be raised apart when a different family adopts each sibling. Some research laboratories (notably one at the University of Minnesota) are in contact with hundreds of pairs of twins who were raised apart, many of whom met for the first time as part of the study.[1]

The results of these studies are startling. Genetics seems to play a huge role in general intelligence; that is, our genes seem to be responsible for something like 50 percent of our smarts. The 50 percent figure is actually an average, because the percentage changes as we age. For young children, it's more like 20 percent, then it goes up to 40 percent for older children, and it's 60 percent or even higher later in life. This increase is the opposite of what you might expect. You might think that genetics would be most important in small children, because even if their environments are different, they haven't been exposed to them for very long, whereas older adults have lived in their environments for decades, so those environments ought to have had more impact. The data don't fit the pattern, however, making us even more likely to suspect that the environment doesn't affect intelligence much.

Other aspects of the data from twins studies, however, show that the environment quite clearly counts for something. If a child was living in a relatively deprived home and then was adopted into a family with greater means, the child's intelligence increased. This increase might have been due to a richer home environment, better schooling, better nutrition, or higher parental expectations, to name just a few possible factors. Other studies using different methods have also indicated that the environment counts for something. Good preschool intervention programs seem to give a modest boost to intelligence, but the effect of the environment in these studies is usually small—maybe 10 IQ points—compared to the effect of genetics.

That was the story until about twenty years ago. Most researchers seemed to have the sense that the range of intelligence was set mostly by genetics, and that a good or poor environment moved one's intelligence up or down a bit within that range.

A real turning point in this work came during the 1980s with the discovery that over the last half-century IQ scores have shown quite substantial gains.[2] For example, in Holland, scores went up twenty-one points in just thirty years (1952–1982), according to scores from tests of Dutch military draftees. This is not an isolated case. The effect has

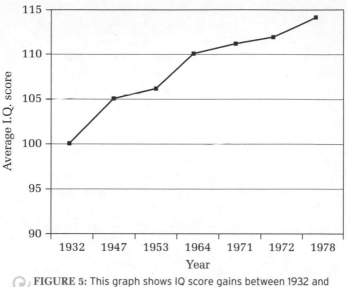

FIGURE 5: This graph shows IQ score gains between 1932 and 1978 in the United States. The "Flynn effect" is strong evidence that the environment has a powerful impact on intelligence, because geneticists agree that the gene pool could not change rapidly enough to account for this change in IQ.

been observed in more than a dozen countries throughout the world, including the United States (Figure 5). Not all countries have data available—very large numbers of people are needed to be sure that we're not looking at a quirky subset—but where the data are available, the effect has been found. The discovery is sufficiently important that it has been named the Flynn effect, after James Flynn, who first described it.

Here's why this evidence is so surprising. If intelligence is largely genetic, we would not expect IQ scores for a whole country to go up or down much over time, because the overall gene pool changes very slowly. But that's not what has happened. There have been huge increases in IQ scores—increases that are much too large to have been caused by changes in genes. Some of the increase may have come from better nutrition and health care. Some of it may have come from the fact that our environment has gotten more complex and people are more often called on to think abstractly and solve unfamiliar problems—the exact sorts of things they're asked to do on IQ tests. Whatever the cause, it must be environmental.

How does this assessment fit with the studies of twins? The twins studies—and there are many of them—consistently show that genetics counts for a lot. But the rapid IQ increase over a short period *can't* be due to genetic factors. How can this paradox be resolved?

No one is completely sure, but Flynn (along with Bill Dickens, his frequent collaborator) has a pretty good suggestion. He claims that the effect of genetics is actually fairly modest. It *looks* large because the effect of genetics is to make the person likely to *seek out* particular environments. Dickens offers the following analogy. Suppose identical twins are separated at birth and adopted into different families. Their genes make them unusually tall at a young age, and they continue to grow. Because each twin is tall, he tends to do well in informal basketball games around the neighborhood (Figure 6). For that reason, each twin asks his parents to put up a net at home. The skills of each twin improve with practice, and each is recruited for his junior high school basketball team. More practice leads to still better skill, and by the end of high school each twin plays quite well—not a future professional, perhaps, but still better than 98 percent of the population, let's say.

Now, notice what has happened. These are identical twins, raised apart. So if a researcher tracked down each twin and administered a test of basketball skills, she would find that both are quite good, and because they were raised apart, the researcher would conclude that this was a genetic effect, that skill in basketball is largely determined by one's genes. But the researcher would be mistaken. What actually happened was that their genes made them tall, and being tall nudged them toward environments that included a lot of basketball practice. Practice—an environmental effect—made them good at basketball, not their genes. *Genetic effects can make you seek out or select different environments.*

Now think of how that perspective might apply to intelligence. Maybe genetics has had some small effect on your intelligence. Maybe it has made you a little quicker to understand things, or made your memory a little bit better, or made you more persistent on cognitive tasks, or simply made you more curious. Your parents noticed this and encouraged your interest. They may not even have been aware that they were encouraging you. They might have talked to you about more sophisticated subjects and used a broader vocabulary than they otherwise would have. As you got older, you saw yourself more and more as one of

FIGURE 6: Who would you select for your team?

the "smart kids."You made friends with other smart kids, and entered into friendly but quite real competition for the highest grades.Then too, maybe genetics subtly pushed you away from other endeavors.You may be quicker cognitively, but you're a little slower and clumsier physically than others.That has made you avoid situations that might develop your athletic skills (such as pickup basketball games) and instead stay inside and read.

The key idea here is that genetics and the environment interact. Small differences in genetic inheritance can steer people to seek different experiences in their environments, and it is differences in these environmental experiences, especially over the long term, that have large cognitive consequences. For that reason, we shouldn't assume that twins have experienced different environments even though they were raised in different households.The fact that their genes are the same may well have encouraged them to seek out similar environments.

Now, why did I take you through this long story about intelligence? Because what we will consider doing for students who seem unintelligent differs depend- ing on the nature of intelligence. If intelligence were all a matter of one's genetic inheritance, then there wouldn't be much point in trying to make kids smarter. Instead, we'd try to get students to do the best they could given the genetically determined intelligence they have.We'd also think seriously about trying to steer the not-so-smart kids toward intellectually undemanding tracks in schools, figuring that they are destined for low-level jobs anyway. But that's not the way things are. *Intelligence is malleable. It can be improved.*

Great! So how do we improve intelligence? The first step is to convince our students that intelligence can be improved.

How Beliefs About Intelligence Matter

Consider two hypothetical students. Felicia seems very concerned about whether she appears intelligent.When given a choice of tasks, she picks the easy one to be sure that she succeeds.When confronted with a challenging task, she quits after the first setback, usually protesting loudly that she is tired, or offering some other excuse. Molly, in contrast, doesn't seem bothered by failure. Given a choice, she picks tasks that are new to her and seems to enjoy learning from them, even if they are frustrating.When a task is difficult, Molly doesn't withdraw, she persists, trying a new strategy (Figure 7).

You have doubtless had Mollys and Felicias in your classroom. What accounts for the differences between them? One important factor is what they believe about intel- ligence. Students like Felicia believe that intelligence is *fixed*, determined at birth; and because it's unchangeable, she's very concerned that she get the "right label," so she picks easy tasks. Felicia's beliefs about intelligence really paint her into a corner. She thinks that smart people don't need to work hard to succeed—they succeed through their superior intelligence.Therefore, working hard is a sign of being dumb.Thus, although it's very important to Felicia to appear smart, she won't allow herself to work hard to be sure she succeeds because she thinks hard work makes her look dumb!

FIGURE 7: If this trivia game allowed players to choose a difficult or easy question, Felicia would choose an easy one to increase the chances that she would get it right and so appear smart, whereas Molly would choose a difficult question in the hopes of learning something. What type of question would you choose?

Molly, conversely, views intelligence as malleable. She thinks she gets smarter by learning new things. Thus failure is not nearly so threatening to Molly as it is to Felicia, because she doesn't believe it says anything permanent about her abilities. When Molly fails, she figures she didn't work hard enough or hasn't learned about this particular topic yet. Thus Molly feels that she's in control of her success or failure because she can always work harder if she fails. Molly sees nothing embarrassing in admitting ignorance or in getting a wrong answer.

Therefore, she's not motivated to pick easy tasks; instead, she's more likely to pick challenging tasks, because she might learn from them. Molly also doesn't think that working hard is a sign of stupidity—on the contrary, she thinks hard work is a sign that one is trying to get smarter.

It sounds like Molly is much more likely than Felicia to succeed in school, and there is good evidence that that's true. Students who believe that intelligence can be improved with hard work get higher grades than students who believe that intelligence is an immutable trait.

Any teacher would rather have a room full of Mollys than a room full of Felicias. Where do students get their ideas about intelligence and ability? Children's understandings of intelligence have different aspects. A child must understand that his ability affects how well he does things, he must develop beliefs about his own ability, and he must understand that he has different ability levels for different types of tasks. Explaining how children come to deeper and deeper understandings of these issues is quite complex. Many factors contribute, but one factor in particular has been studied intensively: how children are praised.

In a classic study on the effect of praise, the experimenters asked fifth graders to work on some problems in which they were to find patterns (Figure 8).[3] The first set of problems was fairly easy so that the students would solve most of them. The students were then praised for their success. All were told, "Wow, you did very well on these problems. You got *[number of problems]* right. That's a really high score." Some were then told, "You must be smart at these problems." In other words, they were praised for their *ability*. Others were told, "You must have worked hard at these problems," thus receiving praise for their *effort*. Each student was then interviewed by

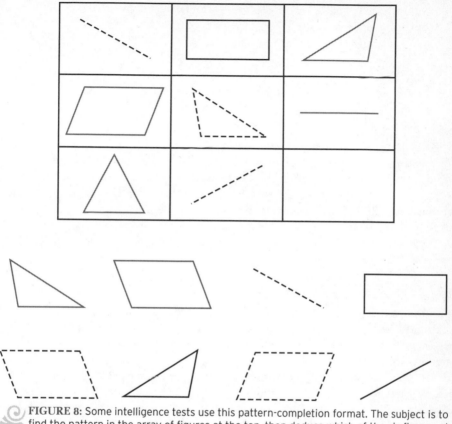

FIGURE 8: Some intelligence tests use this pattern-completion format. The subject is to find the pattern in the array of figures at the top, then deduce which of the six figures at the bottom completes the array.

a different experimenter to learn what the students thought about intelligence. The results showed that those who had been praised for their ability ("you're smart") were more likely to describe a fixed view of intelligence than those who were praised for their effort ("you worked hard"), who were more likely to describe a malleable view of intelligence. Similar effects have been shown in many studies, including studies of children as young as four years old.

Naturally a single experience with an experimenter whom a child doesn't know will not shape his or her beliefs about intelligence forever, but a minor difference in praise—making it about ability or about effort—did affect these children's beliefs at least for the duration of the experiment. It's a reasonable guess that students' beliefs are shaped for the long term by what they hear from parents, teachers, and peers, and by how they see these people act.

What's especially interesting about this work is that it's concerned with praise. How can it be a bad idea to tell a student she's smart? By praising a child's intelligence, we let her know that she solved the problems correctly because she is smart, not because she worked hard. It is then a short step for the student to infer that getting problems wrong is a sign of being dumb.

Implications for the Classroom

What can we do for slow learners? The point of this chapter is to emphasize that slow learners are not dumb.[†] They probably differ little from other students in terms of their potential. Intelligence can be changed.

This conclusion should not be taken to mean that these students can easily catch up. Slow students have the same potential as bright students, but they probably differ in what they know, in their motivation, in their persistence in the face of academic setbacks, and in their self-image as students. I fully believe that these students can catch up, but it must be acknowledged that they are far behind, and that catching up will take enormous effort. How can we help? To help slow learners catch up, we must first be sure they believe that they can improve, and next we must try to persuade them that it will be worth it.

Praise Effort, Not Ability

This principle should be obvious from the research I've described. You want to encourage your students to think of their intelligence as under their control, and especially that they can develop their intelligence through hard work. Therefore, you should praise *processes* rather than ability. In addition to praising effort (if appropriate), you might praise a student for persistence in the face of challenges, or for taking responsibility for her work. Avoid insincere praise, however. Dishonest praise is actually destructive. If you tell a student, "Wow, you really worked hard on this project!" when the student knows good and well that she didn't, you lose credibility.

Tell Them That Hard Work Pays Off

Praising process rather than ability sends the unspoken message that intelligence is under the student's control. There is no reason not to make that message explicit as well, especially as children approach upper elementary school. Tell your students how hard famous scientists, inventors, authors, and other "geniuses" must work in order to be so smart; but even more important, make that lesson apply to the work your students do. If some students in your school brag about not studying, explode that myth; tell them that most students who do well in school work quite hard.

Persuading students of that truth may not be easy. I once had a student who was on the football team and devoted a great deal of time to practice, with little time left over for academics. He attributed his poor grades to his being "a dumb jock." I had a conversation with him that went something like this:

> DTW: Is there a player on the team who has a lot of natural ability but who just doesn't work very hard, goofs off during practices, and that sort of thing?
>
> STUDENT: Of course. There's a guy like that on every team.
>
> DTW: Do the other players respect him?

STUDENT: Of course not. They think he's an idiot because he's got talent that he's not developing.

DTW: But don't they respect him because he's the best player?

STUDENT: He's not the best. He's good, but lots of other guys are better.

DTW: Academics is just the same. Most people have to work really hard at it. There are a few who get by without working very hard, but not many. And nobody likes or respects them very much.

Academics is not always analogous to sports, but in this case I think the analogy holds, and for whatever reason, it has usually made sense to my students, even the nonathletes.

Treat Failure As a Natural Part of Learning

If you want to increase your intelligence, you have to challenge yourself. That means taking on tasks that are a bit beyond your reach, and that means you may very well fail, at least the first time around. Fear of failure can therefore be a significant obstacle to tackling this sort of challenging work, but failure should not be a big deal.

My first job after college was in the office of a member of Congress. I didn't see the Big Boss very often, and I was pretty intimidated by him. I remember well the first time I did something stupid (I've forgotten what) and it was brought to his attention. I mumbled some apology. He looked at me for a long moment and said, "Kid, the only people who don't make mistakes are the ones who never do anything." It was tremendously freeing—not because I avoided judgment for the incident, but it was the first time I really understood that you have to learn to accept failure if you're ever going to get things done. Michael Jordan put it this way: "I've missed more than nine thousand shots in my career. I've lost almost three hundred games. Twenty-six times I've been trusted to take the game-winning shot and missed. I've failed over and over and over again in my life. And that is why I succeed."

Try to create a classroom atmosphere in which failure, while not desirable, is neither embarrassing nor wholly negative. Failure means you're about to learn something. You're going to find out that there's something you didn't understand or didn't know how to do. Most important, *model* this attitude for your students. When you fail—and who doesn't?—let them see you take a positive, learning attitude.

Don't Take Study Skills for Granted

Make a list of all of the things you ask students to do at home. Consider which of these things have other tasks embedded in them and ask yourself whether the slower students really know how to do them. For older students, if you announce that there will be a quiz, you assume they will study for it. Do your slower students really know how to study? Do they know how to assess the importance of different things they've read and heard and seen? Do they know how long they ought to study for a quiz? (At the college level, my low-performing students frequently protest their low grades by telling me, "But I studied for three or four hours for this test!" I know that the high-scoring students study about twenty hours.) Do your slower students know some simple tricks to help with planning and organizing their time?

These concerns are especially important for students who are just starting to receive serious homework assignments—probably around the seventh grade. There is a period of adjustment for most students when homework is no longer "bring in three rocks from your yard or the park" and turns into "read Chapter Four and answer the even numbered questions at the back." All students must learn new skills as homework becomes more demanding—skills of self-discipline, time management, and resourcefulness (for example, knowing what to do when they're stumped). Students who are already behind will have that much more trouble doing work on their own at home, and they may be slower to learn these skills. Don't take for granted that your slower students have these skills, even if they *should* have acquired them in previous grades.

Catching Up Is the Long-Term Goal

It is important to be realistic about what it will take for students to catch up. In Chapter Two I pointed out that the more we know, the easier it is to learn new things. Thus, if your slower students know less than your brighter students, they can't simply work at the same pace as the bright students; doing only that, they will continue to fall behind! To catch up, the slower students must worker *harder* than the brighter students.

I think of this situation as analogous to dieting. It is difficult to maintain one's willpower for the extended period necessary to reach a target weight. The problem with diets is that they require difficult choices to be made again and again, and each time we make the right choice, we don't get rewarded with the instant weight loss we deserve! When a dieter makes a wrong choice or two, there is a tendency to feel like a failure, and then to give up the diet altogether. A great deal of research shows that the most successful diets are *not* diets. Rather, they are lifestyle changes that the person believes he could live with every day for years—for example, switching from regular milk to skim milk, or walking the dog instead of just letting her out in the morning, or drinking black coffee instead of lattes.

When thinking about helping slower students catch up, it may be smart to set interim goals that are achievable and concrete. These goals might include such strategies as devoting a fixed time every day to homework, reading a weekly news magazine, or watching one educational DVD on science each week. Needless to say, enlisting parents in such efforts, if possible, will be an enormous help.

Show Students That You Have Confidence in Them

Ask ten people you know, "Who was the most important teacher in your life?" I've asked dozens of people this question and have noticed two interesting things. First, most people have a ready answer. Second, the reason that one teacher made a strong impression is almost always emotional. The reasons are never things like "She taught me a lot of math." People say things like "She made me believe in myself" or "She taught me to love knowledge." In addition, people always tell me that their important teacher set high standards and believed that the student could meet those standards.

In considering how to communicate that confidence to your students, we return to the subject of praise. Be wary of praising second-rate work in your slower students.

Suppose you have a student who usually fails to complete his work. He manages to submit a project on time, although it's not very good. It's tempting to praise the student—after all, the fact that he submitted something is an improvement over his past performance. But consider the message that praising a mediocre project sends. You say "good job," but that really means "good job *for someone like you.*" The student is probably not so naive as to think that his project is really all that great. By praising substandard work, you send the message that you have lower expectations for this student. Better to say, "I appreciate that you finished the project on time, and I thought your opening paragraph was interesting, but I think you could have done a better job of organizing it. Let's talk about how."

Thus far we have devoted all of our attention to students' minds, with only an occasional mention of their teacher's cognitive system. But obviously your mind is not qualitatively different from the minds of your students. Beyond tuning your teaching to their minds, can the principles set forth here improve your teaching?

Notes

* The task force was created after *The Bell Curve* was published. As you may recall, *The Bell Curve* is a very controversial book that claims, among other things, that observed differences between the races in IQ test scores are largely genetic—in short, that some races are inherently smarter than others. The leadership of the American Psychological Association felt that there was a lot of misinformation about intelligence in the book, and in articles published in response to the book. The task force was assembled to create a summary statement describing what was actually known about intelligence.

† This is not to say that students don't have learning disabilities. Some do. My conclusions in this chapter do not apply to these students.

Bibliography

Less Technical

Dweck, C. (2006). *Mindset: The new psychology of success.* New York: Random House. Carol Dweck's research has been hugely important to psychologists' understanding of the role of one's attitude toward intelligence in learning and in schooling. This book provides a readable overview of her work from the source herself.

Plucker, J. A. (Ed.) (2003). Human intelligence: Historical influences, current controversies, teaching resources. Available at http://www.indiana.edu/~intell, a website maintained by educational and cognitive psychologists at the University of Indiana, with wide-ranging information about intelligence, biographies of prominent researchers, a frequently-asked-questions page, and so forth.

Segal, N. L. (1999). *Entwined lives: Twins and what they tell us about human behavior.* New York: Dutton. A readable review of twins research and what it tells us about genetic influences on our behavior.

More Technical

Carroll, J. B. (1993). *Human cognitive abilities: A survey of factor-analytic studies.* New York: Cambridge University Press. This book reports the results of Carroll's massive review of testing data, the conclusion of which was the hierarchical model of intelligence, with *g* at the pinnacle and increasingly specific abilities as one moves downward.

Dickens, W. T. (2008). Cognitive ability. In S. Durlauf & L. E. Blume (Eds.), *The new Palgrave dictionary of economics.* New York: Palgrave Macmillan. A brief and understandable overview of how to reconcile apparently large genetic effects and large environmental effects on intelligence.

Dickens, W. T., & Flynn, J. R. (2001). Heritability estimates versus large environmental effects: The IQ paradox resolved. *Psychological Review, 108,* 346–369. A very important article proposing a model that reconciles the apparently large genetic effects with the apparently large environmental effects by suggesting that genetic effects may prompt individuals to seek particular environments.

Lazar, I., & Darlington, R. (1982). Lasting effects of early education: A report from the Consortium for Longitudinal Studies. *Monographs of the Society for Research in Child Development, 47* (2–3). One of many studies showing that environmental interventions (such as changes in schooling) can have large effects on cognitive ability.

Neisser, U., & others (1995). *Intelligence: Knowns and unknowns.* Washington, DC: American Psychological Association. Available at http://www.lrainc.com/swtaboo/taboos/apa01.html. The American Psychological Association Task Force's statement on intelligence; among other things, provides a reasonable definition of the construct.

Schmidt, F. L., & Hunter, J. E. (1998). The validity and utility of selection methods: Practical and theoretical implications of eighty-five years of research findings. *Psychological Bulletin, 124,* 262–274. A review of the evidence showing that intelligence (as measured by standard tests) is related to job performance.

9

What About My Mind?

Question: Most of this book has focused on the minds of students. What about the minds of teachers?

Answer: In Chapter One I outlined the cognitive requirements for students to think effectively: they need space in working memory, relevant background knowledge, and experience in the relevant mental procedures. Throughout the rest of the chapters I detailed principles of the mind that illustrate how those requirements might be met. Your mind is not different from those of your students. The cognitive principle that guides this chapter is

> Teaching, like any complex cognitive skill, must be practiced to be improved.

I have discussed a lot of findings from cognitive science thus far. All of this discussion has focused on the minds of students. What about you? Isn't teaching a cognitive skill? So couldn't we apply these findings from cognitive science to *your* mind?

Teaching is indeed a cognitive skill, and everything I have said about students' minds applies to yours. Let's bring back the picture of the mind from Chapter One (see Figure 1, next page) so I can briefly refresh your memory about the cognitive apparatus that must be in place for any type of effective thinking to occur, including effective teaching.

Thinking is the putting together of information in new ways—for example, comparing the structure of the solar system with the structure of an atom and recognizing that they have some similarities. This sort of manipulation of information happens in working memory, which is often called the staging ground of thought. The information manipulated in working memory might come from the environment (from things we see or hear, for example, such as a teacher describing the structure of an atom) or from long-term memory (from things we already know, for example, the structure of the solar system).

We use *procedures* to manipulate information (for example, a procedure that compares features of objects such as a solar system and an atom). Our long-term memory

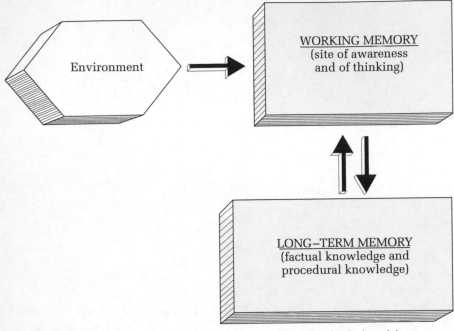

FIGURE 1: The return, and the swan song, of just about the simplest model of the mind possible.

can store simple procedures as in "compare features of these two objects," as well as complex, multistage procedures to support tasks with lots of intermediate steps. For example, you might have stored the procedure to make pancakes or to change the oil in a car or to write a well-organized paragraph.

To think effectively, we need sufficient room in working memory, which has limited space. We also need the right factual and procedural knowledge in long-term memory. Let's think about how teaching fits into this framework.

Teaching as a Cognitive Skill

I have described to teachers how cognitive psychologists talk about working memory: they refer to it as a mental place where we juggle several things at once and where, if we try to juggle too many things, one or more things will be dropped. Teachers always respond in the same way: "Well of course! You've just described my work day." Formal experiments confirm this strong intuition; teaching is quite demanding of working memory.

It's just as evident that factual knowledge is important to teaching. In the last ten years or so, many observers have emphasized that teachers ought to have rich subject-matter knowledge, and there do seem to be some data that students of these teachers learn more, especially in middle and high school and especially in math. Somewhat less well known but just as important are other data showing that *pedagogical content knowledge* is also important. That is, for teachers, just knowing algebra really well isn't enough. You need to have knowledge particular to *teaching* algebra. Pedagogical content knowledge might include such things as knowledge of a typical student's conceptual understanding of slope, or the types of concepts that must be practiced and those that need not be. When you think about it, if pedagogical content knowledge were *not* important, then anyone who understood algebra could teach it well, and we know that's not true.

It's also pretty evident that a teacher makes extensive use of procedures stored in long-term memory. Some of these procedures handle mundane tasks, for example, the procedure for passing out papers or for leading students through the Pledge of Allegiance, or for turn-taking during read-alouds. These stored procedures can also be much more complex, for example, a method for explaining what a limit of a function is or for handling a potentially dangerous student conflict in the cafeteria.

OK, so if teaching is a cognitive skill just like any other, how can you apply what I've discussed to your teaching? How can you increase (1) space in your working memory, (2) your relevant factual knowledge, and (3) your relevant procedural knowledge? You may recall that the cognitive principle guiding our discussion in Chapter Five was *It is virtually impossible to become proficient at a mental task without extended practice.* Your best bet for improving your teaching is to practice teaching.

The Importance of Practice

Until now, I have been a bit casual in how I have talked about practice. I have made it sound synonymous with experience. It is not. Experience means you are simply engaged in the activity. Practice means you are trying to improve your performance. For example, I'm not an especially good driver, even though I've been driving for about thirty years. Like most people my age I'm experienced—that is, I've done a lot of driving—but I'm not well practiced, because for almost all of that thirty years I didn't try to improve. I *did* work at my driving skills when I first got behind the wheel. After perhaps fifty hours of practice, I was driving with skill that seemed adequate to me, so I stopped trying to improve (Figure 2). That's what most people do for driving, golf, typing, and indeed most of the skills they learn.

FIGURE 2: I have a great deal of driving experience, but I have practiced driving relatively little and therefore haven't improved my driving much in the last thirty years.

The same seems to be true for teachers too. A great deal of data show that teachers improve during their first five years in the field, as measured by student learning. After five years, however, the curve gets flat, and a teacher with twenty years of experience is (on average) no better or worse than a teacher with ten. It appears that most teachers work on their teaching until it is above some threshold and they are satisfied with their proficiency.* It's easy to criticize such teachers and to think indignantly, "They should *always* strive to improve!" Certainly we'd all like to think that we are always seeking to better ourselves, but we also must be realistic. Practice, as I'm about to describe, is hard. It takes a great deal of work, and very likely work that infringes on time that might be spent with family or in other pursuits. But I am trusting that if you've read this far into the book, you are prepared to do some hard work. So let's get started.

First, we need to define *practice*. We've said that it's more than engaging in the activity; you also have to try to improve. But how? First, practice entails getting feedback from knowledgeable people. Writers seek criticism from editors. Basketball teams hire coaches. Cognitive scientists like me get written appraisals of our experimental work from expert colleagues. When you think about it, how can you possibly improve unless there is some assessment of how you're doing? Without feedback, you don't know what changes will make you a better cognitive scientist, golfer, or teacher (Figure 3).

It's true that teachers get feedback from their students. You can tell if a lesson is going well or poorly, but that sort of feedback is not sufficient because it's not terribly specific. For example, your students' bored expressions tell you they aren't listening, but they don't tell you what you might do differently. In addition, you probably miss more of what's happening in your classroom than you think you do. You are busy *teaching* and don't have the luxury of simply *watching* what is happening in your classroom. It's hard to think about how things are going when you're in the middle of trying to make them

FIGURE 3: Most of us treat Monopoly as a diversion, but serious players compete in tournaments and are highly skilled. That skill is developed through practice, and practice requires expert feedback. Ken Koury, pictured here, is a U.S. Monopoly player who has served as a coach at the national and international tournament levels.

go well! A final reason it's hard to critique your own teaching is that we are not impartial observers of our own behavior. Some people lack confidence and are harder on themselves than they ought to be whereas others (most of us, actually) interpret their world in ways that are favorable to themselves. Social psychologists call this the self-serving bias. When things go well, it's because we are skilled and hardworking. When things go poorly, it's because we were unlucky, or because someone else made a mistake (Figure 4).

FIGURE 4: People who get in automobile accidents often blame the other driver. At http://www.car-accidents.com people describe accidents they have been in, and most protest that they were not at fault. For example, one driver claims, "The emergency services that attended the scene ruled it was my fault as I failed to give way to her vehicle (which is technically correct), but did not take into account my story."

For these reasons, it is usually quite informative to see your class through someone else's eyes.

In addition to requiring feedback, practice usually means investing time in activities that are not the target task itself but done for the sake of improving that task. For example, aspiring chess players don't just play lots of chess games. They also spend considerable time studying and memorizing chess openings and analyzing the matches that other experts have played (Figure 5). Athletes of all sorts do weight and cardiovascular training to improve their endurance in their sport (Figure 6).

FIGURE 5: Aspiring chess experts cannot simply play a lot of chess. They must also study the game, even memorizing standard game openings. If your opponent starts to play the Giuoco Piano, shown here, and you're unfamiliar with it, you're likely to fall into a trap and lose.

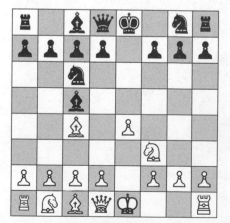

The Giuoco Piano
(or Italian Opening)

FIGURE 6: Tiger Woods is famous for working very hard on his golf game, including running and lifting weights, activities that are not direct practice for golf. At a tournament in Tulsa, Oklahoma, in 2007 the temperature hovered around 101 degrees. Woods was not disturbed by the heat, noting that he maintains a challenging training regimen. He commented, "You should always train hard and bust your butt." Thus, practice for Woods includes activities that are not obviously related to golf.

FIGURE 7: Two heads are generally better than one, and the buddy system is commonly used by young students when they are out on a field trip, as well as by police officers, scuba divers, and fire fighters.

To summarize, if you want to be a better teacher, you cannot be satisfied simply to gain experience as the years pass. You must also practice, and practice means (1) consciously trying to improve, (2) seeking feedback on your teaching, and (3) undertaking activities for the sake of improvement, even if they don't *directly* contribute to your job. There are lots of ways you could do these things, of course. Here I suggest one method.

A Method for Getting and Giving Feedback

There is not, to my knowledge, a method of practice for teachers that has been rigorously proven to be effective. I'm going to suggest a method to get you started, but I encourage you to experiment. I also encourage you to think carefully about a few features of this type of practice that I think are bound to be important.

First, you need to work with at least one other person. Someone else will see things in your class that you cannot, simply because she is not you and thus can be more impartial. (Of course she also has a different background and experiences than you, and that helps.) Furthermore, as anyone who has exercised knows, having a buddy helps you to stick with a difficult task (Figure 7). Second, you should recognize that working on your teaching *will* be a threat to your ego. Teaching is very personal, so taking a close look at it (and inviting one or more other people to do the same) is scary. It's a good idea not to shrug off that concern ("I can take it!") but instead to put measures in place to deal with it.

Step 1: Identify Another Teacher (or Two) with Whom You Would Like to Work

Naturally it will help if this person teaches the same grade as you do. More important, however, is that you trust each other, and that your partner is as committed to the project as you are.

Step 2: Tape Yourself and Watch the Tapes Alone

There is a lot of value in videotaping your teaching. As I mentioned earlier, it's difficult to watch your class while you're busy teaching it, but you can watch a video at your leisure, and you can replay important parts. If you don't own a video camera, you may be able to borrow one from your school. You might want to send a note home with students to let parents know that their child is being videotaped, that the tapes are purely for your professional development and will not be used for any other purpose, and that the tapes will be erased at the end of the school year. (You should check with your principal on this matter.)

Simply set the camera on a tripod in a place where you think it will capture most of the class, and switch it on at the start of a lesson. The first few tapes you make will probably give you important information about logistical matters. You might not be able to tape every type of lesson. For example, you only have one camera, so you'll be able to see only part of the classroom. Also, picking up audio is frequently difficult, so noisy participatory lessons may not work well.

I suggest that you first tape a lesson that you feel typically goes pretty well. It's not easy to watch yourself (and later to critique yourself), so stack the deck in your favor at first. There will be time enough later to examine the things you suspect you don't do so well.

You can expect it to take a class or two for your students to become accustomed to the idea of being videotaped, although this is generally not a concern for long. Then too, it will probably take a couple of tapes for *you* to become accustomed to hearing your voice and seeing yourself move on tape.[†]

Once you have these practical matters settled, you can focus on content. Watch these tapes with a notepad in hand. Don't begin by judging your performance. Consider first what surprises you about the class. What do you notice about your students that you didn't already know? What do you notice about yourself? Spend time *observing*. Don't start by critiquing (Figure 8).

Step 3: With Your Partner, Watch Tapes of Other Teachers

Once you have grown accustomed to watching videotapes of yourself, it's time to include your partner. But don't watch tapes of each other yet. Observe tapes of other teachers. You can find taped classrooms in several places on the Internet, for example, http://www

FIGURE 8: Avid golfers videotape themselves in an effort to learn more about their strokes. Initially that may seem odd: Don't they know what they're doing? To a surprising extent, no. A golfer's stroke is so practiced that it may feel quite comfortable, even though the golfer may, for example, be arching his back in a way that he knows is bad form.

.videoclassroom.org and http://www.learner.org.

The reason to watch tapes of other teachers first is to gain practice in constructive observation and commenting, and to get this practice in a non-threatening situation. Further, you will also get a sense of whether you and your partner are compatible for this work.

What are you looking for on these tapes? It's not productive just to sit down and watch them like a movie, waiting to see what will happen. You should have a concrete goal, such as observing classroom management or observing the emotional atmosphere of the classroom. Many of the tapes featured on Web sites are there for a particular reason, so it will usually be clear why the person who posted the tape thought it was interesting.

This is your chance to practice observing and commenting on a classroom. Imagine what you would say to the teacher you observe. Indeed, imagine that the teacher is there in the room with you. In general, comments should have the following two properties:

1. *They should be supportive.* Being supportive doesn't mean you are there *only* to say positive things. It does mean that even when you are saying something negative, you are supporting the teacher you are observing. *The point of this exercise is not to "spot the flaw."* The positive comments should outnumber the negative ones. I know that principle seems corny, because when listening to positive comments a teacher can't help but think, "He is saying that only because he knows he is supposed to say something positive." Even so, positive comments remind the teacher

that she *is* doing a lot of things right, and those things should be acknowledged and reinforced.

2. *They should be concrete and about the behaviors you observe, not about qualities you infer.* Thus, don't just say, "She really knows how to explain things"; instead say, "That third example really made the concept click for students." Rather than saying, "His classroom management is a mess," say, "I noticed that a lot of the students were having trouble listening when he asked them to sit down."

Step 4: With Your Partner, Watch and Comment on Each Other's Tapes

You should not undertake this step until you feel quite comfortable watching tapes of other teachers with your partner. This means you should feel comfortable in what you say *and* you should feel that your partner knows how to be supportive; that is, you should feel that you wouldn't mind if your partner's comments were directed to you instead of to the unknown teacher on the tape. The ground rules for commenting on the tapes of other teachers apply here as well: be supportive, be concrete, and focus on behaviors. Because this process is now interactive, there are a few additional things to think about (Figure 9).

The teacher whose tape is being viewed should set the goal for the session. She should describe what she would like the other teacher to watch for in the session. It is vital that the viewer respect this request, even if she sees something else on the tape that she thinks is important. If you present a tape hoping to get some ideas about engaging students in a lesson on fractions and your partner says, "Gee, I notice some real classroom-management issues here," you're going to feel ambushed, and you're not going to be motivated to continue the process.

What if your partner keeps wanting to work on trivial things and you notice that there are bigger problems that she's ignoring? If you and your partner make a habit of taping yourselves, there will likely be a time when this issue will come up naturally in the course of discussing something else. You and your partner also might consider agreeing that after viewing, say, ten tapes, each of you will suggest to the other something they might work on that hasn't come up yet.

FIGURE 9: When you watch and comment on videotapes of your partner teaching, it is very important to monitor both the content and the tone of what you say. Something that you may not mean as a criticism may sound like one, and most people's reaction would be simply to shut down.

A final point. The purpose of watching your partner teach is to help her reflect on her practice, to think about her teaching. You do that by describing what you see. Don't suggest what the teacher should do differently unless you are asked. You don't want to come off as thinking you have all the answers. If your partner wants your ideas about how to address an issue, she'll ask you, in which case you should of course offer any ideas you have. But until you're asked, remain in the mode of a careful, supportive observer, and don't slip into the role of the expert fixer, regardless of how confident you are that you have a good solution.

Step 5: Bring It Back to the Classroom and Follow Up

The purpose of videotaping yourself is to increase your awareness of what is happening in your classroom, and to gain a new perspective on what you are actually doing and why, and on what your students are doing and why. With that awareness will almost certainly come some resolve to make some changes. The way to do that is as follows: Make a plan that during a specific lesson you will do one thing that addresses the issue with which you are concerned. Even if you think of three things you want to do, do just one. Keep it simple. You'll have plenty of chances to add the other two things. And of course tape the lesson so you can see what happened.

❧❧

The program I have sketched here is rooted in the cognitive principles I have described. For example, I emphasized in Chapter One that the most important limitation to thinking is the capacity of working memory. That's why I recommend videotaping—because it's difficult to think deeply about your teaching while you're actually teaching. Also, because memory is based on what we think about (Chapter Three), we can't expect to remember later a complete version of what happened in a class; we remember only what we paid attention to in class. In Chapter Six I said that experts see the world differently than novices do—they see deep structure, not surface structure—and the key reason they can see this way is that they have broad and deep experience in their field. Careful observation of a variety of classrooms will help you better recognize classroom dynamics, and careful observation of your own classroom will help you recognize the dynamics that are typical of your own teaching.

In Chapter Two I emphasized the importance of background knowledge to effective problem solving. Background knowledge means not just subject matter knowledge; for a teacher it also means knowledge of students and how they interact with you, with each other, and with the material you teach. Careful observation, especially in partnership with another, well-informed teacher is a good method for gaining that background knowledge. Finally, Chapter Eight painted a hopeful picture of human intelligence—that it can be changed through sustained hard work. There is every reason to believe this is true of teaching.

Consciously Trying to Improve: Self-Management

I've mentioned three components of practice: getting informative feedback, seeking out other activities that can improve your skill (even if they are not practice of the skill itself), and consciously trying to improve your teaching. The last of these components sounds like the easiest to implement. "Sure, I want to improve. Let's go!" But how many of us have made a solemn New Year's resolution only to find ourselves in the second week of January saying, "You know, my birthday is February 4; February 5 would be a *great* time to get serious about this diet." Resolving to do something difficult is easy. Following through is not. Here are a few suggestions that might help.

First, it might help to plan for the extra work that will be required. In Chapter One I pointed out that most of us are on autopilot most of the time. Rather than think through the optimal thing to do moment to moment, we retrieve from memory what we've done in the past. Teaching is no different. It's to be expected that once you have gained sufficient experience you will teach on autopilot at least part of the time. There's nothing wrong with that, but serious work at improving your teaching means that you will be on autopilot less often. It's going to be tiring, and thinking carefully about things you don't do as well as you'd like to is emotionally draining. You may need a little extra support from your spouse and family. You may need to be more vigilant in scheduling relaxation time.

You will also spend more time on teaching. In addition to the hours spent at home grading, planning lessons, and so forth, now you will also spend more time than usual reviewing what you're doing well and poorly in the classroom, and planning how to do things differently than you've ever done them before. If you're going to spend an extra five hours each week (or three hours, or one hour) on teaching, where is that time going to come from? If you schedule extra time for this work, you are much more likely to actually do it.

Finally, remember that you don't need to do everything at once. It's not realistic to expect to go from wherever you are now to "great" in a year or two. Because you're not trying to fix everything at once, you have to set priorities. Decide what is most important to work on, and focus on concrete, manageable steps to move you toward your goal.

Smaller Steps

The program I've laid out is time consuming, there is no doubt. I can well imagine that some teachers will think to themselves, "In an ideal world, sure—but between taking care of my kids and the house and the million other things I'm *supposed* to be doing and am not, I just don't have the time." I absolutely respect that. So start smaller. Here are a few ideas for ways you can work on your teaching that are less time consuming.

Keep a Teaching Diary

Make notes that include what you intended to do and how you thought it went. Did the lesson basically work? If not, what are your thoughts as to why it didn't? Every so often take a little time to read past entries. Look for patterns in what sorts of lessons went well and which didn't, for situations that frustrated you, for moments of teaching that really keep you going, and so on.

FIGURE 10: Self-reflection is an important part of the effort to improve any skill. Maintaining a diary is a great way to be reflective.

Lots of people start a diary but then find it difficult to stick with it. Here are a few tips that might help. First, try to find a time of day when you can write and make it a time that you're likely to be able to maintain. (For example, I'm a morning person, so I know that if I planned to write just before bed, it would never happen.) Second, try to write *something* each day, even if it's only "Today was an average day." The consistency of pulling out the diary and writing something will help make it a habit (Figure 10). Third, remember that this project is solely for *you*. Don't worry about the quality of the writing, don't feel guilty if you don't write much, and don't beat yourself up if you miss days, or even weeks. If you do miss some time, don't try to catch up. You'll never remember what happened, and the thought of all that work will prevent you from starting again. Finally, be honest both in your criticism and in your praise; there is no reason not to dwell on moments that make you proud.

Start a Discussion Group with Fellow Teachers

Get a group of teachers together for meetings, say, once every two weeks. There are at least two purposes to such groups. One purpose is to give and receive social support. It's a chance for teachers to grumble about problems, share their successes, and so forth. The goal is to feel connected and supported. Another purpose, not completely independent of the first, is to serve as a forum for teachers to bring up problems they are having and get ideas for solutions from the group. It is a good idea to be clear from the start about whether your group is to serve the first function, the second, or both. If different people have different ideas about the purpose of the group, hurt feelings are likely. If your group is very goal oriented, you can also have everyone read an article in a professional journal (for example, in *American Educator, Educational Leadership,* or *Phi Delta Kappan*) for discussion.

Observe

What makes students in the age group you teach tick? What motivates them, how do they talk to one another, what are their passions? You probably know your students pretty well in the classroom, but would your students say they are "themselves" when they are in your classroom? Would it be useful to you to see them acting in ways that are not contrived for the classroom or when they are surrounded by a different group of children?

Find a location where you can observe children in the age group you teach. To observe preschoolers, go to a park; to watch teenagers, go to the food court at the mall. You'll probably have to go to a different neighborhood or even a different town, because this exercise won't work if you're recognized.[‡] Just watch the kids. Don't go with a specific plan or agenda. Just watch. Initially, you probably will get bored. You'll think, "Right, I've seen this before." But if you keep watching, really watching, you will start to notice things you hadn't noticed before. You'll notice more subtle cues about social interactions, aspects of personality, and how students think. Allow yourself the time and space simply to observe, and you will see remarkable things.

Notes

[*] Naturally there is variability. There are teachers who always strive to improve and there are teachers who get lazier as time passes. Teachers are no different from anyone else. Another possibility is that, at least for some teachers, improving is difficult because changes in district policy, leadership, and so on make the job something of a moving target.

[†] My father started to go bald at about age forty. He lost hair mostly on the back of his head and it wasn't very noticeable from the front, but by the time he was fifty-five the bald spot was pretty sizable. At that time he saw a photograph of a crowd of people, including himself with his back to the camera. He pointed to himself and said, "Who is that bald-headed gentleman?" It's not easy seeing what the camera sees.

[‡] The wife of a friend of mine teaches seventh grade. My friend told me that walking downtown with her is like being accompanied by a celebrity—everyone knows her, and even the "cool" kids greet her and are excited to get a greeting in return. He also mentioned that she's not reluctant to use her authority. "She puts on that teacher voice and tells kids who are misbehaving to knock it off, and they always do."

Bibliography

Less Technical

Bransford, J. D., Brown, A. L., & Cocking, R. R. (Eds.). *How people learn: Brain, mind, experience, and school.* Washington, DC: National Academy Press. This volume was written by two committees organized by the National Research Council, which included many of the leading scholars on human learning. It is written in an accessible style and includes examples of what the committee took to be lessons in tune with the science of human learning.

More Technical

Ericsson, K. A., Krampe, R. T., & Clemens, T-R. (1993). The role of deliberate practice in the acquisition of expert performance. *Psychological Review, 100,* 363–406. This is the classic article defining practice and outlining the ways in which it is vital to the development of expertise.

Feldon, D. F. (2007). Cognitive load and classroom teaching: The double-edged sword of automaticity. *Educational Psychologist, 42,* 123–137. This article examines the role of automaticity in teaching practice, and the positive and negative consequences of its development.

Floden, R. E., & Meniketti, M. (2005). Research on the effects of coursework in the arts and sciences and in the foundations of education. In M. Cochran-Smith & K. M. Zeichner, (Eds.), *Studying teacher education* (pp. 261–308). Mahwah, NJ: Erlbaum. The American Educational Research Association—the professional organization of academics who study education—commissioned a panel to review what is known about teacher preparation. The result was a comprehensive and unblinking look at the research on this topic. In this chapter, the authors conclude that there is evidence that more subject matter knowledge on the part of the teacher leads to better student learning, but there is persuasive evidence only for the upper grades, especially for mathematics. For other areas there simply are not enough data to be certain.

Hanushek, E. A, Kain, J. F., O'Brien, D. M., & Rivkin, S. G. (2005). The market for teacher quality. National Bureau of Economic Research working paper no. 11154. Cambridge, MA: National Bureau of Economic Research. This study evaluates gains in student learning as a function of many factors. Teacher experience contributes positively to student learning, but only for the first year or two. Estimates vary on how long (on average) teachers improve, but it is seldom longer than five years.

Roese, N. J., & Olson, J. M. (2007). Better, stronger, faster: Self-serving judgment, affect regulation, and the optimal vigilance hypothesis. *Perspectives on Psychological Science, 2,* 124–141. A review of the self-serving bias that puts it into a broader perspective of emotion.

http://www.myteachingpartner.net. My Teaching Partner is a project to help teachers become more reflective about their practice. It involves taping one's class and then talking with a consultant. This project is based at my institution, the University of Virginia, and the guidelines for the project provided much of the framework for the method described here.

Conclusion

Reynolds Price, the well-known author, was one of the few celebrities on the faculty of Duke University when I studied there in the early 1980s. He strode about the campus with a long-stepped gait, often wearing an enormous, bright red scarf. He seemed not unaware that he was watched.

When I took a creative writing seminar with Price, he showed the somewhat forbidding air we students expected from an artist, as well as polished manners and a stock of stories about the famous people he had met. We didn't just respect him, we revered him. For all that, he was quite gracious and took each of us seriously, although it was probably not possible for anyone to take us as seriously as we took ourselves.

Imagine our surprise when Price once told us that any writer should proceed on the assumption that what the reader *really* wants to do is drop his book and turn on the television, or get a beer, or play golf. It was as though he had lit a stink bomb at a swank party. Watch television? Drink a beer? We thought we were writing for a sophisticated audience, for the literate; it sounded as though Price was telling us to pander. Later in the semester I understood that he was just making explicit a principle that should have been obvious: If your writing is not interesting, why should anyone read it?

Years later I see these words through the lens of cognitive psychology rather than literature. Reading is a mental act that literally changes the thought processes of the reader. Thus every piece of prose or poetry is a proposal: "Let me take you on a mental journey. Follow and trust me. The path may sometimes be rocky or steep, but I promise a rewarding adventure." The reader may accept your invitation but the decision-making process does not stop there. At every step the reader may conclude that the way is too difficult or that the scenery is dull, and end the mental trip. Thus the writer must keep in the forefront of her mind whether the reader is being adequately rewarded for her time and effort. As the ratio of effort to reward increases, so does the likelihood that the writer will find herself alone on the path.

I think this metaphor applies also to teaching. A teacher tries to guide the thoughts of the student down a particular pathway, or perhaps to explore a broader swath of new terrain. It may be novel country even for the teacher, and their journeys occur side by side. Always the teacher encourages the student to continue, not to lose heart when he encounters obstacles, to use the experience of previous journeys to smooth the way, and to appreciate the beauty and awe that the scenery might afford. As the author must convince the reader not to drop the book, so too must the teacher persuade the student not to discontinue the journey. Teaching is an act of persuasion.[*]

So how do you persuade the student to follow you? The first answer you might think of is that we follow people whom we respect and who inspire us. True enough. If you have students' respect, they will try to pay attention both to please you and because they trust you; if you think something is worth knowing, they are ready to believe you. The problem is that students (and teachers) have only limited control over their own minds.

Although we like to think that we decide what to pay attention to, our minds have their own wishes and desires when it comes to the focus of attention. For example, you may sit down to read something—say, a report—that you know will be dull but that you nevertheless want to read carefully. Despite your best intentions, you find yourself thinking about something else, with your eyes merely passing over the words. Similarly, most of us have had a teacher whom we liked but did not think was especially effective; he was disorganized, or a little dull, even if also kind and earnest. I said in Chapter One that interesting-sounding content doesn't guarantee attention. (Remember my story about the sex talk from my seventh grade teacher?) The student's desire to understand or to please the teacher is no guarantee of attention either.

So how can a teacher maximize the chances that students will follow her? Another of my college writing instructors answered that question for me when she made this claim: "Most of writing is anticipating how your reader will react." To properly guide the reader on this mental journey, you must know where each sentence will lead him. Will he find it interesting, confusing, poetic, or offensive? How a reader reacts depends not just on what you write but also on who the reader is. The simple sentence "Teaching is like writing" will generate different thoughts in a preschool teacher and a sales clerk. To anticipate your reader's reaction, you must know his personality, his tastes, his biases, and his background knowledge. We have all heard the advice "Know your audience." My professor explained why this is true for writing, and I believe it is no less true for teaching.

Thus, to ensure that your students follow you, you must keep them interested; to ensure their interest, you must anticipate their reactions; and to anticipate their reactions, you must know them. "Know your students" is a fair summary of the content of this book. This maxim sounds suspiciously like *bubbe* psychology. If you weren't aware that you should know your students (and I'm sure you were), your grandmother could have told you it was a good idea. Can cognitive science do no better than that?

What cognitive science can offer is elaboration that puts flesh on the bare-bones slogan. There are particular things you should know about your students, and other things you can safely ignore. There are also actions you can take with that knowledge, and other actions that sound plausible but may well backfire. Table 10.1 summarizes the principle of each chapter in this book, the type of knowledge you need to deploy that principle, and what I take to be the most important classroom implication.

TABLE 1: The nine principles of the mind discussed in this book along with the knowledge needed to deploy them, and the most important implication of each.

Chapter	Cognitive Principle	Required Knowledge About Students	most important classroom implication
1	People are naturally curious, but they are not naturally good thinkers.	What is just beyond what my students know and can do?	Think of to-be-learned material as *answers,* and take the time necessary to explain to students the questions.
2	Factual knowledge precedes skill.	What do my students know?	It is not possible to think well on a topic in the absence of factual knowledge about the topic.
3	Memory is the residue of thought.	What will students think during this lesson?	The best barometer for every lesson plan is "Of what will it make the students think?"
4	We understand new things in the context of things we already know.	What do students already know that will be a toehold on understanding this new material?	Always make deep knowledge your goal, spoken and unspoken, but recognize that shallow knowledge will come first.
5	Proficiency requires practice.	How can I get students to practice without boredom?	Think carefully about which material students need at their fingertips, and practice it over time.
6	Cognition is fundamentally different early and late in training.	What is the difference between my students and an expert?	Strive for deep understanding in your students, not the creation of new knowledge.
7	Children are more alike than different in terms of learning.	Knowledge of students' learning styles is not necessary.	Think of lesson content, not student differences, driving decisions about how to teach.
8	Intelligence can be changed through sustained hard work.	What do my students believe about intelligence?	Always talk about successes and failures in terms of effort, not ability.
9	Teaching, like any complex cognitive skill, must be practiced to be improved.	What aspects of my teaching work well for my students, and what parts need improvement?	Improvement requires more than experience; it also requires conscious effort and feedback.

Cognitive scientists do know more than these nine principles of the mind. These nine were selected because they meet four criteria:

1. As described in the book's introduction, each of these principles is true *all* of the time, whether the person is in the laboratory or the classroom, alone or in a group. The complexity of the mind means that its properties often change, depending on the context. These nine principles are always applicable.

2. Each principle is based on a great deal of data, not only on one or two studies. If any of these principles is wrong, something close to it is right. I don't anticipate that in five years I will write a second edition of this book in which a chapter is deleted because new data have overturned the conclusion.

3. Using or ignoring the principal can have a sizable impact on student performance. Cognitive scientists know lots of other things about the mind that suggest classroom applications, but applying these principles would yield only a modest effect, so it is not clear that it would be worth the effort.

4. In identifying a principle it had to be fairly clear to me that someone would know what to do with it. For example, "Attention is necessary for learning" didn't make the cut even though it meets the other three criteria, because it provides teachers with no direction for what they might do that they aren't already doing.

I know of nine principles that meet these criteria. Three of these principles are concerned with what happens when we encounter a new problem: we're interested in whether it is of medium difficulty, we understand it in the context of things we already know, and like other experiences we remember the aspect of it that we think about. Three of the principles pertain to expertise: expert thinking requires factual knowledge, requires practice, and is different than a novice's thinking. Two of the principles bear on differences among students: their basic mechanisms of learning are more similar than different, and although students differ in intelligence (regardless of how one might define that term), intelligence can be changed through hard work. These eight principles apply to your mind as well as to your students' minds. The ninth principle I highlighted in particular: teaching must be practiced to be improved.

I have claimed that these principles can make a real difference, but that claim is not meant to imply that applying the principles is easy. ("Just take my secret tips and boom! You're a great teacher!") All of the principles listed in Table 10.1 must be leavened with good sense, and any of them can be taken too far or twisted out of shape. What then is the role of cognitive science in educational practice if it cannot offer firm prescriptions?

Education is similar to other fields of study in that scientific findings are useful but not decisive. An architect will use principles of physics in designing an office building, but she will also be guided by aesthetic principles that are outside of science's realm. Similarly, knowledge of cognitive science can be helpful in planning what you teach and how, but it is not the whole story.

Not the whole story—but I see two ways that cognitive science can be useful to teachers. First, knowledge of cognitive science can help teachers balance conflicting concerns. Classrooms are, after all, not just cognitive places. They are also emotional places, social places, motivational places, and so on. These diverse elements prompt different concerns for the teacher, and they sometimes conflict, that is, the best practice cognitively may be poor practice motivationally. Knowing the principles of cognitive science presented here can help a teacher as she balances the different, sometimes conflicting concerns of the classroom.

Second, I see principles of cognitive science as useful boundaries to educational practice. Principles of physics do not prescribe for a civil engineer exactly how to build a bridge, but they let him predict how it is likely to perform if he build its. Similarly, cognitive scientific principles do not prescribe how to teach, but they can help you predict how much your students are likely to learn. If you follow these principles, you maximize the chances that your students will flourish.

Education is the passing on of the accumulated wisdom of generations to children, and we passionately believe in its importance because we know that it holds the promise of a better life for each child, and for us all, collectively. It would be a shame indeed if we did not use the accumulated wisdom of science to inform the methods by which we educate children. That has been the purpose of *Why Don't Students Like School?* Education makes better minds, and knowledge of the mind can make better education.

Note

*I believe Price would agree that his advice applies to teaching, about which he later wrote this: "If your method reaches only the attentive student, then you must either invent new methods or call yourself a failure." *Feasting of the heart.* New York: Scribners, 81.

Notes

Chapter One

1. Duncker, K. (1945). On problem-solving. *Psychological Monographs, 5,* 113.
2. Townsend, D. J., & Bever, T. G. (2001). *Sentence comprehension: The integration of habits and rules.* Cambridge, MA: MIT Press, p. 2.
3. Simon, H. A. *Sciences of the artificial,* 3rd ed. Cambridge, MA: MIT Press, p. 94.

Chapter Two

1. In Everett's preface to his English translation of Deschanel, A. P. (1898). *Elementary Treatise on Natural Philosophy.* New York: Appleton.
2. Recht, D. R., & Leslie, L. (1988). Effect of prior knowledge on good and poor readers' memory of text. *Journal of Educational Psychology, 80,* 16–20.
3. Bransford, J. D., & Johnson, M. K. (1972). Contextual prerequisites for understanding: Some investigations of comprehension and recall. *Journal of Verbal Learning and Verbal Behavior, 11,* 717–726.
4. Wason, P. C. (1968). Reasoning about a rule. *Quarterly Journal of Experimental Psychology, 20,* 273–281.
5. Griggs, R. A., & Cox, J. R. (1982). The elusive thematic-materials effect in Wason's selection task. *British Journal of Psychology, 73,* 407–420.
6. Van Overschelde, J. P., and Healy, A. F. (2001). Learning of nondomain facts in high- and low-knowledge domains. *Journal of Experimental Psychology: Learning, Memory, and Cognition, 27,* 1160–1171.
7. Bischoff-Grethe, A., Goedert, K. M., Willingham, D. T., & Grafton, S. T. (2004). Neural substrates of response-based sequence learning using fMRI. *Journal of Cognitive Neuroscience, 16,* 127–138.

Chapter Three

1. I'm not trying to be funny. College student really do remember jokes and asides best. Kintsch, W., & Bates, E. Recognition memory for statements from a classroom lecture. *Journal of Experimental Psychology: Human Learning and Memory, 3,* 150–159.

2. Dinges, D. F., Whitehouse, W. G., Orne, E. C., Powell, J. W., Orne, M. T., & Erdelyi, M. H. (1992). Evaluating hypnotic memory enhancement (hypermnesia and reminiscence) using multitrial forced recall. *Journal of Experimental Psychology: Learning, Memory, and Cognition, 18*, 1139–1147.

3. Nickerson, R. S., & Adams, M. J. (1979). Long-term memory for a common object. *Cognitive Psychology, 11,* 287–307.

4. Hyde, T. S., & Jenkins, J. J. (1973). Recall for words as a function of semantic, graphic, and syntactic orienting tasks. *Journal of Verbal Learning and Verbal Behavior, 12,* 471–480.

5. Barclay, J. R., Bransford, J. D., Franks, J. J., McCarrel, N. S., & Nitsch, K. (1974). Comprehension and semantic flexibility. *Journal of Verbal Learning and Verbal Behavior, 13,* 471–481.

6. Dowd, M. (1990, June 2). Summit in Washington: Reporter's notebook; Masters of the sound bite cede match to Gorbachev. *New York Times.* Retrieved June 20, 2008, from http://query.nytimes.com/gst/fullpage.html?res=9C0CE6DE113AF931A35755C0A966958260

Chapter Four

1. Searle, J. (1980). Minds, Brains and Programs, *Behavioral and Brain Sciences, 3,* 417–457.

2. Gick, M. L., & Holyoak, K. J. (1980). Analogical problem solving. *Cognitive Psychology, 12,* 306–355.

Chapter Five

1. Whitehead, A. N. (1911). *An Introduction to Mathematics.* New York: Holt, p. 61.

2. Ellis, J. A., Semb, G. B., & Cole, B. (1998). Very long-term memory for information taught in school. *Contemporary Educational Psychology, 23,* 419–433.

3. Bahrick, H. P., & Hall, L. K. (1991). Lifetime maintenance of high school mathematics content. *Journal of Experimental Psychology: General, 120,* 20–33.

Chapter Six

1. Kaplow, L. (Writer), & O'Fallon, P. (Director). (2004). Paternity [Television series episode]. In D. Shore & B. Singer (Executive producers), *House, MD.* New York: Fox.

2. Chase, W. G., & Simon, H. A. (1973). Perception in chess. *Cognitive Psychology, 4,* 55–81.

3. Chi, M. T. H., Feltovich, P. J., & Glaser, R. (1981). Categorization and representation of physics problems by experts and novices. *Cognitive Science, 5,* 121–152.

4. Chi, Feltovich, & Glaser (1981), 146.

5. Retrieved June 19, 2008 from http://www.carnegiehall.org/article/the_basics/art_directions.html

6. Ericsson, K. A., Krampe, R. T., & Tesch-Römer, C. (1993). The role of deliberate practice in the acquisition of expert performance. *Psychological Review, 100,* 363–400.

7. Simon, H., & Chase, W. (1973). Skill in chess. *American Scientist, 61,* 394–403.

8. "Celebrating Jazz Pianist Hank Jones." (2005, June 20). Interview on *Fresh Air from WHYY.* Available at http://www.npr.org/templates/story/story. php?storyId=4710791

9. Cronbach, L. J. (1954). *Educational psychology.* New York: Harcourt, Brace, 14.

10. Emerson, R. W. (1883). *Works of Ralph Waldo Emerson.* London: Routledge, 478.

Chapter Seven

1. From opening paragraph of chapter fourteen in Tolstoy's *What Is Art?*

2. Armstrong, T. (2000). Multiple intelligences in the classroom (2nd ed.). Alexandria, VA: Association for Supervision and Curriculum Development.

Chapter Eight

1. Flynn, J. R. (1987). Massive IQ gains in 14 nations: What IQ tests really measure. *Psychological Bulletin, 101,* 171–191.

2. Mueller, C. M., & Dweck, C. S. (1998). Praise for intelligence can undermine children's motivation and performance. *Journal of Personality and Social Psychology, 75,* 33–52.

Index

Page references followed by *fig* indicate an illustrated figure; followed by *t* indicate a table.

A

Abstract ideas: difficulty of comprehending, 67; dramatic irony as, 79; using examples and analogies to understand, 69; force = mass X acceleration as, 68*fig*, 69; scales of measurement, 70*fig*–71*fig*; understanding by relating background knowledge to, 68–71. *See also* Critical thinking

Accountability, 20

Acronym method, 59*t*, 60

Adams, H. B., 35*t*

Adaptor/innovator cognitive style, 116*fig*

Algebra. *See* Math lessons

American dollar/Mexican peso exchange, 91

American Psychological Association, 145

Analogies, 69

Analogous problem, 77*fig*–78

Analytic/nonanalytic cognitive style, 116*t*

Assignments: designed to facilitate meaning, 63–64; providing relevant and appropriate, 15–16. *See also* Lessons; Problems

Attention: changing the pace to keep student, 17, 126–127; "know your students" to maintain, 162; meaning used to facilitate, 47–49; role of content in, 8–9*fig*; role of curiosity in maintaining, 9–10*fig*

Attention grabbers, 61–62

Auditory/visual/kinesthetic cognitive style, 116*fig*

Auditory-visual-kinesthetic theory, 118*fig*–121*fig*

Automated mental processes, 84–87, 94, 104

Automatization/restructuring cognitive style, 116*fig*

"Autopilot" behavior, 6

B

Background knowledge: assessing student's, 37; chunking enabled by, 101–102; expertise and associated, 32*fig*, 100; four ways that comprehension is facilitated by, 28; learning importance of, 127–128; as necessary for cognitive skills, 28–32; as necessary for reading comprehension, 20–21, 23–28; relationship between comprehension and level of, 27–28, 73–74; understanding abstract ideas by relating them to, 68–71; working memory space increased through, 83–87, 104–105. *See also* Factual knowledge

Behavior: "autopilot," 6; memory as guiding, 6*fig*

The Bell Curve (Hernstein & Murray), 145

The brain, 7. *See also* The mind

Broad/narrow cognitive style, 116*t*

Bubbe psychology, 122, 123*fig*

C

Calculator procedures, 22*fig*

Card problems, 29*fig*, 30*fig*

Carnegie Hall (New York City), 105*fig*

Catching-up goals, 144

Cavalier poetry, 72*fig*–73

Cheney, D., 51*fig*

Chess match clock, 30*fig*

Chess players: comparing chunking process of novice and expert, 102*fig*; function thinking of expert vs. novice, 101–102; Giuoco Piano (or Italian Opening) move by, 151*fig*; memory of, 30; practice required to improve skill of, 151

Chinese language knowledge, 71–72

Chunking: background knowledge role in, 101–102; cognitive problem solving role of, 30–32; comparing novice vs. expert chess player, 102*fig*; description of, 26; as facilitating comprehension, 26–27; working memory increased by, 26–27, 30, 83, 87, 101–102. *See also* Information

Classroom rules, 74*fig*

Cognitive principles: 1. people are curious but not naturally good thinkers, 3, 163*t*; 2. factual knowledge must precede skill, 19, 163*t*; 3. memory is the residue of thought, 41, 47, 163*t*; 4. understanding in context of concrete knowledge, 67, 163*t*; 5. mental task proficiency requires practice, 81, 163*t*; 6. early vs. late cognitive training, 97, 163*t*; 7. children are more alike than different in terms of learning, 113, 163*t*; 8. intelligence can be changed through hard work, 131, 163*t*; 9. teaching must be practiced to be improved, 147, 163*t*; four criteria for, 164; summary of, 163*t*. *See also* Teaching as cognitive skill

Cognitive skills: automated, 84–87, 94, 104; background knowledge as necessary for, 28–32; chunking role in process of, 30–32; factual knowledge as preceding, 19; folding practice into advanced, 94; implications for the classroom regarding factual knowledge and, 36–38; respecting limits of students,' 15; teaching as, 147–159

Cognitive styles: definition of, 114–115; description of different, 115–118, 116*t*; implications for the classroom of, 126–128; list of specific, 116*t*. *See also* Learning styles

Cognitive work: appeal of, 7–9*fig*, 14; automated process of, 84–87, 94, 104; benefits of early training incorporation of, 97–98; examining scientists' and mathematicians' process of, 98–101; expert's mental toolbox for, 101–105; involved in solving discs-and-pegs puzzle, 12*fig*–13; limited space in working memory impact on, 26–27, 83; providing problems requiring appropriate level of, 15. *See also* Mental (or cognitive) abilities

Coin-flip story, 55–57

Comprehension: contextual information required for, 92–93; difficulty in abstract idea, 67; facilitated by understanding analogous problem, 77*fig*–78; four ways that background knowledge facilitates, 28; knowledge creation vs. readiness for, 107–109; relationship between level of knowledge and, 27–28, 73–74; as remembering in disguise, 68–71; rote memorization without, 58–60, 71–74; teaching strategies to facilitate student, 78–79; understood in context of our concrete knowledge, 67, 163*t*. *See also* Learning; Reading comprehension; Students

Confirmation bias, 121

Context: of information, 92–93; learning styles and, 126

Converging/diverging cognitive style, 116*fig*

Counterfeit pennies, 46*fig*

Cramming, 90

Critical thinking: as evaluating information, 21; factual knowledge required for, 19, 21–22; in terms of functions (deep structure), 101–102. *See also* Abstract ideas; Thinking

Crossword puzzles, 9, 10

Curiosity, 9–10*fig*

D

Darwin, C., 134*fig*

Decision making: "autopilot," 6; sequence of mental processes for problem, 12*fig*–13. *See also* Problem solving

Deep knowledge: description of, 74; relationship between comprehension and, 27–28; setting

realistic expectations regarding, 79; shallow vs., 73; spoken and unspoken teaching emphasis on, 79

Dickens, B., 137

Dickson, E., 125

Discovery learning, 63

Discs-and-pegs puzzle, 12*fig*–13

Diverging/converging cognitive style, 116*fig*

Dramatic irony, 79

Drilling practice: automated mental processes developed through, 84–87, 94, 104; creating long lasting memory through, 87–91; decisions regarding when to use, 94; description of, 81–82; facilitating long lasting memory, 87–91; folded into advanced cognitive skills, 94; implications for the classroom, 93–94; knowledge transfer improved through, 91–93; learning enabled through, 82–87; mental task proficiency as requiring, 81, 163*t*; shoe tying, 84*fig*; spacing effect on, 90*fig*–91, 94; tracking schedules of violin, 106*fig*. *See also* Rote memorization; Studying

Driving: placing blame for accidents while, 151*fig*; practicing in order to improve, 149*fig*

E

Edison, T. A., 107*fig*

Education: connection between the mind and, 1; parroting facts stereotype of, 19

Einstein, A., 35

Emerson, R. W., 35, 110

Emotional events, 44–45*fig*

Environment: intelligence genetics vs., 134–139; mind model on forgotten information, working and long-term memory and, 42*fig*–43*fig*; mind model on working memory, long-term memory, and, 2*fig*, 148*fig*

Everett, J. D., 20

Experts/expertise: accelerated transfer of knowledge by, 100–101; background knowledge associated with, 32*fig*, 100; comparing reading process of novices vs., 110*fig*; comparison of novice chess players vs., 101–102; examining cognitive process associated with, 98–100; how to facilitate student development of, 105–107; implications for the classroom related to developing, 107–110*fig*; learning activities appropriate for students vs., 109; mental toolbox of, 101–105; problem solving approach by, 102–103*fig*; "ten-year rule" of, 107. *See also* Mathematicians; Novices

F

Fact learning: as preceding skill, 19; rote memorization as, 58–60, 71–74; standardized testing of, 20–21; stereotype of, 19. *See also* Learning

Factual knowledge: benefits of meaningful, 38; benefits of reading to basic, 37–38; benefits of shallow knowledge over no, 37; critical thinking as requiring, 19, 21–22; demonstration on increasing, 34*t*–35; evaluating what should be taught to students, 36–37; home environment impact on acquisition of, 38; implications for the classroom regarding, 36–38; incidental acquisition of, 38; memory improved by, 32–36; must precede skill, 19, 163*t*; necessity of, 20–21; quotations from great thinkers denigrating, 35*t*; working memory space increased through, 83–87, 104–105. *See also* Background knowledge; Knowledge

Failure as learning process, 143

Favre, B., 115*fig*

Feynman, R., 125

Field dependent/field independent cognitive style, 116*fig*, 117*fig*–118

First letter method, 59*t*

Flynn effect, 137*fig*

Flynn, J., 137

Footbath meaning, 119*fig*

Force = mass X acceleration, 68*fig*, 69

Forgetting: emotional events and impact on, 44–45*fig*; impact of meaning on, 47–49; mind model showing role of, 42*fig*–43; mind models on environment, working and long-term memory and, 42*fig*–43*fig*; reasons for, 43–44; recall trials using hypnotized subjects and, 43, 44*fig*; repetition impact on, 45–46; teaching strategies used for preventing, 44–48. *See also* Information; Memory; Remembering

Fraternal twins, 135*fig*–136*t*

Full moon hypothesis, 121*fig*

Functions (deep structure) thinking, 101–102

G

Galton, F., 134*fig*

Gardner, H., 122

Gardner's theory of multiple intelligences: claims regarding mental abilities and, 122–125; list of individual, 124*t*; recognizing student's individual intelligence, 127

Geometry. *See* Math lessons

Giuoco Piano (or Italian Opening) chess move, 151*fig*

Golfer's strok practice, 154*fig*

H

Hamlet (Shakespeare), 3

Hard Times (Dickens), 19

Herrick, R., 72*fig*

Holist/serialist cognitive style, 116*fig*

Holocaust Memorial (Berlin), 45*fig*

Home environment factor, 38

House, Dr. (fictional character), 98–100, 101

House (TV show), 98–100

Hypnosis/recall trials, 43, 44*fig*

I

Identical twins, 135*fig*–136*t*, 138

Imagination, 35

Implications for the classroom: of drill practice for learning, 93–94; expertise development and, 107–110*fig*; to facilitate student comprehension, 78–79; of factual knowledge improving cognitive processes, 36–38; of learning styles and abilities, 126–128; of meaning as helping memory, 61–65; of successful thinking as pleasurable, 14–17; summary of, 163*t*; for teaching slow learners, 142–145. *See also* Lessons; Teaching strategies

Impulsivity/reflectiveness cognitive style, 116*fig*

Incidental knowledge acquisition, 38

Information: contextual, 92–93; critical thinking as evaluating, 21; "inside joke," 39; retrieved from working memory and long-term memory, 42*fig*–49; scientific expert's analysis of, 98–101; thinking as new ways of combining, 11–12, 21; which fails to make it to long-term memory, 43–44*fig*; working memory combining and manipulating, 11*fig*, 21*fig*, 26. *See also* Chunking; Forgetting; Remembering

Innovator/adaptor cognitive style, 116*fig*

"Inside joke" information, 39

Intelligence (IQ): debate over *The Bell Curve* on, 145; definition of, 132; Dutch studies on, 136; Flynn effect on, 137*fig*; Gardner's theory on multiple, 122–125, 127; using hard work to change, 131; nature vs. nurture origins of, 134–139; pattern-completion format testing, 141*fig*; significance of beliefs about, 139–142; single model of, 132, 133*fig*; twin studies on, 135*fig*–136*t*; verbal and mathematical model of, 132, 133*fig*

Interest, 8–9*fig*

Interval scale, 70*fig*

Intuitive/reasoning cognitive style, 116*fig*

J

Jones, H., 108*fig*

K

Kinesthetic/auditory/visual cognitive style, 116*fig*

Kinesthetic-auditory-visual theory, 118*fig*–121*fig*

Knowledge: background, 20–21, 23–32; benefits of reading to base, 37–38; computer example of

Chinese language, 71–72; deep, 27–28, 73, 79; evaluating what should be taught to students, 36–37; procedural, 13; readiness to comprehend vs. creating, 107–109; rote, 72; shallow, 27–28, 71–74. *See also* Factual knowledge

Knowledge transfer: barriers to, 74–78; expert vs. novice, 100–101; improved through drill practice, 91–93. *See also* Learning

Koury, K., 150*fig*

L

Laurie, H., 99*fig*

Learning: background knowledge importance for, 127–128; discovery, 63; drill practice as enabling, 82–87; motor, 33; quotations from great thinkers denigrating factual, 35*t*; treating failure as natural part of learning, 143. *See also* Comprehension; Fact learning; Knowledge transfer; Students

Learning styles: implications for the classroom of, 126–128; importance of understanding, 113–114; mental abilities and different, 114–115; visual, auditory, and kinesthetic, 116*t*, 118*fig*–121*fig*. *See also* Cognitive styles

LeBlanc, M., 51*fig*

Lesson diary, 17, 157–158*fig*

Lessons: incorporating mnemonics into, 58–60, 64; math, 55–57*fig*, 85–89*fig*; Pearl Harbor, 54*fig*–55*fig*; reviewing possible student thinking about, 61; science, 98, 103*fig*; structured around a conflict, 64–65. *See also* Assignments; Implications for the classroom; Teaching strategies

Link method, 59*t*

Long-term memory: of chess players, 30; discs-and-pegs puzzle solution using, 12*fig*–13; examples of material in author's, 45*fig*; information retrieved from working and, 42*fig*–49; information which fails to make it to, 43–44*fig*; model of the mind and role of, 11*fig*, 21*fig*, 42*fig*, 82*fig*; practice as facilitating, 87–91; procedural knowledge contained in, 13. *See also* Memory; Working memory

M

Manning, P., 115*fig*

Mathematicians: examining cognitive work of, 98–101; mathematical intelligence of, 132, 133*fig*. *See also* Experts/expertise

Math lessons: automated mental processing in, 85–86*fig*; practice as creating long lasting memory of, 87–89*fig*; Z score transformation, 55–57*fig*

Meaning: designing assignments to facilitate, 63–64; examples of piano pictures and, 48*fig*; footbath, 119*fig*; impact on memory by, 47–49; implications for the classroom of memory enhanced by, 61–65; rote memorization vs., 58–60, 71–74; using stories to enhance, 51–58

Memory: emotional events and impact on, 44–45*fig*; factual knowledge as improving, 32–36; as guiding behavior, 6*fig*; impact of meaning on, 47–49; implications for the classroom of meaning as enhancing, 61–65; mnemonics to help with, 58–60; problem solving using, 28–30; recall trials using hypnotized subjects and, 43, 44*fig*; repetition impact on, 45–46; as residue of thought, 41, 47, 163*t*; rote memorization, 58–60, 71–74; spacing-effect in, 90*fig*–91, 94; storage definition of, 5; teaching and importance of, 42–49. *See also* Forgetting; Long-term memory; Remembering; Working memory

Mental (or cognitive) abilities: description of, 114, 122; Gardner's multiple intelligences and, 123–125; implications for the classroom, 126–128; learning styles and, 114–115. *See also* Cognitive work

Method of loci, 59*t*

Mexican peso/American dollar exchange, 91

The mind: comparing a calculator to, 22*fig*; connection between education and, 1; as not being designed for thinking, 3–7; research-practice gap related to study of, 1. *See also* The brain

The mind models: simplest (working memory and long-term memory), 11*fig*, 21*fig*, 82*fig*; working memory, long-term memory, and environment, 2*fig*, 148*fig*; working memory, long-term memory, environment, and forgotten information, 42*fig*–43*fig*

Mnemonics: common methods for, 59*t*; description of, 58, 60; learning to teach using, 64

Moby-Dick (Melville), 24–25

Monopoly player skills, 150*fig*

Motor learning, 33

Mozart, W., 107

Multiple intelligences: claims regarding mental abilities and, 122–125; list of individual, 124*t*; recognizing individual student's, 127

N

Narrow/board cognitive style, 116*t*

Newton's first law, 121

New York Times crossword puzzles, 9, 10

9/11, 44

Nominal scale, 70*fig*

Nonanalytic/analytic cognitive style, 116*t*

Novices: comparing expert chess players and, 101–102; comparing how experts learn and think vs., 109–110; comparing knowledge transfer of experts vs., 100–101; comparing reading process of experts vs., 110*fig*. *See also* Experts/expertise; Students

O

Oedipus Rex (play), 78

Ohm's law, 68

Olson, A., 135*fig*
Olson, M. K., 135*fig*
Ordinal scale, 70*fig*
Othello (Shakespeare), 78

P
Pattern-completion intelligence test, 141*fig*
Peg word, 59*t*
Penny/counterfeit pennies, 46*fig*
Permission rule, 92*fig*–93
Phelps, J., 135*fig*
Phelps, O., 135*fig*
Piano meaning pictures, 48*fig*
Practice. *See* Drilling practice
Praise, 142, 145
Price, R., 161, 165
Problems: card, 29*fig*, 30*fig*; expert abstract
    knowledge of, 102–103*fig*; providing "relevant,"
    15–16; providing students with appropriate, 15;
    reconsidering when to employ "puzzling," 16;
    rotating disk, 103*fig*; understanding facilitated by
    analogous, 77*fig*–78. *See also* Assignments
Problem solving: chunking role in process of,
    30–32; examining sequence of mental processes
    for, 12*fig*–13; expert approach to, 102–103*fig*;
    memory used for, 28–30; pleasure derived from
    successful, 7–9*fig*, 14; providing appropriate level
    of cognitive work through, 15; tea-ceremony,
    13–14*fig*; three peg puzzle, 11–12*fig*. *See also*
    Decision making
Procedural knowledge, 13

R
Ratio scale, 70*fig*
Reading: benefits to knowledge from, 37–38;
    comparing expert vs. novice's process of, 110*fig*;
    as mental journey, 161
Reading comprehension: background knowledge
    necessary for, 20–21, 23–28; chunking as
    facilitating, 26–27; contextual information
    required for, 92–93; four ways that background
    knowledge facilitates, 28; relationship
    between knowledge level and, 27*fig*. *See also*
    Comprehension
Reasoning/intuitive cognitive style, 116*fig*
Recall trials, 44*fig*
Reeves, K., 134*fig*
Reflectiveness/impulsivity cognitive style, 116*fig*
Remembering: repetition impact on, 45–46; rote
    memorization, 58–60, 71–74; understanding as,
    68–71. *See also* Forgetting; Information; Memory
Repetition, 45–46
Restructuring/automatization cognitive style, 116*fig*
Robot movement, 4*fig*
Romeo and Juliet (Shakespeare), 78

Rotating disk problem, 103*fig*
Rote knowledge, 72
Rote memorization: example computer Chinese
    language, 71–72; of knowledge without meaning,
    58–60. *See also* Drilling practice
Rules: expertise "ten-year," 107; permission,
    92*fig*–93; understanding need for classroom, 74*fig*

S
Scales of measurement examples, 70*fig*–71*fig*
Science (journal), 21
Science lessons: rotating disk problem, 103*fig*;
    traditional approach to, 98
Scientists: background knowledge of, 32*fig*, 100;
    examining cognitive work of, 98–101; mental
    toolbox used by, 101–105
Searle, J., 71–72
Self-reflection, 158*fig*
Serialist/holist cognitive style, 116*fig*
Shakespeare, W., 3
Shallow knowledge: deep vs., 73; description of,
    71–74; relationship between comprehension and,
    27–28
Shoe tying practice, 84*fig*
Skills. *See* Cognitive skills
Skinner, B. F., 35*t*
Slow learners: being realistic about catching-up
    goals, 144; demonstrating confidence in, 144–145;
    how beliefs about intelligence impact teaching,
    139–142; implications for the classroom on
    teaching, 142–145; learning how to help,
    131–132; praise effort of, 142, 145; sending
    message that hard work pays off, 142–143;
    teaching study skills to, 143–144. *See also* Students
Songs (mnemonic), 59*fig*, 60
Spacing-effect in memory, 90*fig*–91, 94
Standardized tests: accountability through, 20;
    factual knowledge tested by, 20–21
Star Wars (film), 52
Stories: Pearl Harbor lesson structures using,
    54*fig*–55*fig*; power of teaching through, 51–53;
    teaching by using structure of the, 53–58; Z score
    transformation lesson and coin-flip, 55–57
Story structure: four Cs (causality, conflict,
    complications, character) of, 52; lesson
    applications of, 53–58; Pearl Harbor lesson,
    54*fig*–55*fig*; Z score transformation, 57*fig*
Students: ability to comprehend vs. creating
    knowledge, 107–109; accept and act on variations
    in preparation by, 16–17; assessing background
    knowledge of, 37; evaluating what knowledge
    should be taught to, 36–37; home environment
    and knowledge acquisition of, 38; improving
    your teaching skills by observing, 159; learning
    activities appropriate for experts vs., 109; learning

styles of, 113–128; providing "relevant" problems to, 15–16; recognizing individual intelligence of each, 127; reconsidering how they think, 3; reconsidering when to puzzle, 16; respecting cognitive limits of, 15; teaching them to think like experts, 105–107. *See also* Comprehension; Learning; Novices; Slow learners

Studying: cramming, 90; teaching students skills for, 143–144; timing of, 90–91. *See also* Drilling practice

Style (teacher), 49–51

T

Tea-ceremony problem, 13–14*fig*

Teachers: accept and act on variations in student preparation, 16–17; guide metaphor applied to, 161–162; keep a lesson diary, 17, 157–158*fig*; observation of students to improve teaching, 159; reconsidering how students think, 3; respecting students' cognitive limits, 15; self-reflection by, 158*fig*; starting discussion group with fellow teachers, 158; style as common characteristic of good, 49–51

Teaching as cognitive skill: cognitive science to improve, 164–165; description of, 148–149; getting and giving feedback to improve, 152–156; importance of practicing, 149*fig*–152; self-management for conscious improvement of, 156–157; strategies for improving, 157–159. *See also* Cognitive principles

Teaching diary, 17, 157–158*fig*

Teaching feedback steps: 1. identify another teacher to partner with, 153; 2. tape yourself and watch the tapes alone, 153; 3. with your partner watch tapes of other teachers, 153–155; 4. with your partner watch and comment on each other's tapes, 155*fig*–156; 5. bring awareness back to the classroom and follow up, 156

Teaching strategies: as answering the question process, 58; appropriate for novice student vs., experts, 109–110; attention grabbers, 61–62; using discovery learning with care, 63; effective for slow learners, 142–145; to facilitate student comprehension, 78–79; how beliefs about intelligence impact, 139–142; importance of memory and role in, 42*fig*–49; including meaning as part of, 47–49; keeping a diary on your, 17, 157–158*fig*; mnemonics, 58–60, 64; used to prevent student forgetting, 44–48; providing problems of appropriate difficulty/relevance as, 15–16; using stories as part of, 51–58. *See also* Implications for the classroom; Lessons

"Ten-year rule," 107

Testing: accountability through, 20; factual knowledge, 20–21; working memory, 75

Thinking: cognitive conditions required for, 3; definition of, 3, 21; examining the mechanics of, 10–14; how your brain saves you from, 7; memory as residue of, 41, 47, 163*t*; the mind as not being designed for, 3–7; pleasure derived from successful, 7–9*fig*, 14; teaching students to develop expert, 105–107; three properties of, 5. *See also* Critical thinking

"Thinking outside the box," 7*fig*

Thinking properties: effortful nature of, 5; slow nature as, 5; uncertain nature of, 5

Tolstoy, L., 121

To the Virgins, to Make Much of Time (Herrick), 72–73

Travel funds calculation, 91

Tribbiani, Joey (TV character), 51*fig*

Trivia game players, 140*fig*

Twain, M., 35*t*

Twin studies, 135*fig*–136*t*, 137–138

U

Understanding. *See* Comprehension

V

Verbal intelligence, 132, 133*fig*

Violinist practice schedules, 106*fig*

Visual/auditory/kinesthetic cognitive style, 116*fig*

Visual-auditory-kinesthetic theory, 118*fig*–121*fig*

Visualizer/verbalizer cognitive style, 116*fig*

W

Whitehead, A. N., 35

Woods, T., 152*fig*

Working memory: automated mental processes to get around limits of, 104; chunking as increasing space in, 26–27, 30, 83, 87, 101–102*fig*; discs-and-pegs puzzle solution using, 12*fig*–13; factual knowledge to increase limited space of, 83–87, 104–105; information retrieved from long-term and, 42*fig*–49; limited space of, 26–27, 83, 86–87; mind model on combining/manipulating information role of, 11*fig*, 21*fig*, 26, 42*fig*, 82*fig*; tea-ceremony solution using, 14; testing, 95. *See also* Long-term memory; Memory

Z

Z score transformation lesson, 55–57*fig*

Credit Lines

Why Don't Students Like School?
Daniel Willingham

Figure 1.1   A, Hollywood robot: Alien cat © Fotolia

Figure 1.1   B, industrial robot: Baloncici © Fotolia

Figure 1.2   A, Hillary Clinton: © Greg Adams

Figure 1.2   B, faucet: Eduard Stelmakh © Fotolia

Figure 1.2   C, pot boiling over: © Ethan Bendheim

Figure 1.3,   supermarket bread aisle: © Daniel T. Willingham

Figure 1.4,   Sudoku and geometry problem: © Anne Carlyle Lindsay

Figure 1.5,   boring slide of motivation model: © Anne Carlyle Lindsay

Figure 1.6,   simple diagram of the mind: © Anne Carlyle Lindsay

Figure 1.7,   Tower of Hanoi game: © Anne Carlyle Lindsay

Figure 1.8,   diagram of mind playing Tower of Hanoi: © Anne Carlyle Lindsay

Figure 1.9,   tea ceremony problem: © Anne Carlyle Lindsay

Figure 2.1 A,   attractive guy: Memo © Fotolia

Figure 2.1   B, slob: Alexey Klementiev © Fotolia

Figure 2.1   C, burglar: jeanphilippe delisle © Fotolia

Figure 2.2,   simple diagram of the mind: © Anne Carlyle Lindsay

Figure 2.3,   calculator: Pakhay Oleksandr © Fotolia

Figure 2.4,   woman typing: Monkey Business © Fotolia

Figure 2.5,   graph of results from a reading study: Based on data from "Effect of prior knowledge on good and poor readers' memory of text" by D.R. Recht and L. Leslie in *Journal of Educational Psychology, 80,* 16-20. Copyright © 1988 by the American Psychological Association.

Figure 2.6,   Wason card problem: © Anne Carlyle Lindsay

Figure 2.7,   Beer version of Wason problem: © Anne Carlyle Lindsay

Figure 2.8,   chess clock:
Greywind © Fotolia

Figure 2.9,   pantry:
© Bernie Goldbach

Figure 2.10,   geologist:
© iStockphoto.com/mikeuk

Figure 3.1,   elaborated diagram of the mind:
© Anne Carlyle Lindsay

Figure 3.2,   figure depicting results of hypnosis study:
From "Evaluating hypnotic memory enhancement (Hypermnesia and Reminiscence) using multitrial forced recall" by David F. Dinges, Wayne G. Whitehouse, Emily C. Orne, John W. Powell, Martin T. Orne, and M.H. Erdelyi in *Journal of Experimental Psychology: Learning, Memory and Cognition, 18,* figure 1, p. 1142. Copyright © 1992 by the American Psychological Association.

Figure 3.3,   what I have forgotten:
© Anne Carlyle Lindsay

Figure 3.4,   thing I remember for no reason:
© Anne Carlyle Lindsay

Figure 3.5   A, birthday party:
© iStockphoto.com/sjlocke

Figure 3.5   B, visit to Holocaust memorial:
Alexander Inglessi © Fotolia

Figure 3.6,   true and false penny:
From "Long term memory for a common object" by R.S. Nickerson and M.J. Adams in *Cognitive Psychology, 11,* 287–307. Copyright © 1979. Reprinted with permission from Elsevier.

Figure 3.7   A, piano moving man:
© Kai Harth

Figure 3.7   B, piano being played:
Friday © Fotolia

Figure 3.8   A, Dick Cheney:
© World Economic Forum, www.weforum.org

Figure 3.8   B, Matt Leblanc:
© Glenn Harris/PR Photos

Figure 3.9,   Mikhail Gorbachev:
© A. Gilbert/PR Photos

Figure 3.10,   US entry in WWII:
© Anne Carlyle Lindsay

Figure 3.11,   alternate lesson, US entry in WWII:
© Anne Carlyle Lindsay

Figure 3.12,   hierarchy for Z scores:
© Anne Carlyle Lindsay

Figure 4.1   A, man batting a ball:
© Michael E. Bishop

Figure 4.1   B, man batting a car:
© Scott Barbour/Getty Images

Figure 4.2   A, football team:
Sergei Ivanov © Fotolia

Figure 4.2   B, horse race:
© Eric R. Poole

Figure 4.2,   thermometer:
Josef F. Stuefer © Fotolia

Figure 4.2,   grandfather and baby:
Stuart Monk © Fotolia

Figure 4.3,   ruler:
Brad Sauter © Fotolia

Figure 4.3,   cereal bowl:
Marek © Fotolia

Figure 4.3,   CD:
soleg © Fotolia

Figure 4.4,   Robert Herrick:
From *Halleck's New English Literature* by Reuben Post Halleck. Published by American Book Company, copyright 1913.

Figure 4.5,   list of classroom rules:
© Shawn Zehnder Lea

Figure 4.6,   boy doing homework from a textbook:
Millymanz © Fotolia

Figure 5.1,   simple diagram of the mind:
© Anne Carlyle Lindsay

Figure 5.2,   child who has just learned to tie his shoelaces:
© iStockphoto.com/HelpingHandsPhotos

Figure 5.3,   picture word mismatch:
© Anne Carlyle Lindsay

Figure 5.4,   code:
© Anne Carlyle Lindsay

Figure 5.5,   graph showing forgetting of course material:
From "Very long-term memory for information taught in school" by J.A. Ellis, G.B. Semb, and B. Cole in *Contemporary Educational; Psychology, 23,* 419-433. Figure 1 on p. 428. Copyright © 1998. Reprinted with permission from Elsevier.

Figure 5.6,   graph from Bahrick & Hall:
From "Lifetime maintenance of high school mathematics content" by H.P. Bahrick and L.K. Hall in *Journal of Experimental Psychology: General. 120,* 20-33, Figure 1, p. 25. Copyright © 1991 by the American Psychological Association.

Figure 5.7,   calendar for studying:
© Anne Carlyle Lindsay

Figure 5.8,   no shirt, no shoes, no service:
© Dan Klimke

Figure 6.1,   Hugh Laurie:
© Chris Hatcher/PR Photos

Figure 6.2,   chess boards with two orders of recall:
From "The mind's eye in chess" by W.G. Chase and H.A. Simon in *Visual Information* Processing, edited by W.G. Chase.

Copyright © 1973 Academic Press. Reprinted by permission of Elsevier.

Figure 6.3,   figure reproduced from chi et al physics experts:
From "Categorization and representation of physics problems by experts and novices" by M.T.H. Chi, P.J. Feltovich, and R. Glaser in *Cognitive Science 5,* 121-152. Figure 1, p. 126. Copyright © 1981 Lawrence Erlbaum Associates. Reprinted by permission of Taylor & Francis Informa UK Ltd., via Copyright Clearance Center.

Figure 6.4,   Carnegie Hall:
© Mike Lee, Mikelee.org

Figure 6.5,   violinists practice:
From "The role of deliberate practice in the acquisition of expert performance" by K.A. Ericsson, R.T. Krampe, and C. Tesch-Romer in *Psychological Review, 100,* 363-400. Figure 9, p. 379. Copyright © 1993 by the American Psychological Association.

Figure 6.6,   Thomas Edison:
Library of Congress Prints and Photographs Collection.

Figure 6.7,   Hank Jones:
© Ronald Weinstock

Figure 6.8,   eye movement data:
From *Fundamental Reading Habits: A Study of Their Development* by Guy T. Buswell, *Supplemental Educational Monographs,* published in conjunction with *The School Review* and *The Elementary School Journal,* No. 21, June 1922. Copyright © 1922 by The University of Chicago.

Figure 7.1,   Peyton Manning:
© Image of Sport/PR Photos

Figure 7.2,   Brett Favre:
© Image of Sport/PR Photos

Figure 7.3   A, clipart figures addition:
© Anne Carlyle Lindsay

Figure 7.3 B, boy listening:
© iStockphoto.com/Steve Stone

Figure 7.3 C, girl with abacus:
Photocreate © Fotolia

Figure 7.4, footbath:
Duey © Fotolia

Figure 7.5, full-moon:
Cesar Andrade © Fotolia

Figure 7.6, picture of my grandmother:
© Daniel T. Willingham

Figure 8.1, two views of intelligence:
© Anne Carlyle Lindsay

Figure 8.2, the dominant view of intelligence:
© Anne Carlyle Lindsay

Figure 8.3 A, Darwin:
Library of Congress Prints and Photographs Collection.

Figure 8.3 B, Keanu Reeves:
© Caroline Bondarde Ucci

Figure 8.4 A, Mary Kate and Ashley:
© Wild1/PR Photos

Figure 8.4 B, Phelps brothers:
© Solarpix/PR Photos

Figure 8.5, graph of US IQ increase from Flynn:
From "The mean IQ of Americans: Massive gains 1932 to 1978" by J.R. Flynn in *Psychological Bulletin,* 95, pp. 29–51. Data are from Table 2, p. 33.

Copyright © 1984 by the American Psychological Association.

Figure 8.6, tall and short basketball players:
© Anne Carlyle Lindsay

Figure 8.7, game night:
© iStockphoto.com/bonniej

Figure 8.8, Ravens progressive matrices:
© Timothy Salthouse

Figure 9.1, simple model of mind:
© Anne Carlyle Lindsay

Figure 9.2, picture of the author driving:
© Anne Carlyle Lindsay

Figure 9.3, Monopoly coach:
© Ken Koury

Figure 9.4, car accident:
Terrence Lee © Fotolia

Figure 9.5, Giuoco piano:
© Anne Carlyle Lindsay

Figure 9.6, Tiger Woods:
© Paul Gallegos/PR Photos

Figure 9.7, firefighters:
Duncan Noakes © Fotolia

Figure 9.8, golfer videotaping self:
© Anne Carlyle Lindsay

Figure 9.9, man and woman arguing:
Ken Hurst © Fotolia

Figure 9.10, woman writing in diary:
Darren Baker © Fotolia